Thoughtful Interaction Design

Thoughtful Interaction Design

A Design Perspective on Information Technology

Jonas Löwgren and Erik Stolterman

The MIT Press
Cambridge, Massachusetts
London, England

First MIT Press paperback edition, 2007

This book was set in Stone Sans and Stone Serif by Graphic Composition, Inc.

Printed and bound in the United States of America.

Library of Congress Cataloging-in-Publication Data

Löwgren, Jonas.
Thoughtful interaction design : a design perspective on information technology / Jonas Löwgren and Erik Stolterman.
    p. cm.
Includes bibliographical references and index.
ISBN 0-262-12271-5 (hc. : alk. paper)—0-262-62209-2 (pbk. : alk. paper)
ISBN-13 978-0-262-12271-9 (hc. : alk. paper)—978-0-262-62209-7 (pbk. : alk. paper)
1. System design. 2. Human-computer interaction. 3. User interfaces (Computer systems)
I. Stolterman, Erik. II. Title.
QA76.9.S88L69   2005
004.2′1—dc22

                                                                                2004049891

10 9 8 7 6 5 4 3 2

Contents

Foreword: The Reflective Interaction Designer

Imagine a small portable device that kids could carry around everywhere and use for reading, writing, mathematics, music, art, and entertainment. Imagine that it can store thousands of articles, letters, notes, poems, recipes, paintings, drawings, musical scores, dynamic simulations, animations, games, and everything else the kids like to have at hand. Imagine that the device is technically matched to human senses— with images of print quality, the sound of a decent hi-fi system, and the interactive control of a musical instrument. This is not a specification of your next laptop computer, but a design vision called Dynabook.

The Dynabook vision was created in the early 1970s by the Learning Research Group at the Xerox Palo Alto Research Center, under the guidance of computer scientist Alan Kay. Back then, computers would fill entire rooms and were anything but personal tools for ordinary people. As a design vision, Dynabook is interesting from several points of view including, of course, that as we now look back at the Dynabook from the new millennium, we can think of it as an extremely innovative information technology design vision.

Dynabook is interesting as a design vision because it was strongly connected to a context, to situations of learning, and was not merely focusing on technology as such. It is also interesting, in its use of a musical instrument as a metaphor, for not being limited to existing applications but creating ideas of entirely new forms of interaction. Moreover, it is interesting because it demonstrates the value of design visions that reach far beyond the contemporary state of technological development. The Dynabook prototype that was implemented was a very impressive computer for its time, with an object-oriented programming environment, a graphical user interface with windows and pop-up menus, a virtual desktop, and a mouse. It also featured tools for text processing, painting, drawing and generating music. Creative and groundbreaking in its design, the Dynabook prototype was also expensive, clumsy, slow, and—in practice—useless.

The Dynabook design vision is about shaping and composing—not in clay, plastic, or metal—but in information technology, the material that the authors of this book aptly call "the material without qualities." An interaction designer takes part in creating a "dynamic gestalt," to use another fruitful concept from the book, a design product that is more closely related to film and theater than to the coffee pots of industrial design or the buildings of architecture. However, the material without qualities is also involved in dissolving the boundaries between material and virtual in the development of smart devices and virtual workplaces.

The authors of this book do not teach ready-to-use methods and techniques for creating design visions. They have another purpose—namely, to write a book prompting thoughtful reflection on what it means to be a good interaction designer and how to be prepared to act professionally in the design situations. What kind of knowledge is this? What kind of design ability is needed to address these concerns?

Does it matter in the creation of Dynabook that its designer, computer scientist and engineer Alan Kay, was also a proficient amateur jazz musician? Did that affect his design ability? What did it mean for Dynabook that the Learning Group was comprised of members with experience in architecture and social anthropology? Did the desktop metaphor and object-oriented programming environment suit the practical context of children and learning? Where did the ideas of the graphical user interface, menus, and windows come from? Was it a lack of design ability that made the photocopying equipment company Xerox unable to develop Dynabook as a commercial product, when companies such as Apple and much later Microsoft were successful in bringing such concepts to the market?

This book is a contribution to the kind of design theory that makes it possible for a designer to learn from earlier examples such as Dynabook, but it gives no certain answers. Design theory is not a scientific theory in the narrow sense of predicting the outcome of an action irrespective of context and situation. Instead, it is concerned with transforming the conditions and potentials for human action, with the intellectual virtue that is nearly forgotten in our technology-obsessed times but that Aristotle viewed as the most important one and labeled *phronesis*. Phronesis refers to an action-oriented and context-dependent design theory based on practical value rationality. It is a practical theory with which designers can develop their sense of ethical and aesthetical judgment and create designs appropriate for their contexts.

In making a contribution to a practical design theory for professional designers, the authors of this book subscribe to a design tradition that owes a great deal to Donald Schön, a leading figure among modern design theorists, and his concept of the *reflective practitioner*. Schön demonstrated in his studies how architects, musicians, psychoanalysts, lawyers, and other professionals listen to the situation "talking back" to them, how they reflect-in-action, and how they develop theories-in-use. This fundamental understanding of what designers do when they design is then applied in an interesting way in this book to a new context—the professional design of information technology.

As information technology researchers, Jonas Löwgren and Erik Stolterman primarily address interaction designers. In my opinion, however, the book is equally relevant for industrial designers, architects, and all other professionals involved in the shaping of our material and virtual realities. The authors' ideas about interaction design are on the forefront of design theory and design studies, and well in line with the design theory of more established design disciplines such as industrial design and architecture.

This book has every chance of contributing to the development of information technology as a design discipline, the education of the reflective interaction designer, and hence to the socially appropriate, ethically defensible, and aesthetically adequate design of the "material without qualities."

Pelle Ehn, Professor of Informatics and author of *Work-Oriented Design of Computer Artefacts*

Preface

The shaping of digital artifacts is an act of design. Design of information technology is not only one of many design processes in society today, but one of the most prominent. In many ways and in many contexts, the design of digital artifacts influences the functions of workplaces, the structure and forms of schools and educational systems, how people communicate and use their leisure time, how organizations develop, and how social and cultural structures evolve. The role and importance of information technology is becoming increasingly visible and acknowledged.

Most digital artifacts around us originate in the information technology (IT) industry, dominated by companies developing hardware, software, and telecommunications. In the academic world, the core fields concerned with the development of digital artifacts include information systems development, software engineering, and computer science. Our aim is to *introduce a design perspective on the creation and shaping of digital artifacts;* our claim is that it is both necessary and rewarding to consider the development of digital artifacts as a design discipline akin to, for example, architecture or industrial design. In our experience, this perspective is quite uncommon in the IT industry as well as in IT academia.

The intention behind this book is to provide material that will stimulate a discussion on how to design digital artifacts and how to think about the design process and the designed product. The fundamental question underlying our work is what kind of knowledge the aspiring interaction designer needs. We want to emphasize the importance of what we call *interaction design* and the responsibility that practicing and future interaction designers have. We discuss interaction design in rather broad terms, including the responsibility for ethical and aesthetical (as well as functional) qualities of digital artifacts. This is at variance with many contemporary job descriptions where interaction design is more narrowly defined in terms of usability and usefulness. This discrepancy is intentional, since we feel that the design perspective we outline has rather far-reaching implications for the everyday practice of developing digital artifacts in the IT industry and in academia.

Furthermore, we argue that the discipline of developing digital artifacts requires a new perspective on design—*thoughtful design*. Thoughtful design is needed since the design challenges we face today are more complex than ever. Research and experience provides us with more and more knowledge and information. But rapid technological development prevents us from experimenting with and learning about all the new possibilities created by new technology and new knowledge. Consequently, designers today have to deal with a reality marked by complexity and change. It is essential that members of the design discipline collectively find appropriate forms for growing and nurturing design knowledge. We believe such a demand can only be met by an approach based on a foundation of design *thoughtfulness*.

We—the authors—have been involved for quite some time in the interaction design training of professionals and students in information systems, computer science, and human-computer interaction. It has been important for us to open up wider perspectives on the design of digital artifacts than those provided by the technical craft view that dominates the field. Of course, a field such as ours needs a literature with a technical focus and an emphasis on methods and techniques for design and development, but we have learned that this technical literature alone is not sufficient. Our aim is to write a book that can help students and professionals think about and reflect on the field using reasonably well-grounded ideas and concepts based on a design perspective. The approach we have chosen is to write a book for thoughtful and critical reflections.

A thoughtful book is not intended to be read as a presentation of self-contained knowledge or practical approaches; rather, it should be seen as fuel for the reader's own thoughts and reflections. We aim to critically examine and challenge prevailing ideas in the IT industry and IT academia on what interaction design is and what it ought to be. When we write about the "how" of interaction design, we do not address *how to do* interaction design but rather *how to think about* interaction design. Hence, this book is not a complete manual on interaction design. It has to be complemented with other material where necessary skills, methods, and techniques are introduced.

In the interplay between author and reader, the better part of the work falls on the reader. The reader has to relate the material presented to her own ideas and experience. In other words, the reader's knowledge is constructed through active effort. The work of knowledge construction consists of reading and thinking, as well as discussion and debate. It is our hope that this book can stimulate discussions on digital artifacts and interaction design processes.

The field of interaction design has strong relations to several established academic fields concerned with information technology, including human-computer interaction, systems development, information systems, computer science, and software engineering.

We aim at a level of generality that makes our ideas relevant to readers from all these fields. There are, of course, differences among the fields, which, among other things, entail different understandings of design and design practice. Again, we pass on the work of doing the necessary adaptations to the reader.

We envision that this book will be used primarily in higher education, particularly within information technology–related disciplines. It may also be used in other academic fields where the aim is to develop an understanding of interaction design and digital artifacts in general. Finally, we also hope to provide IT professionals with an interesting read and some grounds for reflection on their practice.

We are grateful to many people for their contributions to our work. Håkan Edeholt, Bill Gaver, Vadim Gerasimov, Ylva Gislén, Mikael Jakobsson, Nina Lundberg, and Håkan Mannerskog provided valuable information and material. We are also thankful to two anonymous reviewers from The MIT Press. Our colleagues and students at Malmö University and Umeå University have helped us sharpen our thoughts and articulations over the years through questions, comments, and criticism. We are also deeply grateful to Harold Nelson for being an inspiration to us and for providing some of the ideas fundamental to this book. Thank you all for engaging in the thoughtful practice of interaction design.

1 | Introduction

We live in an artificial world. It is a world made up of environments, systems, processes, and things that are imagined, formed, and produced by humans. All these things have been designed, and all new things have to be designed. Someone has to decide their function, form, and structure, as well as their ethical and aesthetical qualities. In this artificial world created by humans, information technology is increasingly becoming not only a common but also a vital and fundamental part. Our designed world is full of *digital artifacts,* that is, designed things built around a core of information technology. We can find them in our workplaces, in our meeting and public spaces, and in our homes. Digital artifacts have a direct impact on our everyday lives.

Even if digital artifacts are based on technical systems, they influence our lives at individual as well as social levels. In the artificial landscape, digital artifacts constitute the environment and "nature" in which we live. They help or hinder us in almost all of our professional and everyday activities, and they influence our individual and social developments. This means that IT professionals and others involved in the design of this new environment take on a huge responsibility. To design digital artifacts is to design people's lives.

All design work results in a product of some kind. The product can be abstract or concrete. It can be something small or big, something seemingly important or unimportant. Irrespective of its constitution, the outcome of a professional design process is the result of a conscious action of a designer. This does not mean, however, that all properties and characteristics of the design process outcome are the results of intentional design decisions. Many qualities of a designed artifact are more or less unintended side effects or consequences of mistakes or lack of knowledge. The complexity of design situations prohibits completely rational approaches, which means that there can never be a perfect design process with a perfect outcome. Every digital artifact designed by an interaction designer is in some respects imperfect. Using imperfect technical artifacts causes frustration and stress, and people today are frequently dissatisfied with the digital artifacts they want to use or have to use.

It seems as if the whole business of designing digital artifacts suffers from a lack of knowledge or some kind of limitations that lead to designs that people are not happy with. Why is this? This book is built on the assumption that interaction design—which we shall define in what follows as the shaping of use-oriented qualities of a digital artifact for one or more clients—is in itself an extremely complex and difficult task. It is a unique process that cannot be prescribed or even described exhaustively. There are many books in the field purporting to address the problem by introducing methods and techniques for creating better designs. We maintain, however, that normative approaches are not enough. In order to handle the complexity of interaction design, there is a need for a reflective mind—what we would label a *thoughtful designer.*

Thoughtful interaction design is built on a thorough understanding of the design process, design ability, the designed product, and design as part of a larger context. Being thoughtful is about being reflective. To reflect means that you use your critical mind to examine your role as a designer; it requires you to examine the purpose, outcomes, and benefits of doing design in different ways, and using different methods, tools, guidelines, or theories. Being thoughtful is about caring for your own design ability, the designs you produce, and how the world will be changed by your design ideas and decisions. A thoughtful designer is someone who takes on design as a serious and important task and who tries to become a designer with the ability to create fascinating, authentic, and useful digital artifacts.

A thoughtful designer is part of a larger culture, which we call *design as knowledge construction.* In many design disciplines, emphasis has been firmly placed on the produced artifacts. The professional knowledge of design, on the other hand, has been considered more or less tacit, which is reflected for instance in the traditional design school structures of master-apprentice learning and the importance of portfolios and exhibitions. We agree that design practice and design learning are strongly dependent on these elements; however, we want to introduce the notion of a complementary perspective in which the main "products" are not artifacts, but knowledge. Design knowledge is primarily intended for other members of the knowledge construction culture—including not only designers, but also critics, clients, users, and so on—to share, debate, challenge, extend, reject, and use. This requires *articulation,* not necessarily in the form of written or spoken words, but in forms that can be appropriated and assessed by others. Parts of this book illustrate possible forms of articulation; other parts discuss the issues of what it means to be a thoughtful designer in a knowledge construction culture.

Being thoughtful is not easy, however. Interaction design is a complex process full of dilemmas and contradictions. One of the most challenging aspects is that interaction design is concerned with *digital* artifacts. The technology constituting our design material is changing so rapidly that there never seems to be time for reflection or for a more thoughtful approach. Why reflect when the things you work with are gone tomorrow and you have to deal with new technology? To a certain extent, this is a valid objection, but at the same time the core of being a designer does not necessarily change as rapidly as the material. We believe not only that there is a possibility to find a reflective position in the midst of changes created by evolving technology, but also that it is essential.

When dealing with material we know well, it is possible to work with the qualities of that material. Knowing a material well also entails knowing the drawbacks. For instance, we know that wood rots, iron rusts, and that concrete is inflexible once molded. However, we do not always have such detailed knowledge of the materials we use. Design becomes more complex when we combine different materials that each have specific qualities. It becomes very difficult when the material is a composition of both technical artifacts and social systems. If a design process aims to create an information system in an organization, then individuals, groups, and teams can be seen as kinds of material. The challenge is to design the social "components" together with the technical components as a systemic whole. Such situations challenge our design ability through their nearly infinite complexity.

Designers of digital artifacts face a particular difficulty. The material they use—that is, the digital technology—can in many ways be described as a *material without qualities*. It is certainly true that the basic technology itself has some fundamental properties. For example, it is based on electricity and on a specific kind of logic, and it normally has quite well-known features, such as a gray desktop box with a screen and keyboard attached to it. On a more general level, there are qualities we might now think of as inherent in digital material. Examples include the facilitation of many-to-many communication and the medium's dualistic nature as spatial and temporal. However, history demonstrates that most of these material qualities of digital material are constantly challenged by new technological breakthroughs and new innovations in how to use the material. Over the years, we have learned to be open to new understandings of the major defining qualities of this specific technology. So, to some extent we have to consider it a material without qualities. As a consequence, the design process becomes more open, with more degrees of freedom and therefore more complex.

Our thoughts on digital technology as a design material and its qualities, including the rhetorical notion of information technology as a material without qualities, have been stimulated by many sources, including the classic novel *The Man without Qualities* by Robert Musil. In this book, Musil discusses the relationship between thinking and creativity. Of course, Musil had no knowledge of our modern information technology when he wrote the book in the 1920s and 1930s, but his general ideas are still valid. We believe that his work has helped us formulate certain aspects of design that are traditionally not well developed in our field. In chapter 7, we further develop this relation to Musil's work.

If we accept the idea that information technology is difficult to grasp as a design material, then certain design issues come to the fore. As designers of digital artifacts, we might be closer to the conditions of the author and the writer than we are to designers working with more traditional materials. The material of the author and writer is language. Language is a material nearly without inherent qualities, perhaps similar to information technology in that respect. It is possible to create almost anything with language as a material: novels, manuals, instructions, prayers, fantasy worlds, poems, and constitutions. The responsibility for what is created is fully in the hands of the creator—the designer. Similarly, the design of digital artifacts is largely open and unbounded. This leaves us with a situation where the designer wields significant power, and with such power comes responsibility. It becomes important to ask questions about what is good and what is bad design, and about the goals to which an interaction designer should lend her skills.

1.1   What Is Good Design?

A book on design of digital artifacts is, of course, about the design of *good* digital artifacts. But what does good mean? Can it be measured or analyzed? Our basic assumption is that good is determined by many factors. To begin with, the digital artifact has to be evaluated in relation to a situation. Even though certain aspects of a digital artifact might be independent of the context, its most crucial qualities are always deeply context-dependent. An extremely fast and efficient digital artifact is hardly good design if it is not understood by its users. Outstanding user interface intelligibility is pointless if the basic functions of the artifact fail to satisfy the users' needs. An intelligent and adaptive artifact with exceptional problem-solving capabilities is worthless if it is too slow.

The good of a particular digital artifact also has to be judged in relation to the intentions and expectations present in the specific situation. This means that the artifact users' competence and skills in judging quality has a great impact on how the artifact is assessed. With a group of novice users, a sophisticated and complex artifact might be seen as bad, while a simple one might be seen as very useful.

"Good" is also defined in relation to societal laws, regulations, agreements, and contracts, and in relation to ideological considerations such as democratic, cultural, and environmental ideals. It is therefore obvious that we cannot reach a simple definition of what constitutes "good design." Such a definition is too complex to formulate once and for all. This is, however, not an argument for refraining from trying to come up with a definition. Working with design means that you continuously need to define and redefine what you think of as good design. It is a never-ending process of thoughtful reflection.

Thinking about good design is also essential for any designer who wants to improve her design ability. Since there can never be checklists or guidelines capable of determining what good design is, the designer needs highly developed *judgment* skills. This enables the designer to approach each situation in the unique way it demands. What ultimately determines the goals to strive for in a design process is formed by the individual designer's judgment—there is no other way. It might be possible to interpret this as a way to avoid the question of what good design is. Our hope, though, is that a thorough reading of this book will provide a basis for a designer who wants to enter the ongoing process of attempting to answer the question. We cannot offer any shortcuts.

A designer's most important task is to develop her judgment, by critically and independently formulating her own assumptions and beliefs. This does not mean that a designer is left all alone with all the work. There are ways to support the development of design ability.

The way we have chosen to help the designer is to present ideas and concepts that can be used for intentional reflection. We consider this to be the way of the thoughtful designer. It is a critical and reflective approach. The thoughtful designer sees her own ability as something that has to be designed. The thoughtful designer understands that theories, concepts, and ideas about design are practical intellectual tools. The thoughtful designer dares to challenge her own thinking and assumptions as a way to develop her competence and design ability.

1.2 Core Concepts

In our text, we try to keep the number of core concepts low. We have also tried to stay close to an everyday understanding of the concepts by avoiding advanced and complex definitional procedures. However, there are a few core concepts that require short introductions, since they are used throughout the book. These concepts are: interaction design, design process, design situation, and digital artifact.

Interaction design refers to the process that is arranged within existing resource constraints to create, shape, and decide all use-oriented qualities (structural, functional, ethical, and aesthetic) of a digital artifact for one or many clients.

This definition will be elaborated in connection with our discussion of design ability in chapter 3, but we may note here that it implies a rather broad scope. The words *create, shape, use-oriented,* and *digital artifact* provide hints on how the intellectual tradition of interaction design is composed. First, it is a design discipline, which means that concepts and theories from other design disciplines and from the transdisciplinary academic field of design studies are relevant in understanding and developing interaction design. The main overall motivation for this book is the need for an elaboration of what it means to assume that interaction design is a design discipline. Secondly, interaction design has a strong relation to the academic field of human-computer interaction, where the human use of digital artifacts has been studied and enhanced for over thirty years. Finally, the concentration on digital artifacts implies that all fields concerned with constructing and developing digital material contribute to the intellectual tradition of interaction design in various degrees. These fields include computer science, information systems, and software engineering.

To treat all of these fields as parts of the intellectual tradition of interaction design means that they provide concepts, ideas, and perspectives for our presentation. Our contribution lies in the selection of what material to appropriate and how to fashion it into a more or less coherent whole.

The *design process* begins when the initial ideas concerning a possible future take shape. The process goes on all the way to a complete and final specification that can function as a basis for construction or production. In some cases, the final specification is identical to the final product. We do not distinguish between processes that lead to construction of new technology and processes that lead to the composition of an artifact by assembling readymade components or configuring an off-the-shelf product. In both cases, the work constitutes a design process.

Design is always carried out in a context. The concept *design situation* refers to the situation that is both the reason for the design process to be initiated and the context within which the design work is carried out. One simple case is when an organization perceives the need for new information technology support. They ask someone to act as a designer and work with the people in the organization. In this scenario, the organization more or less becomes the design situation. In other cases, the limits of the design situation are not as clear-cut. For instance, when design is performed for a mass market on the Internet, the delimitation of the design situation becomes more complex. Another example is when design is carried out for products that people will use in their homes, their cars, or carry in their shirt pockets. A designer is always charged with figuring out the situation at hand, what should be considered to be part of the design situation, and what can be left out. The design situation therefore becomes a core concept in interaction design. The situation is the starting point for the design, as well as the more or less malleable target for interventions through design. In other words, the design situation evolves along with the design process. The "now" that exists when the design process starts is not unaffected by the design work and its outcomes. Design amounts to standing in the "now" with the task of studying possible futures, or ways in which the design situation might evolve due to our intervention.

The result of an interaction design process is what we choose to call a *digital artifact*. An artifact refers to "something made by humans." This concept is normally used to denote physical objects, but it can be used in a broader sense as well. We use "digital artifact" in this book to refer to artifacts whose core structure and functionality are made possible by the use of information technology. Moreover, we limit our studies to digital artifacts that operate in rather close relations with humans in social contexts. For instance, we will not address automated processes or fully embedded components unless they have a direct relation to users. This follows from our focus on interaction design and use-oriented qualities as opposed to information technology design in general.

Digital artifacts are commonly referred to by such terms as systems, programs, or products. In our text, we will occasionally use these terms in order to reflect the common language in the domain we happen to be discussing. They are, in general, to be regarded as synonyms to digital artifacts without any more precise connotations intended.

There are many roles and many people involved in design. The ones we will be mentioning most frequently are the designer, the client, and the user. We have tried to keep the meaning of these roles as simple as possible. A *designer* is any person who actively takes part in the shaping of the digital artifact. A *client* is a person or an organization contracting with the designer. The client typically pays for the design work and makes final decisions about whether the results are acceptable. A *user* is a person who will be using the digital artifact when it is implemented.

Of course, more elaborate schemes of roles are prevalent in professional IT practice. There, we typically find that our generic "designer" role is divided into a number of specializations, such as information architects, graphic designers, interface programmers, and so on. Similarly, our generic categories of "clients" and "users" are often refined to include, for example, legislators or user organization representatives. The intention behind our using a more simple set of roles is that the arguments we present reside on a more generic level, and are therefore applicable to several specialized roles after suitable appropriation and adaptation.

1.3 What Is Design Theory?

This book can be viewed as an attempt to contribute to a design theory; that is, it contains ideas about the essence and nature of design work that are intended to support designers in becoming more proficient. But what is design theory and to what extent can it be of any practical use? These questions can only be answered in relation to some basic assumptions about design work.

Our basic assumption about the design process is that its form, structure, and qualities are not given or ruled by laws of nature. Design work is given form and structure by designers' own thoughts, considerations, and actions. Its character is influenced by people's habits, traditions, and practice. This means that *knowledge for design* should, to a large extent, be thought of as *knowledge about design*. Knowledge about design concerns differences in design traditions and practices, limitations in the design process, and the nature of design thinking.

Design theory can be seen as knowledge that can liberate the designer from preconceived notions and conceptions of how the design process can and should be performed.

Liberation is not enough, however. As a designer, you might also need help in creating order and meaning in a complex world. This can be done by making the complex less complex by organizing, structuring, and categorizing. Hence we identify a second purpose of design theory—to function as a conceptual tool that will help us create some kind of order in a chaotic world of practice.

Design theory is also knowledge focused on creating new conditions for design, different patterns of thinking and acting, new design examples, and a general understanding of the conditions for creative and innovative work.

There are, of course, many different definitions and understandings of what design theory is and what it should be. In some cases, design theory is seen as a way to specify the outcome of the design process. For instance, there are several design theories advocating an environmental approach. They are formulated with the goal of influencing design work in the direction of more environmentally sound products. Other theories are based on ideological foundations, oriented, for instance, toward making the design process more democratic. Every theory is formulated with an intention and a purpose. This makes it impossible to assess them by simple comparisons. Theories might all be good at supporting their specific purposes, but still be exceptionally different in character and nature.

Our definition of design theory is based on our intention to discuss design in a way that helps interaction designers improve their design ability by exercising thoughtful design. The definition is therefore focused on design as skill, knowledge, and competence. Our definition of design theory is also process-oriented, with an emphasis on design thinking and design action.

1.4   A First Sketch of the Design Process

To design is to create something new. Design is not the same as problem solving in the mathematical or logical sense. Based on the actual meaning of the words *problem* and *solving,* problem solving implies that certain problems exist and that they are solvable. In most areas, problem solving also implies that it is possible to determine if a problem is solved or not. Most important, problem solving implies that a solution is either right or wrong. However, in design there are no correct answers. Every design proposal is formulated in a close relationship with a changing and growing understanding of the situation (the *problem*). Since this is an ongoing process, it is never possible to determine whether a design proposal is right or wrong. Still, we may note that a designer's current understanding of a design situation is commonly referred to as the "problem," and her ideas on how to proceed are called "solutions." We will adhere to this convention, but we would like to emphasize that the words mean different things in design than they do in formal logic.

Every design process is unique. The preconditions for design work change from one occasion to the next. This means that design work is impossible to predict. If the outcome *can* be predicted, it is by definition not a design process. Every design process is affected by the people responsible for carrying out the work and by existing conditions, such as available staff, tools, and time. The process is also a consequence of the specifics of the design situation at hand. The combination of these three elements—the designer, the resources, and the situation—is always unique, which makes every design process an *ultimate particular* (Nelson and Stolterman 2003), that is, an ultimately unique instance of a design process. Even though this process might have a lot of characteristics in common with other design processes, it is still never possible to fully prescribe or predict. Ultimately particular processes create specific conditions for the designer.

For instance, design is about uncertainty. To participate in design work means that you, as a designer, play a part in a venture that involves great risks. Design involves chance; it forces you to challenge the unknown and to create the not-yet-existing.

Design is very much an ethical activity. Every design process is a combination of actions, choices, and decisions that affects people's lives and possible choices for action.

As such, design is deeply influenced by values and ideals. In every design, no matter how small, there are always choices that in different ways will lead toward or away from those values. There is an ever-present ethical dimension in design, manifested in the most practical choices and decisions.

Design is also an aesthetical activity. Design processes fill our world with artifacts that influence our lives not only by their functionality but also by their form and the way we experience them in use situations. The importance of aesthetical aspects in design cannot be overestimated. We are all living in a world almost completely artificial and designed, and every new addition, every new design adding to this world, has an impact on how we experience the whole. Every design is a change of our life world; the designer influences our overall experience of the world as a pleasant or ugly place to spend our lives in.

Design is also a political and ideological activity. Since every design affects our possibilities for actions and our way of being in the world, it becomes a political and ideological action. With designed artifacts, processes, systems, and structures we decide our relations with each other, society, and nature. Each design is carrying a set of basic assumptions about what it means to be human, to live in a society, to work, and to play. When looking at large infrastructural designs, such as the way we organize society and companies or large technical systems, most people realize how they affect the way we can live our lives. We would like to point out that the same also holds true in a small-scale perspective. Every digital artifact restricts our space of possible actions by permitting certain actions, promoting certain skills, and focusing on certain outcomes. To some extent, the user has to adapt to the artifact. Since all designs influence our lives, they become manifestations of political and ideological ideas. People often dismiss the relation between ideology and design as insignificant, in terms of impact as well as importance. We believe this to be a mistake. The role of digital artifacts has to be recognized and measured in relation to the way they have a real impact on our lives.

This view of design, this first sketch, leads to a realization that design includes *responsibility*. Since design is unique, ethical, aesthetical, political, and ideological, it puts pressure on the designer. Even if we, as designers, think that we are only designing artifacts that are extremely small in relation to an almost infinitely complex reality, we cannot escape our responsibility. The most minute, seemingly insignificant, change of the whole can have large and unexpected consequences. Someone might argue, "As a designer I am only satisfying my client, so the client has the responsibility." It is a common situation that a client hires a designer to get help with difficult decisions in a design process. The client has the overall responsibility for the outcome, but a designer is still responsible for the result she produces and hands over to the client. It is important to acknowledge the complex relationships between the client, the designer, and the user in the design work.

1.5 The Amazing Design

In every design process, there are situations when the designer is "forced" to be creative—to be able to see people, things, and situations in a new way, and to be able to handle contradictions, dilemmas, and conflicts. At the same time, the designer needs the ability to cooperate, understand other people's views, and present and argue for her own ideas and proposals. Given all of these considerations design is challenging and exciting, but also difficult enough to induce anxiety and stress.

Personal engagement and personal expression are vital aspects of good design. A designer has to be prepared to engage in the process not only as a skilled professional, but also as a creative individual. A job where you have to be engaged and where you have to find ways to express your own ideas is stimulating, of course, but it can also be highly demanding.

In most cases design is a very practical and concrete activity, or at least an activity that will have very practical consequences. Design is about shaping the world we live in by creating the conditions, opportunities, and restrictions that will make up that world. Design means that you influence people's work, leisure, and everyday life (including travel, economy, communication, entertainment, and so on). From this perspective, design is an amazing activity—it enables people to engage in creating the reality in which they spend their lives. A designer has a chance to do something of importance.

Design is also amazing since it deals with profound and existential issues in a very tangible way. As a designer, you have to think about the relation between what *can* be done and what *ought* to be done. Design reveals, in its very practical activities, deeply philosophical questions concerning how people can and should live their lives, as well as questions about the environment in which we live. A designer has to think about how the artificial environment where we spend most of our time should be designed. Design forces us to challenge the present and makes us think about the basic conditions of our society. This holds for interaction design as well as for any other design field. Digital artifacts contribute to shaping the way people can live their lives; they become important parts of people's everyday environment.

Design is about will and desire. It is driven by a will for change. Almost any attempt to make a change will face some kind of resistance. This means that the person who pushes for change must be brave and prepared to take on the resistance in a suitable way. To do this, the designer needs to be convinced of the strength of her proposal and to trust her judgment. Facing this kind of resistance can be exciting since it leads to ongoing learning and development, but it can also be frustrating and create doubt and insecurity.

On the whole, design is a diverse and complex activity, full of contradictions and dilemmas. Being a designer is demanding, but it is also something that can be extremely fascinating, exciting, and rewarding.

1.6   Everyday Practicalities of Design

In this introductory chapter, we have stated that design can be both amazing and frustrating. The frustration is not only a consequence of the fact that fundamental ethical, aesthetical, and functional considerations in a design project might seem overwhelming. Design is also carried out within social and organizational contexts that have particular limitations and restrictions. On a practical level, there is only a certain amount of resources and time at the designer's disposal. There will always be demands and preconditions that cannot be changed. There might be an unpredictable client or decision maker. There are an infinite number of conflicting wishes, requests, and demands. There can be power struggles and conflicts. All of these considerations belong to the *everyday practicalities* of design. Situations where a designer can choose and create the most ideal way to carry out the design work are extremely rare, to say the least.

To be a designer does not mean that you have to get rid of all obstacles. The real task for the designer is to develop something of lasting quality in the most suitable and creative way given the existing conditions. To do this, the designer has to challenge existing conceptions and restrictions that are based on false assumptions. Blaming a poor design on the preconditions and the situation is not a way to avoid responsibility, even though it may be a way to explain certain decisions and results. Having limited resources and time can sometimes even stimulate creative and innovative thinking. Being successful in design means being able to handle the everyday practicalities, and to deal successfully (or at least adequately) with difficult technical and social contexts.

1.7   Design and Society

Every design, however small, is a part of what can be seen as the largest design project of them all—the joint design of the world as a place for human life. Design is one of the more active processes in this attempt to make the world a better place. As we have stated earlier, in the light of these dynamics, every design has technical, social, ideological, and political consequences.

So what is expected of a designer? The client who contracts with a designer is driven by needs and wishes. The designer, however, has other considerations as well. For a professional designer, it is not enough to make the client happy. A designer is also a citizen in a society and a member of a group that possesses specific professional knowledge. Consequently, the designer has the power to change and influence the development of society, which implies significant responsibility. It is a responsibility that transcends the particular conditions of the project and the contract with the client. For instance, an architect who only considers the wishes of the client without caring for other societal goals, such as an overall city plan, or the character of the surrounding environment, will be subject to severe criticism.

An interaction designer participates in this ongoing discussion about the development of information technology and its role in the society. Participation does not have to be in the form of public appearances and debates, but it is unavoidably manifested in the digital artifacts that are designed and produced. Every profession has its own internal debates about and control of what constitutes proper professional behavior and good quality. In many cases, the most knowledgeable and severe criticism of a design project may come from colleagues.

To be the designer of the city library information system can be exciting but also revealing, since your work will be open to inspection by anyone who visits the library. Criticism of digital artifacts is not an established practice, as is the case in architecture, industrial design, and other more visible and established design fields. This may change since interaction design is gradually becoming one of the most influential design fields in contemporary society. Interaction design is the source of an increasing number of products that make up people's everyday lives. A more developed discipline of interaction design criticism may appear in the near future. We would welcome such a development.

Whether design is seen as amazing or frustrating, or from a narrow or a broad point of view, any designer has to develop her own understanding of its essence and character. Difficult questions have to be posed; dominant conceptions have to be challenged. This is something every thoughtful interaction designer has to do. We hope that this book offers some of the necessary tools for this critical and reflective venture.

1.8   Book Overview

As we have stated, this book primarily addresses the IT industry and IT academia. Its purpose is to introduce a design perspective to familiar materials and processes and to provide conceptual tools to help the reader ponder the implications of this perspective.

One of our basic assumptions is that many of the important aspects and questions on design are generic and therefore applicable to most design fields. This assumption plays out in the text in several ways. In many cases, we discuss theories and philosophical dimensions of design without clearly stating *what* is being designed. The connection to interaction design is mostly expressed in the examples we use, which are all about the design of digital artifacts. In this way, we hope to create a broad general understanding of design and a more specific preparedness for interaction design.

Chapter 2 is about the design process, its nature and character. We outline a view of the process that differs somewhat from the typical assumptions underlying the literature on methods and techniques in the IT field. The chapter covers the development from initial idea to final specification. The design process is also discussed as a social process where the role of the designer in relation to other participants and stakeholders is examined.

At the very core of interaction design is the designer herself. Chapter 3 considers what constitutes a thoughtful designer. We also discuss some ways for a designer to develop her design ability.

In chapter 4 we examine a selection of methods and techniques for interaction design. The chapter is meant to support critical reflection on design methods and techniques rather than to provide how-to guidelines. We have selected methods and techniques for consideration based on their correspondence with our general perspective on design, which means that they represent contributions from several academic fields involved in the intellectual tradition of interaction design.

Chapter 5 moves on to the outcome of the design process, that is, the digital artifacts as designed products with certain qualities. The view of the design process and the designer's ability that was outlined in previous chapters hinges on a repertoire of exemplars, a sense of quality, and a language for articulating the use-oriented qualities of digital artifacts. Chapter 5 illustrates how these requirements can be met.

The preceding chapters are largely oriented toward an insider's perspective on interaction design. In chapter 6, we zoom out to consider the large-scale conditions for design. We relate interaction design to other design disciplines, design history, and the technological developments in our field.

In the last chapter, chapter 7, the basic ideas of the book are revisited. We return to Robert Musil and his novel *The Man without Qualities* in order to draw out the main themes of our exposition.

Interaction design is a heterogeneous field drawing on several academic disciplines. The amount of potentially relevant literature for a thoughtful interaction designer is overwhelming. Consequently, we conclude the book with an annotated bibliography, which is intended to provide some useful guidance in the diverse literature of interest to our field.

2   The Process

There are many ways to describe the uniqueness of design, and many theories explaining what design is really about. Such theories usually focus on a specific aspect of design, such as creativity, teamwork, management, social aspects, aesthetic or ethical aspects, or analytical or visual thinking. Some have even tried to capture the whole design process in a complete model or methodology. In the information technology (IT) field, there are many such theories, all possibly valuable and useful. But they can never be comprehensive or complete in any sense. Anyone who tries to "use" or "follow" these theories or models must understand their inherent limitations.

We believe that the design process is too complex and diverse to fully describe in any universal or general way. At the same time, however, we realize that a designer needs a description, model, or theory that can help her plan, organize, navigate, and evaluate her work. All this leads to the conclusion that in order to be able to "use" explicit theories and models, the designer has to remain critical. The designer needs to be critical toward any description of the design process, and to appropriate aspects of it rather than adopt it completely. This is the *thoughtful design stance* advocated in this book. The designer has to rely on her own reflective and critical mind, based on a thoughtful understanding of how design can serve a purpose.

Our description of the design process will not be in the form of a method, techniques, or distinct phases. We will try to portray the process by focusing on some aspects that are not usually addressed in IT design methodologies. Our purpose is to show how these aspects are to a great extent the basis for a thoughtful understanding of the design process. They form a set of starting points from which theories and methodologies can be evaluated and examined, appropriated, and brought to use.

Our main focus is on the early parts of the design process. This is where the designer gets involved in design work, establishes a preliminary understanding of the situation, navigates through available information, and initiates all necessary relationships with clients, users, decision makers, and so forth. Based on all this, she creates a design proposal.

In the first section of this chapter we present a brief overview of the scope of the design process from initial idea to final specification (see figure 2.1). We then discuss the design process as a *thinking* activity and as a *social* activity. We conclude with some comments on how the process can be organized and managed.

2.1 From Vision to Specification

A design process begins in the moment when a designer is "thrown into," or thinks about, the environment where she is supposed to act, or in the moment when she is assigned to a particular design task. This is usually the moment when the designer is exposed to the background material, a problem statement, a list of requirements, or a task description for the first time. In some cases, it might be the designer who initiates the design process.

We want to emphasize that the design process begins earlier than what is usually realized. In traditional methodologies, particularly within fields such as information systems development and software engineering, the process does not formally start before a plan is in place and there have been several meetings about what is supposed to be done. However, the actual design work has begun much earlier. This is especially true in regards to the *design of the design process,* which may well be the most important design work in a typical project. In the design of the process, which takes place very early in a project, it is decided to what extent the process will focus on early phases, creative and innovative work, new technology, the organization in question, users, the needs of the client, analysis, and specification. These early decisions create the "container" and the conditions for the subsequent process.

Our message is that this kind of design of the design process requires *thoughtful design.* It entails reflecting on the larger picture, the overall role of the design work, the approach to be used, the need for skills and competence, and so on. Dealing with such complexity demands a critical and reflective mind—the mind of a thoughtful designer.

Before focusing on the actual design process, we have to touch upon some fundamental aspects of the process. They are fundamental because they cannot be separated from the process and do not belong to a particular phase or activity. They are present throughout the process. One of these fundamental aspects is the *recurrent leaping between details and the whole,* or between the concrete and the abstract. In many cases, the designer has strong initial ideas about what should be done, or what constitutes an innovative solution, but is also facing a very chaotic situation that requires a practical solution. It is then necessary to move rapidly and repeatedly between the world of ideas and the concrete reality of the design situation. Sometimes, this process can seem cum-

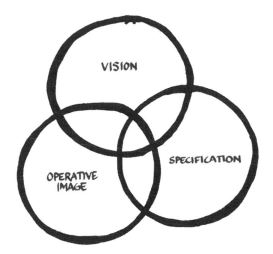

Figure 2.1
The three abstraction levels of the design process influence each other in a fully dynamic dialectical process.

bersome and an obstacle to creating a good design process, but it is in fact a necessary and natural part of design work. Accepting this reality and dealing with it is better than hiding behind a model of design work that appears rational or logical.

Another fundamental aspect is that any design process is characterized by *dilemmas*. A dilemma is not a problem in the logical sense, since it does not have one given solution. In fact, it does not have a solution at all in the most basic sense of the word. Instead, we know that something is a dilemma when we realize that the situation involves choices that all lead to unsatisfactory solutions. The complexity of design and the nature of dilemmas make creativity fundamental. In a dilemma situation, there is no chance that we could simply find a solution within the existing framework of the situation, because there is no solution hidden in the situation. Instead, a dilemma can only be resolved by a creative leap, by transcending the limitations of the present. Since design is inevitably concerned with dilemma situations, creative thinking becomes one of the fundamental aspects of the process. So, both the leaping between details and the whole and the creative transcendence of given boundaries have to be seen as underlying all the other aspects of the process we will discuss in this chapter.

We distinguish among three levels of abstraction in early design work: the vision, the operative image, and the specification. When a designer is confronted with a design situation, a *vision* emerges. If the designer is experienced, an initial vision will probably emerge very early in the process, especially if the situation reminds her of similar situations from previous design experiences. Even if we view the vision as something emerging, it comes from the mind of the designer. However, we want to point out that a vision is not necessarily a conscious and deliberate decision. On the contrary, it often seems to be an intuitive, immediate, and almost instinctive reaction to the situation at hand.

The way we define a vision is not as a solution or a specification. It should be thought of as a *first organizing principle* that helps the designer to structure the initial attempts to respond to the situation at hand (Nelson and Stolterman 2003).

A vision can take on different forms. It can be a preliminary idea about a basic technical solution or an infrastructure, a thought about an essential function in a new design, or an image of a certain style or form. At this early stage, the vision is only in the mind of the designer and it is usually sketchy and diffuse.

As an example, we can imagine a designer who meets a new client for the first time. The designer is told that she is expected to create a new solution for the company's internal database of all employees. The client tells the designer how things work in the present situation and why they are considering a new system. The basic argument is that they have several systems that do not communicate, which means that when information about an employee is changed, it has to be updated in many different places. Depending on who the designer is, different visions might emerge. To one designer the vision might be a "unified database," to someone else an "improved user interface," and to yet another a "technical infrastructure." These or other visions will follow the designer through the design process and influence her analysis, studies, ideas, thoughts, and proposals.

A problem, and at the same time a strength, of a vision is that it is *elusive* and *contradictory.* In the early stages of design, there will be several visions "fighting" to be realized. The early design process is more or less a chaos of conflicting visions, of details struggling to become part of a whole, of practical circumstances causing "damage" to abstract ideas. A typical example is the vision based on the idea of a specific form and the use of a specific material. As is often the case, it might turn out that the envisioned form cannot be implemented with the envisioned material. So, even if the vision actually guides the design process, it might also be contradictory.

Contradiction is not necessarily a bad property of a vision. In fact, the strength of the vision may lie in its contradictory nature. Within a contradictory vision, different and opposing ideas can be held together and support the designer in her subsequent work. The fact that a vision can simultaneously be diffuse and detailed, abstract and concrete, makes it a conceptual tool that helps the designer in working with complex real situations where many demands and desires struggle to be fulfilled. Ultimately, the vision is the designer's first organizing principle.

During the next stage of the design process, which typically lasts a relatively short time, the designer develops an initial version of the *operative image*. The operative image is a first externalization of the vision. It starts out as a diffuse image and is usually captured in simple sketches, sometimes with the help of metaphors or analogies. As the process continues, the operative image is given more defined shape and becomes a more solid foundation for design work. This development unfolds as a dialectical play between the situation at hand and the operative image, and between the operative image and the vision. Since all three of these things can be quite different in character, structure, and level of detail, the dialectic relationships function as an "engine"—catalyzing or releasing energy that can be transformed into new ideas.

The tensions among the situation, the vision, and the operative image have to be overcome, which "forces" the designer to be creative. An important implication of our conceptualization of the design process so far is that it facilitates or necessitates creativity. This is in contrast with views of design where creativity is seen as the starting point of the process. For designers, our message might be helpful. It says that design is not necessarily a process where a person sits down and waits for the creative spark or insight that will tell her what to do. Instead, it says that a designer has to delve into the situation, and all its dilemmas and complexity, with an open mind. If she is sincere in her approach, she will come up with a vision and can start working on an operative image. When the designer has reached that point, the complexity in the relationships between the situation, the vision, and the operative image will "force" creative work, which then tends to come naturally in response.

The operative image is probably the most important part of the design process. It has the function of bridging the abstract and elusive vision to the concrete and complex situation. Both the vision and the view of the situation will change over time. When new details are added to the operative image, the situation will look different. They will also influence the vision and vice versa. What finally decides how this process will move forward is the designer's ability to refine the operative image.

The operative image is usually stabilized at the time when more visible and "productive" design work begins. In the structured work following the initial phase, the operative image will be put to test. It will be challenged by new conditions, restrictions, demands, and possibilities. The image becomes increasingly detailed and complete.

Many times a designer will feel that the operative image has to be changed into something inferior—that is, the distance from the original vision increases instead of decreases. This usually happens due to changing conditions or the fact that the designer actually decides to alter the vision. As the designer learns more about a situation, new ideas and possibly new visions will arise.

A defining quality of the operative image is that it is operational. This means it will have an explicit form that enables manipulation, simulation, and visualization. Perhaps most important, an operative image enables communication. The operative image will become ever more detailed through all these procedures and is eventually transformed into a specification of the final design.

In the example mentioned earlier where the vision took the form of a "technical infrastructure," the first operative image can be created with simple structural sketches that capture the relation between parts and the whole. Initially, the sketch is crude and can hardly be called a design. Perhaps consisting of simple lines representing an envisioned structure, the sketch can still be used in discussions with other designers and participants. If the designer instead started with an "improved user interface" as the vision, the process would have taken a different path. The operative image could then be realized in sketches of screen layouts and a structure of user functions. It is not possible to say that one way is wrong and the other is right, since that would require a well-defined problem with a solution that could be measured in terms of correctness. In real design situations this is never the case. In this example, both a technical infrastructure and an improved user interface are possible operative images and can only be judged as good or bad in relation to a vision, the particular design situation, and the overall purpose of the design process.

When the operative image is sufficiently detailed, the person formally responsible for the design process makes a decision that it will function as a *specification* of the final design. After this point, another process begins which can be labeled the construction process. During this stage, the task is to produce a concrete and final artifact, based on the specification. Even in this step, many new design issues will appear, since new demands, problems, and opportunities will arise. There is no clear division between design and construction. In the design process, there will always be considerations based on constructional issues, and in the construction process new design situations inevitably come up. In the previous example, the final specification will probably be closely related to the predominant vision. In the case where the vision is based on the idea of a new infrastructure, the final specification might be focused on the envisioned technical platform and how the present system might be moved and adapted to the new infrastructure. In the case of a vision based on an improved user interface, the specification will probably be built around the specific interfaces and focused on how the present system can be adapted to the new form.

At this stage, it is important to state again that we are not talking about a linear process nor an iterative process. Instead it is a *fully dynamic dialectical* process. The vision, the operative image, and the specification influence each other continuously.

The fact that all of this happens at the same time does not in itself prohibit an understanding of the design process. To the contrary, our highly relational and reciprocal description corresponds well with the image of the design process given by many professional information systems designers (Stolterman 1991). Practicing designers usually find it very difficult to separate certain steps or phases of the design process. To them, it is all about a process where you move from a complex and open situation to a more focused and operational one.

It is this web of relationships in constant change and development that we call the *design process*. In different parts of the process, the designer makes choices on how to acknowledge and handle the complexity of the process. To an artist, working in a highly creative process, the dynamics of the process might be the dominant experience. The artist modifies sketches, which lead to new ideas about the artwork, which in turn affects the ideas the artist want to express, which influences subsequent sketches, and so forth.

In other processes, such as in engineering, most participants would agree that complex and dynamic relationships between the vision and the operational image receive full attention in the very early phases of the process, while they are later suppressed in favor of a much more controlled process. In a field such as engineering, the idea is to stabilize the specification as soon as possible, by fighting changes and influences that might challenge it.

The way that a generative task is approached—whether as an engineering problem, an artistic exploration, or an intentional design process—is a choice that has important consequences for how the design process can and will be conducted. Even though we cannot judge one of these three approaches as generically better or worse than the others, we do know that the responsibility lies with the designer. In every design situation, even when taking into account all restrictions and limitations, there are still an unlimited number of possible visions and operative images. A design situation can never be restricted to the extent that there is only one solution, because if that were the case, it is, by definition, not a design situation.

2.2 Design as a Thought Process

So far, we have described design on a more conceptual level, but it is also a process of thought in the mind of the individual designer. When we focus on design as a thought process, we do this from the perspective of thoughtful design. This means that we will not take a prescriptive approach, but rather introduce certain aspects of design thinking that might seem strange and perhaps irrational. The idea that underlies this chapter is that to be good at design, you have to understand what seems to be the "nature" of design thinking. Of course, there is no "natural" way to do design, but there are recurrent and common characteristics in the design process. The perspective of thoughtful design implies that the first prerequisite for change and development in design thinking is to have a deeper understanding of design as such. Armed with this kind of knowledge, it is possible to start "designing" your own way of design thinking.

2.2.1 The Problem and the Solution

One of the most fundamental things to know about design is that an understanding of the design situation is established in parallel with the first design proposals. At the same time a designer starts to formulate a problem—that is, a specific interpretation of the design situation—a solution is also formulated. Note here that we use the word *problem* to refer to a designer's current understanding of a design situation, and the word *solution* to refer to the designer's idea on how to shape her intervention in the situation. This is in line with common usage of the terms in design, but different from the logical notion of a problem as an exhaustive specification and a solution as an answer that can be either right or wrong.

A common idea in IT fields such as information systems, software engineering, or human-computer interaction is to assume that the timeline demands the problem to be clearly defined before a solution can be devised. However, we have already mentioned that a vision is formed at the very first contact with the design situation. This vision will change, develop, be criticized, and maybe rejected in favor of some other vision, but it is certainly present and is going to affect the thinking and decisions of the designer. The vision even influences what the designer chooses as a foundation for the work and what is deemed important enough to require analysis. In a design situation, there is never enough time to examine and analyze everything with equal care. Decisions and choices have to be made, and the vision influences all of these decisions and choices.

It is also not possible to finalize a description of the design situation without simultaneously working with a solution proposal. There is no way a designer can say that she understands the situation before having struggled with ideas for solutions. Through this work, new insights on the character and nature of the situation are gained. In this sense, the search for design solutions is also a way of revealing the design situation.

Donald Schön has influenced many design thinkers with his ideas on the nature of practical, action-oriented knowledge. In his work, Schön (1987) focuses on professional design fields where there are no right or wrong answers, only actions and consequences. He discusses what knowledge is needed and how it is used and creates an outline for an idealized design process that looks like this:

▪ It starts in a situation where the actor applies common concepts, strategies, and interpretations of what she sees and formulations of what she is planning to do. The actor does not spend a lot of time and energy in the determination of what strategies and interpretations to use. It could be argued that the knowledge is "tacit" in the sense that the designer will probably not be able to describe it, only to act in accordance with it.

▪ Then something happens: A well-known action leads to a result that in one way or another surprises the actor.

▪ The surprise makes the actor reflect on what happened and what caused the unexpected result. The reflection is more or less conscious, but maybe not expressed in words. The actor tries to relate what she sees to similar situations in her previous experience.

▪ The actor's reflection is a questioning of the familiar assumptions that were the basis for her decisions and actions. In this new situation, she can rethink her strategies for action, create new interpretations, and formulate new agendas for what to do.

▪ The new ideas are used as a basis for improvised experimentation, where the actor tries new actions to explore the unexpected result, test her understanding, or evaluate new ways of doing things. These experiments can create new surprises.

Schön's description of this chain of events is not strange or difficult to comprehend, and it helps us to understand some important aspects of what it means to approach a design situation. Schön describes this approach as a kind of *conversation* between the designer and the situation. The designer asks questions of the situation—through actions or "design moves" rather than words. She listens to the replies and adapts her further actions accordingly. This can be understood as the designer's way of testing her vision against the situation.

If design is understood, in Schön's terms, as *reflection-in-action* and *reflection-on-action,* it is easier to understand why the problem and the solution have to evolve in parallel. While trying to solve a problem the way we currently understand it, we create situations that will surprise us; that is, we will *learn* something we did not know. These surprises, this learning, form the basis for the questioning and development of new creative solutions. This kind of learning cannot be achieved without working with solutions, since we need them to find out if we are moving in the desired direction. Another argument for this kind of experimentation with solutions and creating surprises is that it reveals the knowledge that we might possess in tacit, or at least hitherto unarticulated, forms. It forces us to find out things, not only about the situations in question, but also about our own knowledge and ourselves.

So design should be seen as a conversation with the situation and as experimentation where we as designers have to be good "listeners" and "readers" of the situation.

The psychologist James Hillman (1996) talks about the *authentic attention* needed to fully grasp the reality around us. The relevance of this concept for our discussion is that a designer needs to understand the situation she is supposed to change with her design. The notion of authentic attention involves a special way of approaching reality with *carefulness* and *concern*. If a designer does not take this approach, important knowledge that can and will affect the success of a proposed design will be lost.

Carefulness and concern help the designer to recognize alternatives and to be prepared for unexpected events and insights. First of all, they show how the designer's own actions are a natural part not only in a learning process, but also in a knowledge creation process. In this sense, *good design work is knowledge creation and production*. Its ways and conditions are different from those of research, but it is a powerful way of producing knowledge.

As designers, we have to be aware that we can, and have to, work with several different visions and operative images in our exploration of a design situation. We have to accept that there are no problems to take for granted and no given solutions to be deduced. We create "problems" and "solutions" at the same time and in parallel, in a process where they coevolve.

For example, assume that an interaction designer is confronted with a situation where the client has a problem: The internal network used in the client's company cannot manage the present demand for communication capacity. Based on such a problem statement, the solution is obviously an increase in the capacity of communication channels. But if the designer questions the problem-as-stated, other solutions may appear. For instance, the designer might investigate the situation underlying the original problem statement and find that changing the design of the information management procedures currently in use can drastically reduce the need for communication capacity. In this new situation, the problem is no longer the capacity of communication channels, but rather the ways in which the company manages information needs and information flows. This new "solution" does not only indicate what could be done, it also helps to create new knowledge about the present situation.

Being a designer who works like this requires *courage*. It takes courage to avoid the simple solutions, to challenge the present situation, to oppose simplistic interpretations of what makes a proper solution. A common reaction is to question why a designer should spend time and money on exploring a design situation when the problem is already obvious. Such a reaction is not based on a proper understanding of design. A thoughtful designer is someone who knows the limitations and opportunities of design and understands how to handle them in a unique design situation. It is someone who understands that design is a thinking process, which means that almost everything of importance in a design process is a result of thinking rather than preconditions, limitations, or "obvious problems." If necessary, a thoughtful designer takes on the responsibility of educating the client, users, or anyone else involved in the process, in order to better facilitate a thoughtful design process.

2.2.2 The Process and Levels of Abstraction

From a distance, a design process might look like a straight line from the abstract to the concrete—that is, from the vision, via an increasingly detailed operative image, to a complete specification and a final product. But, if we take a closer look at this "straight line," we will find that it shows a completely different structure. The path moves up and down, from abstract ideas about a vague vision to very concrete work on a specific detail. What seemed to be a straight line is only the mean value of the process over time.

The path of the design process over time is illustrated in figure 2.2. The up and down movement can be interpreted as a consequence of reflection-in-action and reflection-on-action. Design moves result in surprises, forcing the designer to reconsider her basic assumptions. A surprise may occur during work on a concrete detail of the project and overthrow decisions already made at a more abstract level.

The path of the process shows that design is not about logical calculation or deduction from a given situation to a given solution. Empirical design studies show that designers' sketches in the early phases of the process are extremely *ad hoc* and appear random to the observer. In these sketches, one can find attempts to visualize fundamental structures or forms. At the same time, there are sketches showing the very specific solution of a detail or the choice of a certain material. For instance, when a designer is thinking about a new digital artifact, her first sketches might be details describing the

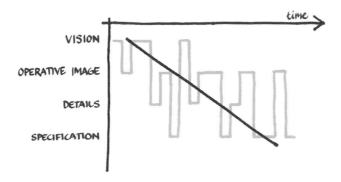

Figure 2.2
The design process as a whole moves from vision to specification, but the path is not straight and linear.

layout of specific screens, simple boxes and lines representing the overall information flow, or a sketch of the actual physical room where the artifact will reside. To an observer, this mix of sketches at different levels might seem irrational, but for the designer, they all connect and influence each other.

The apparently erratic path of the design process might seem unreliable, perhaps even scary to the inexperienced designer. Since the up and down movement and changes in course are not an explicit part of most design methodologies, the inexperienced designer might feel as if they are "wrong." The truth is that change happens in every design process. There is nothing wrong with it; rather, it is a consequence of the concepts we have introduced earlier in this chapter. It is a sign of the way in which a designer approaches a situation, explores possible actions, and expands available knowledge.

2.2.3 Questioning

We have already touched upon the necessity for the designer to ask questions and critically examine assumptions and preconditions. In design work aiming at innovation, this becomes even more important. Asking questions is not only a way to learn more about the preconditions; if done seriously, it is a way of challenging the whole understanding of the existing situation. When a client tells a designer to solve a problem, a fundamental reaction is to ask why.

The "why question" challenges old ideas that have settled over time and opens up new avenues of thought. On many occasions, it may sound a bit silly to ask why, but this can be seen as a sign that the question has actually reached an assumption that is elevated to truth status by tradition. To challenge the truth always sounds a bit silly, but a designer should not be afraid of looking silly sometimes. It might be necessary if you really want to understand the conditions of a design situation. Here is a small example:

Client (C):   I need a digital calendar. Can you design one for me? What would it look like?

Designer (D):   Why do you need a digital calendar?

C: I can't fit all my meetings in the small calendar I have now, and I still want a calendar that is small enough for my pocket.

D: Why can't you change your work so you don't need to go to all those meetings?

C: Well, it is my job. . . . I just have to.

D: Why do you need to carry your calendar in your pocket?

C: I don't want to go back to my office between every meeting.

D: Wouldn't it be a good idea to organize your work so you could have a short break in your own office between meetings?

This conversation may sound a bit embarrassing to most people. The designer asks seemingly unnecessary questions, but in some cases the answers can uncover unseen and alternative solutions. The role of the designer changes with this approach. Instead of being someone who only reacts to the ideas of a client or user, the designer becomes an actor in a larger social context. This also changes her relationships towards clients, decision makers, users, and other stakeholders. It is not necessarily true that the client or the user knows everything. This approach of questioning becomes a way to challenge the very reason for the design process to take place. When that happens, it opens up many new designs and alternative solutions. The design is no longer a problem-solving activity, but a truly creative and innovative process.

2.2.4 Degrees of Freedom and External Representations

Many designers find it frustrating not to be able to start from scratch. This frustration is caused by a wish for the ideal situation where nothing is given and the creation of the whole and its details is open and unbounded. However, such wishes are based on a romantic ideal that never exists. Moreover, if such a situation could exist, it would actually not be an ideal but more of a designer's nightmare. A common assumption is that it is easier to design with more degrees of freedom. It turns out that facing a design situation where everything is possible requires an enormous effort from a designer. Everything has to be designed; every precondition, goal, restriction, and limitation have to be created and decided. Nothing is given.

An independent artist is probably the one who lives closest to an unbounded creative situation. Many artists have considerable freedom from external requirements about what to do, how to do it, when to do it, and why. At the same time, however, we know that artists usually restrict themselves quite forcefully by choice of material and form of expression. To make the choice to express a feeling by carving a specific form from a rock, without the use of high technology or colors, restricts the artist significantly. Such choices are not made to limit creativity, but rather to cultivate it. When everything is possible and nothing is given, creativity has no friction, nothing to work with, nothing to build on. Creativity is strange in that it finds its way in any kind of situation, no matter how restricted. Metaphorically speaking, the same amount of water flows faster and stronger through a narrow strait than across the open sea.

Designers always work within restrictions and limitations. Examples of such restrictions, typically imposed by external forces, are budget, time limits, and resources available to the design process. One task for the designer is, of course, to seek ways to manage restrictions and maybe sidestep them in creative ways. A good designer is therefore someone who has the ability to work in a highly restricted situation and still be able to create surprising and satisfactory solutions and designs.

In order to cope with a complex design process, a designer needs to *externalize* the actual design thinking through representations: sketches, drafts, models, and the like. Design research has shown that most designers use some kind of external representations, such as sketches, in their work. These external representations are carriers of the first ideas, of the thoughts that emanate from the vision. They are the first seeds that will form an operative image. Many designers start sketching at the same moment they are introduced to a design situation. The sketching does not necessarily follow any plan or method. In most cases, it is a way to create material to work with.

One explanation for this behavior can be found in the writings of Schön. As we outlined earlier, Schön suggests that there is an ongoing conversation between the designer and the situation. The representations (sketches, drawings, and so on) can be understood as tools for thinking and as mediators in the dialectic relationship between the vision, the operative image, and the situation.

With the external representations, the designer carries out a dialogue about the design situation and solution ideas. The lines on the paper or the shadows in the model give the attentive designer rich information. It is easier to evaluate ideas when they are objectified and externalized. They move out of the vague and abstract realm, start to live their own lives, and have conversations with the designer. As long as ideas reside in the mind, it is difficult to see their limitations and spot their incoherencies. Sketching is a way for designers to bring their thinking out in the world and expose it to inspection, contributions, and criticism by others. At the same time, sketches become tools for the designer to further develop her ideas.

Even though sketching has different characteristics in various fields of design, it is possible to recognize its three basic purposes: (1) to form ideas, (2) to communicate with oneself, and (3) to communicate with others.

Forming Ideas   Sketches can be used to stimulate creative thinking, by opening up new possibilities and combinations of ideas. In many cases these openings and combinations can be difficult to see without external representations. Sketching can also be used to structure one's thinking, test the logic of a proposition, outline restrictions, dependencies, and relations, and handle many proposals at the same time. In sketching to form ideas, speed and lightness of hand are often of the essence. Many designers use thumbnail formats in order to keep the sketches fast—and sketchy.

Communicating with Oneself   When ideas are externalized, that is, brought into the world, it is possible for a designer to view her own thinking in a new way. She has something to react and respond to, and is relieved of the hard task of being proactive and inventive from scratch. It becomes possible to reflect upon something that exists. The sketch works as a conversation partner by presenting resistance, drawing the designer's attention to previously unseen properties, revealing obstacles and openings, and talking back to the designer.

Communicating with Others   Perhaps the most obvious purpose of a sketch is to function as a tool for communication with others. Sketches express our thoughts and a design team can work together by developing something that they can all see and discuss. Even if the sketch is not understood or interpreted by all members of the team in a uniform way, it still serves as a focus for further critique and discussion.

The importance and understanding of sketching in the design process can hardly be exaggerated. Practicing sketching, developing new sketching techniques, and inventing new externalization tools are fundamental in design learning. It is the way designers present ideas, form suggestions, test their proposals, and communicate their visions. It is at the core of the design process.

2.2.5 Exploring Design Possibilities

In discussions of design, the terms *convergence* and *divergence* are often mentioned. These concepts are used to capture two basic approaches in design thinking. Divergence is an approach where the designer expands her thinking to cover broader issues, find more alternatives, and explore more opportunities. It is a process that creates more information and options. Convergence is about focusing on a specific solution or a synthesis of several ideas. Convergence creates a deeper understanding and a more detailed and narrowly focused proposal. Since the final outcome is usually an artifact, a system, or a specification, the design process always ends in a convergence phase with the focus on one specific solution. This, however, does not mean that the whole design process is a continuous convergence from the broad initial situation to the narrow final solution. Rather, a design process is driven by the will to learn as much as possible about different opportunities existing in a particular situation.

Moving forward in a design process usually means that the designer has to explore as many possibilities as time and resources allow. Consequently, the early design work is often primarily a divergent activity, where several ideas are developed instead of focusing on a single one. The aim is to explore the spaces of possible designs and problem formulations.

Divergent thinking—considering several ideas in parallel—has an important practical advantage. In a design process, it is not uncommon for a designer to "fall in love" with a favorite idea and defend it by refuting all criticism from other team members. Sometimes people push their own ideas farther than they deserve to go. The design process can degenerate into a case of personal pride where nobody wants to lose. By working with several ideas in parallel, however, it is possible to avoid this trap. A more desirable situation is where ideas are not closely related to individual participants, but exist in their own right as alternative or complementary proposals. Recognizing the possibility that there might be several equally satisfying solutions in a design process is necessary in thoughtful design. To be thoughtful is to acknowledge your own limitations and to welcome possibilities presented by others. A thoughtful stance is characterized by a will to explore design possibilities, even when an apparently sufficient proposal already exists. Innovative ideas and creative solutions take time, in particular when it comes to finding out how new ideas can be integrated into an existing situation.

2.2.6 Capturing the Design Situation

Every design addresses a specific context. A new design will become a part of an already existing reality. All qualities of a new design have to fit the environment where it will be placed and used. For this to happen, a designer needs to have knowledge and insight about the context where a design will end up. In this sense, a designer is a researcher exploring the reality that constitutes the design situation.

Whenever we try to study the world around us, two aspects become crucial. One aspect is our understanding of what constitutes reality—our ontology—and the other is what we believe is possible to know about reality—our epistemology. These two notions significantly determine how we will approach the study of the existing reality. Our ontology influences what we consider to be important aspects and dimensions of reality and our epistemology determines in what way we believe it is possible to acquire knowledge about reality.

For instance, if we believe that the world consists of layers where the underlying layer determines and explains the one above (e.g., that psychology can explain sociology), we have an ontology that tells us how the world should be approached and studied in order to be understood in a correct way. Questions of possible ontological and epistemological assumptions have been studied in philosophy for centuries. These discussions have influenced how scientific research is carried out today; they have also been influential in determining what are considered good ways of exploring a design situation.

is a need for a diverse set of competences, which is typically hard to find in one individual. Consequently, the design process is almost always a *social process*. As a social process, it has to be managed and organized. All people involved need to know what to do, when to do it, and with whom they need to work. Issues of responsibility, accountability, and power invariably emerge. The design process must therefore be seen not only as a process of thinking, but as a management challenge as well.

A simple way of sorting out the stakeholders involved in design projects is to introduce a three-layered structure (see figure 2.3). At the *core,* we will find the professional designer together with the users and clients directly involved in the work. The *periphery* includes the users and clients not actively participating in the actual work, together with all other stakeholders. The *context* is the surrounding environment and society at large that is not directly involved in the design process, but still influences it in indirect and complex ways.

The idea of three circles of involvement is, of course, oversimplified, but it highlights the complexity of managing the design process. It is, for instance, not possible to manage design by focusing only the core circle alone. Successful design requires a recognition of the intricate relationships between the circles, as well as managing the processes within each circle.

First of all, the design process has to accommodate the fundamental aspects we have already discussed, such as the relation between the vision, operative image, and specification. All parties involved in the process—that is, all circles—will influence the development of the final design. There is a need to manage these relationships in a way

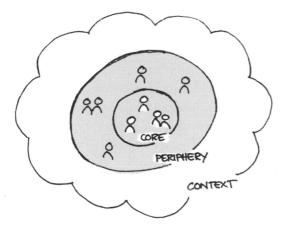

Figure 2.3
The three circles of involvement.

that acknowledges the role of the vision, that honors the integrity of all involved parties, and that leads to a final design in a reasonably predictable way. We will briefly outline how that can be done by discussing how to care for the vision, how to deal with relationships and roles, and how to see the process as a project.

2.3.1 Caring for the Vision

When IT development projects increase in size and complexity, it is common to divide a project into parts or modules based on the structure of the imagined final design. After the initial phases where the vision and first operative images are created, a first attempt is made to divide the system into subsystems or modules. The subsystems are then given to different teams for further development. This approach is powerful and efficient in principle, but it is difficult to employ in a satisfactory way. For instance, subsystems are frequently identified based on technical considerations. A typical example might be one subsystem for data storage, one for data entry and maintenance, and one for search and presentation of database contents. Such a division is unfortunately not likely to coincide with the users' perspective, where it might be necessary to enter data and search in the context of the same task. If the two subsystems are developed by different teams without close coordination, it is likely that the users will find them inconsistent and inconvenient to use.

Managing the design process by dividing the system into smaller parts requires an initial design of the whole system in the way that a user will experience it. All designers working in a project need to have a similar understanding of the vision and the wholeness of the system. It is also important to have a continuous and lively discussion around the operative image, since it will develop and influence the vision during the project. A common experience is that it is difficult for a design team to share and develop a vision and an operative image together. Potts and Catledge (1996) studied a rather large software project for almost a year and describe the creation of a shared vision and its evolution into a final specification as a process of nonmonotonic convergence. This is to say that there were periods of incremental detailing, but between those periods the team was forced to rethink and reformulate its basic vision.

Other studies show that successful design teams use a diverse set of strategies to disseminate and share the fundamental ideas that constitute the basis for a system. One method is to facilitate informal communication across organizational borders. This has been seen as an approach to handle insecurity and change in a design project (Kraut and Streeter 1995). Informal communication can be supported by having design teams share offices and common spaces, by sharing information channels such as email or conference systems, or by using methods that force people to meet across teams and groups. All of these strategies create opportunities for informal communication that can help the total design project hold together its ideas and development trajectories.

Yet another strategy is to appoint a "super designer." This person, who might be called a systems architect or lead designer, has the ultimate responsibility for taking care of the vision. In some cases, this task is given to a small group of designers. It is not unusual to find a person or group of people taking on this responsibility without formal appointment, based merely on their experience or informal status (Curtis, Krasner, and Iscoe 1988).

Perhaps the most common approach for managing a vision within a project is to write documents of various types, such as project-specific design rules, specifications, and descriptions. Documents have some obvious advantages but also severe limitations. Documents and text have to be interpreted by the readers and it is apparent that even if people work in the same project, it is not easy to reach full agreement on abstract notions such as visions and ideas solely through the use of text. It is also a fact that people, including skilled professionals, are very poor at documenting their work, even though they know how much work it will save in the long run. This probably has to do with the relation between short-term efforts and long-term paybacks and with the division of responsibility between the individual and the organization. To the individual, it creates more overhead work to write documents describing her own ideas and work than the immediate benefits motivate. For the organization, on the other hand, a well-documented process and outcome might be worth more in the long run than the individual realizes at the moment when the documentation has to be done. It appears to be difficult to care for the vision in a design project by means of documents, both as a technique (Poltrock and Grudin 1994) and in terms of motivation. Still, an enormous amount of time and resources are spent in large projects on documentation as a way to care for the process itself—as a management tool—and for the evolving vision.

2.3.2 Relationships and Roles

In a design process, there are many different actors interested in the process and in the outcome of the process. A thoughtful designer has to be clear on her own role and position in the process. To act as a designer, with the responsibility for the outcome of a process, is to be in a delicate position. It is not possible to describe all possible positions a designer might find herself in, but what we can do is to outline a few idealized types. Idealized types are thought experiments or theoretical constructions that have no strict correspondence with existing entities, but serve as grounds for reflection.

The role of a designer, in the design process, is shaped by her relation to the client and the user. In the strictly formal sense, the client represents the reason for the design process. This does not mean that clients actually know what they need or want, nor that they know what the intended users of the digital artifact need or want. The client may not even be an active participant in the process. Another issue is that the client's ideas do not necessarily coincide with the user's ideas. For a designer, this is often manifested in a dilemma with contradicting needs and requirements, which plays out as a very practical issue. Who should the designer listen to? Which of the two parties' requirements and needs are important enough to influence the design work? When should a statement by a client or a user be taken literally, when should it be interpreted as a sign of an underlying message to be explored, and when should it simply be disregarded?

In some interaction design situations, it is hard to identify the primary user. For instance, in a system for a car dealership, is the "true" user the car salesperson or the customer? Should the designer aim for a system that supports the salesperson as much as possible, or is it more important for the system to satisfy customers, even though it may entail more work and perhaps more frustration for the salesperson? This dilemma shows the difficulty in determining roles in the design process.

A thoughtful designer has to understand that accommodating people's roles and their relative importance in a design process is itself a design task. A skilled designer recognizes and knows when and how to involve different partners in the process, such as users, clients, decision makers, and others. This is a complex design task. Even if a designer can identify who should be involved, it is quite common that people decline to participate in the process. The reason can be lack of time, lack of interest, or any other practical or political reason. From the perspective of the designer, the forming of the relationships with people involved in the process can be understood as a form of social intervention. The designer enters the social context of a workplace, an organization, a home, an interest-based community, or a group of friends. In that process, the designer becomes an important player. Throughout the history of design, there have been debates about the possible positions and actions for a designer in terms of social intervention. Dahlbom and Mathiassen (1993) present three roles an interaction designer can take, more or less in the form of idealized types. The roles are based on traditional, but still important, historical and philosophical ideas. The three roles are: computer expert, socio-technical expert, and political agent.

The *computer expert* offers technical expertise and expects clients and users to specify what they want her to produce. The computer expert knows a lot about technology and how to build digital artifacts, while the users know their field and are assumed to be able to judge the qualities of the artifacts in use. Being a computer expert entails a certain humility, in the sense that she view her expertise as restricted. It is the job and responsibility of others to decide the outcome of the process. The traditional assumption within IT development of a complete and detailed requirement specification, finalized early in the process and used to guide design work and verify the outcome, fits well with the computer expert role in a design process.

Socio-technical experts view their responsibility in different way. To them, it is necessary to include social aspects in the design work to achieve a good system and satisfy users. It is, according to socio-technical experts, not always a technical solution that is needed, since many problems can be caused by social or organizational factors. Therefore, they see it as their task to develop an understanding of underlying problems. Socio-technical experts try to reveal what kind of information is needed, what social roles exist, and what expectations future users have. In socio-technical approaches, it is required that users participate in the process. The socio-technical experts need to cooperate with users to be able to fully understand their situation, needs, and expectations. The experts' attitude is to be engaged and cooperative. They master technical as well as socially oriented methods and know how participative design and cooperation with users can be conducted. This position also incorporates the view that an expert is there to solve problems for a user, and that the context and relationships they work with are based on ideals of consensus and harmony. Participation and cooperation creates a common understanding focused on the best possible solution for all parties involved.

Political experts argue that the most important aspect of design is to take a stand in the ongoing struggle that is the design situation. To them, the crucial question is who the users are. When this is determined, the task is to work to empower the chosen users by helping them to develop their resources, technical tools, and knowledge. To a political expert, any digital artifact is by itself an intervention in a play of powers where the designer cannot be neutral but has to choose sides and work for one group and against some other group.

The political expert cannot determine if a digital artifact is good without asking who it helps. Evaluating a particular artifact can only be done in relation to the interests of an actor or group of actors. It follows that groups with different interests cannot agree on the quality of a digital artifact. Therefore, it makes no sense to search for the most agreeable solution; design work should instead be done in close relation with a chosen group sharing values and interests.

Dahlbom and Mathiassen (1993) discuss some classical examples where designers have chosen to take on one of these roles. Historically, the field of digital artifacts has been dominated by designers who take on the role of computer experts. More recently, research as well as professional practice has evolved in directions such that designers take on the role of the socio-technical expert. The political role is less common, even though it can be argued that many digital artifacts today, when implemented in a context, catalyze changes in power and social order. The artifact becomes a carrier of politically significant outcomes, even if it was not designed with such intentions.

Our short presentation of the three roles is not meant to be used in any way other than as a reflective tool. We believe that a designer in any design situation faces choices that bear some relation to these three idealized types or to other designer positions on a similar level of abstraction. A thoughtful interaction designer reflects on the position that any specific situation requires, even if it does not result in one of the distinct roles as we have described here.

2.3.3 Design as a Project

Since designing is a complex process, it has to be organized and managed. How this should be done depends on the specifics of the situation. There are, however, some characteristics that hold enough general validity to deserve a brief discussion.

There are several reasons for finding ways to manage the design process. Someone in the organization conducting a design process is usually responsible for its outcome and adherence to given time and resource limitations. For anyone who has that responsibility it is necessary to keep track of people and manage communication, cooperation, documentation, and so on. A designer also has personal reasons to consider organization and management. For instance, there is a desire to put one's skills to the best possible use, have the right resources and the right amount of time, and to be relieved of unnecessary and time-consuming administrative work. The client needs to have knowledge about the process in order to handle implementation planning properly. The client may also want to create decision points along the path of a project. Moreover, other stakeholders in a design project often have their own reasons for some kind of organization and management of the process. For example, managers in departments adjacent to the client's may need to coordinate their own activities with development of the new system.

Interaction design inherits a rich history of methods, models, and methodology from fields such as human-computer interaction, systems development, and software engineering. Most of those tools are intended to support the coordination, organization, and management of what we would call "the design process." We do not introduce them in detail here, since they are well covered in the literature (see, e.g., Fitzgerald, Russo, and Stolterman 2002, for a comprehensive discussion). Instead, we will concentrate on the larger context of the process-as-project.

Following Grudin (1991), projects aiming at developing digital artifacts can be divided into three broad categories, each with its own characteristics. The categories are contract development, product development, and in-house/custom development.

Contract development is formally initiated by a client, who decides to do something about a perceived problem or need and asks development companies to make bids for a solution. The real origins of contract development may, of course, be that a resourceful salesperson from a development company convinces a potential client of the existence of a problem or need. In either case, it is common to set up a competitive situation where interested development companies have to propose solutions, present how they would go about in achieving these solutions, and how much it would cost. The client selects the most favorable bid and contracts are drawn up between client and developer to specify what is to be delivered, at what time, and at what price. Then, it is up to the development company to meet the terms of the contract.

Product development, on the other hand, is initiated by a development company. It may have detected a market demand and decided to develop a product to meet the demand. Another typical scenario starts with an idea for a new product and the related work of creating a market, need, or demand. There is no obvious client; development is oriented towards a broad market that may be more or less precisely defined.

In-house development refers to a situation where developers and intended users belong to the same organization. Typical examples are IT departments of large corporations developing systems for internal use. In-house projects are often less formal, since there are established contacts between the parties involved and sometimes even a shared budget. The cooperation often lasts for long periods of time, taking the form of ongoing enterprise support rather than individual projects with fixed delivery dates. Systems developed in-house are tailored to the intended use contexts within the organization, even though they can sometimes form the basis for products and services addressing the customers of the organization.

The nature of design work is affected by project type. In contract development, the core element is the business relation between client and developer. It is quite common to outline a product in the contract, thereby reducing the design possibilities significantly. Unfortunately, these decisions are not always made from a design perspective. They may be taken loosely and based on financial or internal political reasons rather than on proper design work.

Product development ought to accommodate significant elements of unrestricted design work, but in many companies it turns out that management and marketing departments lay out directions for new products. The designer's skills are not necessarily used in the development of ideas for new products and services, and interaction design in industrial product development sometimes deteriorates into the design of user interfaces for a given set of functions.

The less formal nature of in-house development often affords a more flexible design process. The possibility to view development as a continuous process is particularly interesting. Chances are good that a designer will be able to learn how her ideas work in a practical context and gain important insights for future work.

It is not difficult to come up with project categories beyond the three outlined by Grudin. For instance, contracting situations can often evolve into less formal structures similar to in-house development, based on long-standing business relationships between a client and a developer. Another example is the deployment of cross-media services where, for example, a development company develops and runs a web site related to a recurrent TV broadcast. The rapid development of our design material (digital technology) and its contexts implies the further emergence of yet other categories. Our point is not to identify the specifics of the different categories, but rather to show that a category—whether intentionally chosen or not—affects the way in which design work can and will be carried out. Most decisions influencing the general nature of the project are taken higher up in the organizations involved. Many designers perceive this as an obstacle to their own understanding of the best ways to work. At the level of a single project, most participants wish they had the power to make more decisions, including strategic ones. This is, however, rarely possible. Design processes are set in larger organizations with their own motives and strategies. There is always a tension between the larger organizational context and the individual project.

This leads to the conclusion that "real" design is about finding ways to design a project within these preconditions and limitations—by accepting them or trying to change them. A design project is itself designed and depends on creative and innovative thinking for its success.

2.4 Designing the Design Process

This chapter has briefly touched on some of the more vital aspects of the design process. It is hopefully clear that the process is of such complexity that it is impossible to capture all of its important characteristics in a book, let alone a chapter. Our aim has been to show the breadth of issues a designer will face in preparing and navigating through a design process.

We find that there is no clever way of defining away the intricacy of design. Any such attempt is in itself a form of design. Since every design process itself has to be designed, someone will shape it, decide what has to be done, and how it should be carried out. Unfortunately, this is the task in a design process that typically receives the least attention. Many books and articles are written about the design process, methods are developed, and project models are invented. Much work is devoted to prescribing how to organize and manage the process. The issue of designing the design process, however, is not as well addressed. It is usually assumed that the solution is to use a predesigned model or method. For purposes of managing the design process, this solution may be adequate. But if we assume that the design process has to be created, invented, and designed, then other aspects appear as crucial.

Thoughtful design has to be based on a realization and understanding of the fundamental aspects of the design process described in this chapter. A thoughtful designer knows that almost nothing is given or true when it comes to what and how to design. It is also obvious that the complexity of the process demands conceptual clarity from the designer. The thoughtful position is to view the whole situation as a design task: to design the design process.

3   The Designer

It is impossible to discuss what design is all about without focusing on the designer. Like all creative activities, design is extremely dependent on who is actually doing the work. Since the designer is at the core of design, we must ask: What is a designer and what does it take to be a good one? Is it possible to learn to be a good designer? The image of the designer that we present in this chapter is based on research findings from various sources, as well as our own experience as designers and design teachers. Our aim is not to give a comprehensive explanation of human behavior in design, but merely to introduce some ideas and thoughts that we find helpful in the process of becoming a thoughtful designer.

So who is this designer we now focus on? To us, anyone participating in design work that includes the use-oriented shaping of digital artifacts is in principle an interaction designer. Even though this chapter might be valuable to all kinds of designers, we focus on people who engage professionally in the design of digital artifacts. We do not, however, differentiate between the specific aspects of interaction design. We believe the ideas presented are valuable to any designer involved in the design process, whether in more technical or social issues, in early or later phases of the process, and irrespective of the specific genre of digital artifacts or the domain where the design will be implemented. Differences do exist, to be sure, and on certain levels they determine what the designer needs to know to accomplish her task. Our notion of a thoughtful designer and her conceptual tools addresses a more general level where the differences are less significant.

In this chapter we discuss two fundamental questions concerning the designer: (1) What is it that characterizes design ability? (2) How is it possible for a designer to develop that ability?

We will in fact start by giving away the conclusion: The possibility of a designer succeeding in a specific situation is determined by the extent to which she is *prepared*. A good designer is not the one who best follows the prescriptive steps of a method or technique, or the one who knows "the solution" in advance. Rather, a good designer can approach, appreciate, and assess a complex and unique design situation. Based on a creative idea, she can compose a design that fulfills and possibly surpasses the functional, structural, aesthetical, and ethical demands of the situation. This way of putting it comes across as a bit complicated; we aspire to explain and elaborate it throughout this chapter.

Every design situation is unique and demands unique solutions. Dealing with a situation in a unique way means acknowledging that there are no recipes to follow, no standard solutions. Instead, the designer needs to be prepared to develop the aspects constituting design ability in advance of the situation where they are needed. In the actual moment when a design decision has to be made, when a creative idea is needed, there is almost never enough time to approach that situation in a complete and comprehensive way. The designer has to trust her design ability, including her ability to make good judgments.

The chapter is divided into two parts, based on the questions presented earlier: What is it that characterizes design ability, and how is it possible for a designer to develop that ability. We will show some possible answers and, we hope, give the reader a basis for developing a personal understanding of herself as a designer. A thoughtful designer reflects on her own strengths and weaknesses and intentionally changes them in positive ways.

3.1 Design Ability

Every designer needs knowledge and skill related to her specific profession. Having knowledge means understanding the vast amount of specific information and techniques existing within any design field. Skill concerns the necessary craftsmanship. Both knowledge and skill are needed if a person wants to be a good designer. We will not address the details of interaction design skill and craftsmanship here, since it is highly genre-dependent and covered in the corresponding literatures (see bibliography). Instead, we will focus on a more general understanding of design ability.

There are, of course, many possible answers to the question of what design ability is about. As a starting point, we will use the definition of interaction design that we presented in the introduction.

Interaction design refers to the process that is arranged within existing resource constraints to create, shape, and decide all use-oriented qualities (structural, functional, ethical, and aesthetic) of a digital artifact for one or many clients.

This definition offers a set of concepts that can be used to frame the abilities needed for interaction design, as follows:

- *Creating* and *shaping* demands creative and analytical ability.
- *Deciding* demands critical judgment.
- Working with a *client* demands rationality and ability to communicate.
- Design of *structural qualities* demands knowledge of technology and material.
- Design of *functional qualities* demands knowledge of technology use.
- Design of *ethical qualities* demands knowledge of relevant values and ideals.
- Design of *aesthetic qualities* demands an ability to appreciate and compose.

How can these abilities be developed? Can they really be learned or are they a reflection of innate talent? We will present some general ideas that can function as a basis for a more personal approach to these questions. Our purpose is not to present a general method that will turn the reader into a professional designer. Since each person is unique when it comes to dispositions and talents, everyone has to develop her own way of becoming a good designer. It is ultimately a question of *designing oneself as a designer.*

If you know that you find it easy to come up with new ideas and solutions, and that you are not afraid of new situations, then you may not need to strengthen your creative ability. If you have a reliable sense of quality or a clear sense of what is right and wrong, there are probably other aspects of your design ability that you need to develop. In this section, we present arguments for why it is important to make a conscious effort to develop your design ability and offer some ideas on how it can be done.

We will not discuss all the design-oriented abilities mentioned in the definition above. For instance, issues concerning insights about technology use and functional qualities are addressed to some extent in chapters 4 and 5, as well as in the significant body of literature in human-computer interaction and information systems. Moreover, knowledge about structural qualities of information technology—the essence of fields such as computer science and software engineering—is more or less outside the scope of this book. It is important to note that these aspects are equally fundamental to interaction design, even though we do not address them here. The choice we have made is simply to focus on design aspects that are less frequently treated in existing information technology texts.

3.1.1   Design Ability and Design Intelligence

Much effort has been devoted to the task of identifying the most important design ability. This is an impossible endeavor, of course, because of the strong influence of the specifics of the situation at hand. In spite of that, we propose to characterize design ability in general as a *constructive intentional intelligence*. This definition emphasizes two major qualities in a designer's competence. First, it points out that a designer is supposed to be constructive, in the sense of being creative and innovative. Second, it puts a strong emphasis on being intentional, that is, consciously trying to achieve change in the world. It is possible to view constructive intentional intelligence as a specific kind of intelligence used by designers in design situations (Cross 1995). Such an intelligence is in many ways different from what we traditionally assume intelligence to be and definitely dissimilar from what is measured in IQ tests.

We are all familiar with the traditional notion of intelligence. It is usually equated with being logical and having strong problem-solving and analytical skills. All of these abilities are of course important for a designer, but design intelligence is also about creativity, composition, judgment, and intentional change.

Being analytical—that is, having the skill to divide things in smaller parts in a logical way with the purpose of understanding their inner workings—is an ability so universal it is probably needed in any human endeavor. This is certainly true for design. In addition to having analytical skills, however, a designer must also be able to create synthesis. Design is about creating more complex things from less complex ones. It is about building larger compositions based on knowledge and information about smaller parts. Such holistic thinking is always present in design.

A designer is involved in a task of creating something whole. The thing that is supposed to be designed, the digital artifact, is not only a thing in itself with its structure and functions; it is also something that has to fit into a larger context. Being able to see how these designed wholes can be put together, based on incomplete information about the separate qualities of the components, is a major part of design intelligence.

Whereas traditional intelligence is relevant for proving the correctness of software code at an increasingly detailed level, design intelligence as we define it is needed for a task such as designing a support system for medical staff to manage X-ray images. In the first case, it is possible to imagine how knowledge can be built around the correctness of code. We can develop an approach to determine program correctness with increasing precision over time. The problem is general and abstract enough to make it amenable to analytical intelligence. The second case, creating a support system for medical staff, requires broad knowledge about information technology, diagnostic radiology, X-ray imaging technology, the professional skills and practices of the medical staff, the characteristics of the workplace, and other specific conditions of the situation at hand. This is a typical design situation in the sense that the available information will always be incomplete, but design decisions have to be made nonetheless. Dealing with such complexity in creating something appropriate for the situation at hand is a task that demands design intelligence—that is, a constructive intentional intelligence.

Another aspect of design intelligence is the ability to recognize and judge the quality of a design. This kind of overall quality judgment evaluates all the qualities mentioned in our definition of interaction design: structural, functional, ethical, and aesthetic. All dimensions must be judged as part of the overall judgment. It is not possible to simply measure each quality separately and add them together; the overall design is not a simple sum of distinct qualities. The whole is always more than the sum of the parts; it can only be measured by well-informed judgment.

Design intelligence is also about imagination and the ability to envision future situations based on existing ones. Every design starts out as an idea, to be sure, but where does the idea come from? There are strong indications that designers benefit from a rich *repertoire of examples,* exemplary models of related design ideas that are sometimes called formats. Many theories of design and design methods describe the early ideational work as a matching process between the designer's repertoire and the situation at hand. Design processes are shown in empirical studies to be driven by initial exemplars structuring and shaping the work. In addition, studies show that creativity in the sense of being able to produce innovative solutions of high quality is strongly dependent on the domain. For instance, there is no reason to expect an accomplished productivity applications designer to be particularly good at designing games.

Another level of analysis points to the existence of examples, or formats, that are strong enough to reproduce and prosper in the intellectual ecology of ideas constituted by the community of design-as-knowledge-construction. Consider the game Tetris, which will be discussed in depth in chapter 5. The basic idea for the game is very simple and easy to describe, yet it has proven inspirational for literally thousands of new designs. The original Tetris idea has been subject to every variation, elaboration, and modification imaginable. In that sense, it is easy to see it as a strong format.

The way for a designer to construct an effective repertoire, however, is largely unknown. We might assume that the evidence discussed earlier in this section, together with other observations such as the emphasis traditionally put on product studies and collaborative critique sessions in design schools, indicate the importance of building and developing a rich repertoire. Unfortunately, there is no systematic knowledge on what constitutes a good example or format from a design ability point of view, or how best to build a repertoire. We are left only with the general conclusion that a repertoire is a crucial component of design ability. The approach we take in chapter 5, providing examples of digital artifacts and their use qualities, is our suggestion on how components of a repertoire can be articulated and disseminated for appropriation in a culture of design as knowledge construction.

Once an idea exists, it has to be transformed into something explicit and something external to the designer's imagination. It has to be given a form, perhaps as a model, map, sketch, diagram, image, or text. The process of transforming ideas into an explicit form is not only necessary to make communication possible; it is also a vital aspect of the design process itself. Design intelligence is the ability to work with the material, with the sketch or model, to reach a final design.

It may seem as if we define design ability as something special and unique, but at some level it is an everyday ability that all of us share. It is not the case that some people are born with design ability and some are not. We engage in design—we create, synthesize, shape, and envision future situations—all the time. We decorate our homes, build and rebuild our houses, change our cars, buy clothes, and design our time and our interests. Nowadays this largely means that we make our choices among ready-made consumer products, but we still design in the sense of shaping the wholeness that becomes something specific. Each of us designs our lives and ourselves. However, even if design on this level is a natural part of life, the distribution of talent varies. Some people are more creative and have the ability to use their imagination efficiently, some are better at seeing how things fit together in compositions, others excel at assessing the functional feasibility of a design idea, and so on.

We discuss design ability on a general level and the aspects we consider are similar for most designers, regardless of their professional field. But, at the same time as we focus on the universal aspects of design, there are also specific abilities determined by the specifics of a professional domain. An architect, an organizational consultant, a graphic designer, and an industrial designer all have particular demands dictated by their respective fields of expertise. This has to be recognized and respected. But it also needs to be analyzed. What is it that is demanded from these designers and why? Educators continuously debate what it is that manifests the core competence of a profession, and how to best stimulate and develop that core. In architecture, for instance, different opinions have been voiced on what is the core of architectural ability. Is it an artistic core, an engineering core, or a core built on social awareness? How the core is viewed is, of course, significant for considerations of how to educate an architectural student. Design of digital artifacts has been debated in similar ways, with a focus on what constitutes the core of design ability in the field. Is it the ability to create good software? The ability to solve complex logical problems? Perhaps the ability to interpret and understand future users?

A designer develops her ability within an existing tradition, with its own understanding of what constitutes the discipline's core. Much like the design profession as a whole has to critically examine its preconditions and traditional core, every designer has to critically examine the ideas about what represent necessary design skills. This is not only relevant over time, but it is something that has to be done each time a new design situation is approached.

A design field changes over time. New tasks appear carrying new demands and challenges created by new hopes and desires. Taken together with more concrete changes—such as new material, technology, and additions to the body of knowledge of the field—we find that traditional assumptions concerning competence are constantly undermined. It is also common that style and preferences change over time, thereby influencing what is thought of as good design. Consequently, design ability becomes a moving target.

In design education, it is possible to influence design ability negatively as well as positively. Many studies demonstrate how different approaches to education change students' ability to design and their ways of approaching a design task. Among other findings, it has been observed that architects, engineers, and researchers all approach situations in different ways. Their way of doing things is not only a consequence of personal traits, but can be traced back to common ways of thinking and acting in a particular design field that are shaped by their professional education (Lawson 1980).

How we will think and act as designers is not only predisposed by how well our design abilities are developed; it is also a product of our own understanding of who we are as professionals and how we perceive our role as designers. This means that to act as a designer, you have to be able to think about yourself as a designer.

In the following sections, we will discuss in more detail some of the aspects of design ability we have briefly mentioned. The aim is to support the reader in her own examination of what it means to view oneself as a designer, and to make the case that "oneself as a designer" leads to the notion that it is possible to "design oneself." Becoming a good designer is to some extent a design endeavor, and not an easy one. It demands a thoughtful, constructive, and intentional ambition.

3.1.2   Rationality and Communication

It is commonly understood that a designer should be rational. Most people would say that is true, maybe without paying detailed attention to what it means to be "rational." We must take a closer look at the concept of *rationality*.

We usually consider a process to be rational: (1) when it is possible to understand—that is, when we can see why the process has been enacted in a specific way, and (2) when the enactment is in line with our own values. This means that in order to declare a process to be rational, it has to be possible to understand the actions and decisions in the process as based on reasons, and that these reasons coincide with our own means of assessing actions.

Rationality is a multifaceted concept used in many senses and with many connotations. There is an everyday interpretation of what constitutes rational work. For instance, it has to be efficient, economical, logical, and correct. The criteria for assessment of rationality depend on the domain and people involved. In some instances, rationality is only an economical question of costs and earnings. In other situations, an action may be deemed rational within an ecological and sustainable approach, based on environmental ideals. If logic is the criterion, rationality is a matter of consistency, contradictions, and paradoxes. To some, rationality lies in acting according to an appreciation of religious beliefs.

The values underlying the everyday understanding of rationality have become "invisible" over time and "rational behavior" is seen as a universal logic, legitimate in all circumstances. Consequently, the meaning of rationality has become increasingly shallow (Rescher 1988).

According to Rescher, the everyday understanding of rationality is too narrow, since it is almost entirely based on economic values. This has led to a situation where economic criteria dominate conceptualizations of rationality in all areas, even those where economic aspects are minor or even nonexistent. This way of understanding rationality has also had a huge impact on how people think about design and what is considered to be a good design process. We want to argue that rationality is the intentional reason and motivation that makes an action understandable, and that motivation is a result of (consciously or unconsciously) chosen values.

If rationality is open for interpretation, how is it possible to know if you are rational? Is it possible to measure rationality in some way? Sometimes we are fooled by the apparent simplicity of a task and accordingly apply an overly simple rationality to it. A dishwasher may be understood as a tool that makes washing dishes more rational: it is fast, efficient, and saves time. But when public awareness of environmental issues grows stronger, that understanding might be challenged. If the efficiency that the machine stands for is based on the use of environmentally harmful detergents and a great deal of energy, it may not seem as rational anymore. This example demonstrates the close relation between our values and what we interpret as rational.

All this means that a designer has to have a solid understanding of the complexity involved in being rational. When a designer works with a client, she has to be able to appreciate the client's understanding of rationality, in relation to her own understanding of it. A basic appreciation of that relationship is fundamental to the communication between designer and client. Rationality is therefore not only a matter of how to do things, but a precondition for good communication.

Communication in design is vital in many respects. There are usually many different parties involved in the actual design process. Some are more active in the early stages, some in the later stages. Ultimately, communication is at the core of the whole process. In the early stages, designers, decision makers, users, and others will be involved in some kind of creative generation of ideas. This is explorative work where possible solutions are discussed and tested. One of the most important skills here is to make ideas "visible"—that is, to give them form and structure in ways that allow the participants to "see" them, analyze them, and evaluate them. If nobody understands a new idea or a new vision, it does not matter how good it is. The ability to externalize ideas and visions is vital to any designer.

Externalizing an idea, making it "visible," also makes it accessible for criticism, development, expansion, revision, and possible discard. It is sometimes assumed that there is a conflict between the creative generation of ideas and making them explicit, since idea externalization may lead to delimitation of possibilities and influence further ideas in a specific direction. However, the conflict between internal insight and external representation creates a tension that is necessary and useful for the design work that follows. It is through external representation that ideas become real and the design process moves forward.

The notion of communication of design ideas is particularly difficult when it comes to digital artifacts and interaction design. As we will discuss in subsequent chapters, we still lack the languages to fully describe the qualities of digital artifacts.

The ability to communicate ideas and to argue for a particular design is important not only for the sake of communication itself; it constitutes an intrinsic part of being rational. If you fail to make yourself understood you are not considered rational. Motivating a design according to reason is a great challenge to designers in every design project.

3.1.3 Creative and Analytical

Nearly every design situation requires analytical skill from the designer. At the same time, the designer needs to be creative. These two abilities are sometimes seen as opposites and even regarded as "enemies." We tend to superficially categorize people as either creative or analytical. There might be some truth to this simple dichotomy, but there are also strong connections that tie creativity and analysis together. One of the connections is that both skills require an imaginative mind.

In order to perform any kind of analysis, there are many questions to answer and many decisions to be made. One has to decide what needs to be analyzed, why there is such a need, how it should be analyzed, and what to expect from the analysis. In this process, the designer has to be able to imagine what will happen depending on the choices that are made, possible outcomes, and the value to place on them. Since the situation at hand in a design project is infinite in its complexity, analysis can become endless. Any aspect or detail of a design situation can, in principle, be analyzed forever. There is no natural end to the analytical process. It is always possible to say "we need to know more," and there will always be more to know. But design is limited by time and resource restrictions, and the need for analysis has to be controlled. Therefore analytical thinking depends on creative thinking. The designer makes creative decisions concerning what is relevant enough to analyze.

Conversely, in order for a creative mind to be useful, it needs to be able to distinguish between good and bad ideas, and to know a sustainable and workable idea from a misguided one. Pure creativity is therefore not what is most needed in design. Producing ideas is not difficult if there are no restrictions. Creating ideas that are relevant, appropriate, and capable of being realized, and at the same time are new and radical, however, can be very difficult. This means that creativity has to be balanced with analytical thinking.

As a designer, it is never possible to be strictly creative or strictly analytical. There are no situations during the design process that require only one of these abilities. A design process is about being creative and analytical at the same time, more or less all of the time. Studies of professional information system designers strongly corroborate this view of the relation between creativity and analysis (Stolterman 1991). We might even claim that the dynamic tension between creativity and analysis is at the core of design and therefore at the core of a designer's ability.

3.1.4 Values and Ideals

Design, like any other human activity, attracts people with diverse backgrounds, diverse knowledge and experiences, and diverse social and psychological traits. In the meetings that are part of design work, these differences have a strong impact on what will happen. As a creative activity, design naturally leads to confrontations and conflicts between opposing ideas, intentions, and knowledge. Most decisions and judgments are ultimately based on personal values and ideals.

Consider a simple example of values and ideals in interaction design: designing a support system for a car dealership. Depending on whose perspective you take, different underlying values will come to the surface, in the sense that different qualities of the digital artifact stand out as more or less valuable to a particular party involved. For the company, the guiding quality might be efficiency in the sales process. The customer might prioritize correct and complete information, including all costs involved. For the salesperson, the guiding value is perhaps a better work situation with more customer contacts and less administrative work. A designer has to deal with all of these values and wishes. At the same time, it is clear that it is not possible to fully comply with all of them, especially since some of them are contradictory in nature. This creates a field of tension within which the designer has to navigate.

In addition to values held by different participants involved in the process, there are also other values and ideals influencing the designer. Every society has a foundation of basic values that might be quite homogenous and stable in certain domains, while more dynamic and elusive in others. There are situations where a designer is challenged by questions concerning values on, for instance, what constitutes a dignified workplace or what is acceptable when it comes to working conditions in general. In some cases, these questions might even concern what is right or wrong from a legal standpoint, such as if the client wants a sales-support system that hides costs from the customer.

What responsibility does a designer have in these situations? What are the ethics of design? Each of us working in fields where we are supposed to change the world in some way has to face these questions. To a designer, they may seem intrusive from time to time. There is no simple way to get out of ethical dilemmas. There are no general rules, other than the meta-advice of establishing ethical awareness. As with other design abilities, it is more a matter of being prepared than having a specific recipe or procedure for how to act. It is important to participate in ongoing debates and critical examinations of what can be seen as legitimate tasks for design. It is about building your internal compass, your own thoughtful ethical position.

3.1.5 Aesthetic Sensibility

Within the IT industry and IT academia, the aesthetic aspect of digital artifacts has not been dealt with in a significant extent. This is not unique to interaction design, but quite common in design fields with a strong element of technological tradition. Functionality and efficiency are prioritized over aesthetics. It is common to assume that aesthetic aspects are rather superficial—related solely to shape, form, and color. However, the aesthetic qualities of digital artifacts go far beyond the surface. One of the most fascinating aspects of a digital artifact is that it must be understood aesthetically as an experience over time. When you use a digital artifact, you do things, the artifact responds, you act back, and so on. It is an unfolding story. The artifact gradually reveals its *dynamic gestalt* (see further discussion in chapter 5). Gestalt can be understood as the overall image, the emergent dynamic whole, something changing over time. In this sense, when it comes to the aesthetic experience, a digital artifact is perhaps most closely related to time-based media such as film and performance.

To design something is to create something not yet existing. In the design process, the designer needs to be able to imagine the gestalt of the artifact. The artifact has to be *composed*. It is in a composition that ideas are given form and brought together with what already exists. Composition is about "putting things together" in a way that makes sense and creates a whole that has a gestalt including all that is needed and desired. To be able to imagine a gestalt, to see the whole, is a crucial design ability.

This skill can be understood as the ability to *see something as something* and to see how a composition becomes the expression of a balance between different demands on a design. Function, structure, and form have to be juggled in an interlocking balance. Design is never only one or the other of these aspects, but all of them at the same time.

A digital artifact will never be better than its gestalt, the totality of its composition. The quality of an automated teller machine (ATM), for instance, is not determined only by the efficiency of the transaction or the intelligibility of the user interface. If the users do not trust it, if they do not find the use situation acceptable, then the composition as a whole will lose its value and fail to live up to expectations.

The notions of gestalt, composition, and the whole may seem abstract and difficult to grasp. An alternative approach might be think of it as the total aesthetic dimension of a digital artifact. It is by composition and in the creation of the gestalt that the designer shapes the overall aesthetic experience that follows with the use of an artifact. Sensibility to aesthetic aspects of balance, harmony, rhythm, and relationships concerning whole versus details, function versus beauty, and efficiency versus usability, is also at the core of being a good designer. A designer's aesthetic sensibility has to be developed and extended by constant challenges and criticism, to avoid becoming mannerism and simplistic "style."

Aesthetic sensibility is in many ways how a designer expresses her personality in design. It is the trademark of a specific designer and her skills.

3.1.6 Judgment

We have already stated that a designer is constantly faced with situations that require *judgments*. In everyday life, we usually distinguish between situations where we can act according to a plan or method and others where we have to act based on our own judgment. The usual answer to a question where no straightforward procedure can be offered is, "Well, use your best judgment." The problem with judgment, in a superficial sense, is that it is not possible to prescribe. It turns out that this is the very definition of judgment. Judgment is the skill used in situations that cannot be fully described, specified, and prescribed. If it were possible to prescribe judgment, then we would not need it. Design, more than most other activities, depends on judgment. The reason for this is that design always takes place in complicated situations that prohibit the acquisition of complete information, and hence preclude fully rational action.

Since design is about the not-yet-existing, it will always be the case that the designer cannot obtain complete information. It is, by definition, impossible to know everything about something that does not exist. And things that do not exist cannot be calculated or derived from what is; they result from our intentions and desires (Nelson and Stolterman 2003). This means that judgment is an inevitable aspect of design.

The fact that design rests on judgment also means that we can never expect a design process to lead to the optimal or correct design. Design can only lead to a sufficient or *adequate* design. Adequate does not mean that the design could really have been better; it means that designers have to accept that any design is affected by the situation at hand. To be able to recognize an adequate design is at the core of what design is all about. This ability forms the basis for the designer's judgment, which in turn makes it possible to understand what is reasonable in relation to goals, limitations, restrictions, and resources.

Throughout a design process, different judgment situations appear. There is no singular type of judgment, different situations demand different types of judgment (the rest of this section is based on Nelson and Stolterman 2003). For a designer, it is of utmost importance to recognize situations when judgment is needed and also what kind of judgment is called for. When a designer knows that she is actually using her judgment, that it is both allowed and important, and that there are several different types of judgment, she can approach her design tasks more confidently. She can accept the demands put on her, and understand that she has to act even though she will never have complete information or knowledge.

Design processes involve judgment on behalf of the client as well as on behalf of the designer. Basically, the client has three types of judgments to make. The first is to decide whether or not the task at hand should be approached as a design task. There is always the possibility to approach the task as, for instance, an engineering process, a problem-solving process, or a scientific process. A client always has the right not to choose design as the preferred approach. If design is chosen as the approach, the client also has to make a judgment about which criteria will be used for evaluating the final design. The third judgment the client has to make concerns the overall purpose of the design.

A designer has to acknowledge that she always has to work with—or sometimes in opposition to—the judgments of the client. To some extent, these judgments create the context for the design work. As a designer, you have to recognize the judgments of the client as preconditions, but at the same time critically examine and challenge those judgments. A good client understands that the expertise of a designer might help in viewing the purpose of the design and the evaluation criteria in new ways. So even if these judgments are in the hands of the client, the designer can take part in the process.

In addition to the client's judgments, the designer has to face other aspects of the design situation, all of which demand her consideration. We will briefly discuss some design situations that demand different forms of judgment. Our purpose is not to give a complete description of judgment and its different types, but merely to indicate the importance of judgment in the complex conglomerate of aspects that constitute design ability. We would also argue that judgment can be approached in a more rational way than what is usually the case. Examining different types of judgment is a way to improve your judgment ability and to make situationally appropriate judgments.

When a designer first approaches a design situation, there is usually not a concrete idea about the nature of the final design. This is not to say that there are no ideas (see the discussion of vision in chapter 2). Specific functions, forms, or materials may be envisioned, but there is no composed whole. This situation is difficult to handle. The designer has to be able to start working with a situation that is extremely complex and underdetermined.

One of the first things that happens is that the designer creates a *frame*. The frame is the result of a judgment that sets provisional limits for the design and determines what should be considered to be inside and outside the scope of the design. It is similar to the situation where a photographer chooses what will be in the picture and what will be outside.

Another familiar analogy is when students are given an open assignment to write an essay on a subject of their own choice. To the inexperienced student, this freedom can be intimidating, since there are many choices to make just in order to get started. She has to choose a topic, perspective, message, style, layout, and so on. These decisions can only be seen as judgments, which means that the answer to the student's question of "How should I do this?" would be that "It depends . . . ." It depends on the student's abilities and what her goals are. So the student has to make her own judgments, which can be an unsettling process. The framing judgment creates the foundation for the design work that follows. It is one of the most important judgments in a design process.

Another type of judgment has to do with *composition*. To be able to judge what is a suitable composition is many times more important than being creative. Composition has to do with the overall wholeness of a design. It is usually about "putting things together," or composing all aspects and parts into a whole that has a certain balance and integrity. We have discussed composition earlier in this book and will only state here that the ability to make a judgment on composition is one of the vital aspects of design work. It is hopefully apparent that the two types of judgment mentioned so far are very different. Judgment has to be related to the purpose of a specific activity. Setting the frame is different from composing the whole.

A third type of judgment is *navigational judgment*. Throughout the design process, the designer faces situations where she has to choose between a range of alternatives.

This type of judgment does not demand creativity in coming up with new solutions. There are already several alternatives at hand, from which one has to be chosen in order to move the process along. Making this kind of choice, based on necessarily incomplete information, is very difficult and will depend on the designer's navigational judgment.

The types of judgment we have presented here are only examples (a more complete discussion of design judgments can be found in Nelson and Stolterman 2003). We believe that a thoughtful designer has to be reflective and critical of her own skills. The ability to make good judgments is one of the least noticed skills in design. Most designers would agree that judgment is important, but it is usually not examined or even recognized as something capable of examination, let alone something that can be intentionally developed. The purpose of our brief discussion is to make judgment visible and something worth examining. This leads to the more general question of how design ability can be developed.

3.2   Developing Design Ability

In this chapter, we have discussed what characterizes design ability. This raises new questions—in particular, the question of how design ability can be developed. We will argue that developing design ability is all about *preparing for action*. Design ability is not about finding the correct ways of doing things, the definitive method, or the perfect tools. Since design is always about acting in unique situations, it is impossible to for mulate generally applicable rules or methods that will always work. The designer has to be able to apply general knowledge in a specific situation. Design is all about being prepared and able to make good judgments.

First of all, a designer has to be confident that she will be able to make good judgments in a unique situation. She has to trust that good judgment leads to good actions and decisions. We might describe this phenomenon as trusting the *right feeling*. It might sound unreliable and irresponsible to put your trust into a feeling, but in design practice, there is nothing else to turn to. It is important, though, to understand that trusting the right feeling does not mean blindly following your feelings or impulses. The right feeling is a profound concept, bringing together many subtle and diffuse considerations present in any design situation. It can be seen as a placeholder for an advanced understanding of the core of design ability.

The right feeling can be understood as an everyday label for the ability we use in a specific situation when we do not have the time, opportunity, or capacity to comprehensively analyze and rationally examine the full complexity of the situation in order to make a decision and a choice. In design situations, this kind of time restraint is always going to be the case. The ability we refer to might be labeled as intuitive. Intuition is distinguished in its capacity to create an overview or a feeling of context and coherence. Intuition helps us to deal with complexity when we cannot make a rational decision in a deliberate and intentional way.

The kind of intuition we discuss here—the feeling that we can trust in a design situation—is not something that anyone has in any situation. It comes from long and serious preparation. Intuition in this sense is not the same as chance or guesswork; it is not a question of sitting down and "waiting for intuitive guidance." We think of intuition in a similar sense to the performance of an improvising musician. Musicians learning to improvise must reach a stage where they can play without having to plan their actions. There is not enough time to analyze each situation rationally and decide how to play in relation to the other musicians. The musicians have to trust their intuition. This kind of intuition is not something given or innate, but a skill that must be learned and developed over a long time. The purpose of all the preparation is to reach a stage where the musicians do not have to think about *how* to play, only *what* to play. In the unique moment, there are no rules or guidelines to guide improvisation. The musicians have to trust the right feeling.

We cannot prescribe design, and we cannot present guaranteed methods for developing design ability. Design is in itself the result of a design process and has to be treated as such. What we can offer are some ideas and suggestions on how to approach the task of developing design ability. How they work is, of course, dependent on the person and the situation, and a designer must use her judgment and knowledge to adapt them. More specifically, we would like to introduce four approaches that may serve as useful tools for design ability development:

- a sense of quality
- a developed language
- reflective thinking
- retrospective reflection

Designers need ways of navigating the design process and making decisions about which direction to pursue. A well-developed *sense of quality* can play an important role. The sense of quality has many facets. A designer must have a sense of structural, functional, ethical, and aesthetic aspects of design. There are other quality dimensions related to the different forms of judgment we mentioned previously. A sense of quality has to be developed, continuously challenged, and improved. In principle, there are two main ways to go about doing this: to focus on the process or on the product.

If we focus on the *process*, then the most important aspect to develop is an understanding of the quality of the process. This means that a designer should experience many processes and make all possible mistakes in order to gain experience. Through such an approach, the designer will learn to recognize general patterns in unique situations and recognize what patterns of actions to apply to each situation. An understanding of quality consists of paying close attention to patterns that keep reoccurring throughout the design process. This is similar to the musician's way of practicing by playing different songs in different variations, over and over again.

If the focus is on the *product* instead of the process, the sense of quality is tied to the qualities of designed products. This can be developed by paying close attention to the specific qualities of good and bad examples of design. Over time, such studies will lead to a sense of quality— a recognition of what determines good quality in a specific type of design. The basic idea is that a sense of quality when it comes to products will help to guide the designer in understanding what needs to be done in the process and enable her to plan the process in a way that leads to good products. For a musician, this might mean spending a lot of time listening to music that she really appreciates, while trying to examine what it is in her favorite music that makes it so good.

To an interaction designer, these two approaches will lead to very different ways of developing design ability. One approach entails spending time doing and practicing the process, while the other entails examining and evaluating already designed digital artifacts. To the thoughtful designer, however, the two approaches are not mutually exclusive. A thoughtful designer will understand that the right way to develop design ability can only be judged in relation to what it is supposed to promote. A designer needs to develop a sense of process quality as well as product quality. There is a time and place for both approaches in the preparation of thoughtful design work.

To develop a sense of quality more or less requires a development of a *language*. A designer needs a well-developed language in order to be able to express design ideas and design qualities. A sense of quality is not enough if that sense cannot be expressed in some kind of language. Note, however, that the language we talk about here is not necessarily limited to words. The contents of the repertoire we discussed earlier—examples, formats, exemplary models—also form "words," or perhaps the concepts behind words, in a design language.

Design is a social process, which means that communication with other participants is crucial. Moreover, a language is necessary in making ideas and thoughts more precise and well-crafted. It is usually not possible for a designer to refer to her "feeling" without more rational arguments to support or criticize her idea. Design disciplines have made significant efforts to develop design languages such as concepts for product semantics; in chapter 5, we will give some examples of what it might mean to develop such a language within interaction design in the field of digital artifacts.

A third, and more personal, way of improving your design ability is to study your own thoughts and actions. This requires *reflective thinking*. An important contribution to the field of design is the work of Donald Schön. In *Educating the Reflective Practitioner* (Schön 1987) and other books, he shows the efficiency of well-developed reflective thinking in the shaping of a creative design ability. He argues that the technical rationality dominating research and science today is not suitable for the chaotic and complex reality facing a designer. The quality of practice needs to be challenged through continuous reflective thinking. Schön's concepts of reflection-in-action and reflection-on-action summarize the basic idea of continuous reflective thinking. A practitioner has to reflect in her actions by separating herself from the actions and by judging the outcomes of the actions.

In addition to reflecting on one's own actions and thoughts, a designer can benefit from reflecting upon other designers' actions and thoughts. However, this is not easy to achieve in practice, since the matter for reflection is hidden in the minds of fellow designers. It is very difficult to "peek" into another designer's mind to see the assumptions and sense of quality that guide her towards a result. What we can access, however, is the tangible outcomes from other designers' actions and thoughts—that is, their designs. An interaction designer encounters many digital artifacts every day; each of these can be examined and analyzed with respect to the original designer's own ideals and ideas. We can always ask the question "What ideals and what thoughts might have guided the designer to create a product with these qualities?" This simple thought experiment can be called *retrospective reflection*.

Retrospective reflection can never reveal the ideas and ideals behind a specific product with certainty, but it will force the reflecting designer to come up with arguments and ideas that *could* explain a specific design. In such a way we can train our design thinking by doing it backward. Retrospective reflection does not lead to a recipe for how to approach design tasks, but it might help us in developing the necessary language and sensibility to design quality.

The approaches we have presented here should not be seen as straightforward methods or techniques. They will not lead to simple answers or quick fixes. Our aim is simply to inspire the development of design ability by outlining basic approaches that are hopefully useful. It is the closest thing to "instruction" that we can think of when it comes to developing design ability. We have to remember that design ability is first and foremost the ability to be a thoughtful designer.

As we said earlier, every designer needs her own approach to developing design ability. This is a design task in itself that has to be done in a thoughtful way. It is neither a simple choice of techniques nor a matter of acquiring the necessary information or knowledge, but rather a question of *assuming responsibility for one's own professional mind*. This is a very demanding process. To approach your own design ability as a design project takes effort, time, and energy. Conceptual tools such as the ones we have suggested—striving for a sense of quality, developing a language, practicing reflective thinking and retrospective reflection—may facilitate the process.

A thoughtful designer knows that we are talking about a lifelong design project of developing individually as a designer. It is about preparing for action and building the right feeling, so that when challenges appear in practical design work, intricate decisions can be made in the moment. The paradox of design ability is that a thoughtful approach, being slow and time-consuming in itself, will ultimately lead to design ability that enables the designer to act promptly in complex situations based on her intuition and judgment.

In all design fields, there is a natural interest in how-to aspects. When they are addressed in the literature, it is usually in the form of design methods. This book is not devoted to the actual procedures and practicalities of doing design. Instead, we are focusing on the way to reflect upon these aspects. However, we do have a chapter on methods and techniques. The reason is simply that a thoughtful designer needs to reflect on the role that methods and techniques play in the design process.

What do we mean by methods and techniques? Simply put, a method refers to a description of a way of working or a recipe for action. A method is always based on a specific purpose and specific values, and it translates them into an actable procedure. A technique is smaller in scope and ambition than a method and is frequently related to a particular form of expression or execution, as in the visual arts where pencil and charcoal can be categorized as techniques. A method may comprise several steps to be carried out in different techniques, or allow for the choice of different techniques in accomplishing a certain outcome.

In the field of information systems, one might come across the more or less tacit assumption that we can build better systems by developing better methods and simply adhering to them. We argue that this is a fallacy; the result of a process is never better than the capability of the people involved in carrying out the process. The implication for interaction design is that a designer's abilities ultimately determine the quality of the final system. This view means that methods and techniques must be seen as vehicles for developing the designer's abilities. By describing and characterizing modes of working that have led to desirable results in the hands of others, we can offer the reader the opportunity to develop her own practices. The choice of methods and techniques must always be made in relation to the situation at hand and the people involved.

One of the most important contributors to design methodology is John Christopher Jones, who published an exhaustive collection of design methods in 1970 under the title *Design Methods: Seeds of Human Futures* (Jones 1992). In the introductory chapters, he outlines different conceptualizations of the designer and the consequences of these conceptualizations on the choice of methods. If the designer is envisioned as a *black box* that produces creative solutions without being able to explain or illustrate what goes on in the process, then there needs to be a focus on methods to facilitate and support such hidden inexplicable creative processes. The other extreme is the designer as a *glass box,* where every step in the design process is rational, and capable of being described and disseminated. Glass box methods are highly systematic and tend to assume a sequential process and the decomposition of large problems into sets of smaller problems.

A third possible conceptualization of the designer, according to Jones, is as a *self-organizing system* who has the capability to look for ideas and solutions as well as the capability to assess her own process. This conceptualization leads to methods with strong elements of metacognition that support the designer's reflection upon work process and strategy. This is also the conceptualization we prefer: the designer as a reflective practitioner, with the ability to act and the ability to reflect in and on her actions.

For us, describing a method is a way to give designers insights into practices and ways of working that they would perhaps not have thought of otherwise. A method is never simply used, but rather appropriated: the designer has the responsibility of assessing the nature and role of a method, its possible outcomes, and underlying values, and then to add it to her toolbox and apply it skillfully in relevant situations. All these steps require intentional and critical judgment, as well as the self-awareness of making decisions about which methods and techniques to employ.

That is why the emphasis of this chapter is placed on *ways of thinking about* methods and techniques, and not on providing context-free procedures of how-to information. More specifically, we want to illustrate a design-theoretical way of thinking about methods and techniques in interaction design. To this end, we discuss a set of methods and techniques that we find relevant for interaction design. This discussion includes methods from general design methodology, from design disciplines such as industrial design, and methods more specifically oriented toward the creation of digital artifacts. Standard methods from the fields of information systems, human-computer interaction, and software engineering are not included in this chapter, since we concentrate on providing a design-oriented complement to the dominant practices in the respective fields.

As a way to support the reader's appropriation of the methods and techniques we describe in what follows, we introduce five main headings: inquiry, exploration, composition, assessment, and coordination. In comparing these headings with the general concepts of vision, operative image, and specification outlined in chapter 2, note that the ones we use here are more activity-oriented. The reason for this is simply that the sources of methods and techniques that we sample in this chapter are typically oriented towards activities and actions, which necessitates a structuring principle of the same nature. Throughout the discussions to follow, it should be self-evident how the structure of this chapter relates to our more general discussion of the design process in chapter 2.

Inquiry corresponds to the aspects of design work that are mainly oriented toward finding out about a design situation, both in terms of what the situation is currently like and what it could be like in a possible future. *Exploration* is a general label for the work involved in moving through the spaces of possible solutions and problem formulations. *Composition* refers to the methods and techniques involved in crossing the gap from a more general vision to an increasingly specific operative image. *Assessment* is the critical examination of a design idea, concept, specification, prototype, or artifact. *Coordination* is the meta-level of our structure: involving methods and techniques intended to facilitate the design process, particularly the coordination between multiple participants in the process.

The design-theoretical way of thinking about methods and techniques for interaction design consists of both our selection of methods to present and the five-heading categorization that provides clues as to the intentions or main characteristics of the selected methods. It is our understanding that such a design-theoretical approach to methods and techniques is also the approach of the thoughtful designer.

4.1 Inquiry

In many ways, the design process as a whole can be said to be about learning and inquiry. Nevertheless, the early stages of a design process are most clearly oriented towards finding out more about a present design situation. The better part of the methodology literature in the fields of information systems and human-computer interaction addresses cases where the use situation already exists, typically in a workplace, and where the designer's initial task is to learn as much as possible about this situation. This is an honorable goal, of course, but it tends to overlook the crucial difference between existence and potentiality, or between that which exists and that which could exist. In other words, many methods prescribe a detailed analysis of workflows and information pathways of future users' current work and organization.

What we need to recognize, however, is that the situation being analyzed is a complex mixture of the temporary and the timeless. New digital artifacts have the potential to transform much of what is currently understood as good practice, but not all of it. If the analysis of a design situation is not sensitive to this distinction, there is a risk that the outcome of the design process fails: either by merely proposing computer-supported versions of current manual tasks, if the transformative potential of the new technology is anxiously underexploited, or by proposing insensitive innovations where the timeless qualities of the current practice are overlooked. Design takes place at the delicate balance between what exists and what could exist, and it would be presumptuous to attempt to predict the future by merely analyzing the current situation. A better basis for decision is obtained by experimenting repeatedly with the dialectical relationship between the present and elements of a possible future.

In a nutshell, this means that inquiry at early stages of a design process is extremely hard. It is essential, of course, to provide an initial understanding of the design situation, but inquiry does not end after the first steps of a design process. It proceeds in the continuous reframing of design ideas and problem formulations that are a core characteristic of design. In fact, inquiry becomes easier the further on we move into the design process. In this sense, it is hard to distinguish between inquiry and exploration, as we see in this chapter.

However, as we move further along in the design process, we also move closer to the end when the final result is due. By necessity, it takes longer to realize an artifact in all its details than to come up with an idea of its core qualities and characteristics. A reasonable compromise is to arrange the processes of inquiry to be sensitive to this dilemma. Field techniques used to study the design situation should be built around the distinction between what is and what might be. A designer must be encouraged to broaden her inquiry through quick and inexpensive techniques that complement expensive and time-consuming fieldwork. We describe two methods of inquiry here that seem to fit these criteria rather well: *contextual inquiry* and *why-why-why*. In addition, the *future workshop* method we describe later could also be seen as a method of inquiry.

4.1.1 Contextual Inquiry

Contextual inquiry was formulated in the field of human-computer interaction in the late 1980s as part of a user-oriented systems development method called *contextual design*. It is presented by Beyer and Holtzblatt (1997) as a set of principles and techniques based on the idea that systems design should be grounded in the work of future users, but also aim to enrich the work through the new possibilities offered by information technology.

A contextual inquiry consists of interviews combined with observations, where the goal is to construct a rich picture of the actual work situation: roles, responsibilities, problems with the work and existing tools, and so on. Contextual inquiry is guided by three principles.

Context   Start with the real work situation, not with what people say they do.
Partnership   Future users are experts in their work and should be jointly responsible for the inquiry.
Focus   Everybody focuses on something different in the same situation; it is important to be aware of this fact and actively try to extend the total focus of the inquiry.

An interview is best performed when the person to be interviewed is working on her daily tasks, the interviewer is right next to her, and the two discuss what is happening and what it means. The interviewer does not only take down what the interviewee says, but also what she does if there are any problems, if the tools used in the work cause disturbances or distractions, and to what extent the tools support the work. Several people are interviewed in this way in order to cover as many roles and viewpoints as possible. The results are analyzed as a whole in order to establish a focus, interpret the information, structure the interpretations, and gradually approach a vision of the new system to be developed.

4.1.2   Why-why-why?

In order to keep a broad perspective during inquiry-intensive phases of a design process, it is essential to question and move beyond the problem as it is currently perceived. One way of doing this is to ask a series of why-questions and build a chain of reasoning backward from the original formulation. Assume, for instance, that we are involved in a project with a local hospital where the handling of X-ray images seems problematic. There is a manual X-ray archive, which works like a library for interlibrary loans, where all the images are stored. Medical staff and others authorized to access X-ray images do so by filling out request forms and, after a day or two, the requested images arrive via internal mail unless they are already on loan to someone else. Let us further assume that the project we are engaged in was initiated by a dissatisfied physician:

Physician (P):   I am not happy with the way X-ray images are currently handled at this hospital.
Designer (D):   Why?
P: Because I have to order my images several days in advance.
D: Why?
P: I never know in advance how long it will take to get them.
D: Why?
P: If the images I want are on loan to someone else, then I have to wait until they return them.

D: Why?

P: There is only one copy of each image.

Note that the why-chains can branch off in different directions, depending on how the why-question is interpreted and whose perspective is assumed in answering:

P: I am not happy with the way X-ray images are handled today.

D: Why?

P: Because I get the wrong images sometimes.

D: Why?

P: Because the X-ray archive staff makes mistakes.

D: Why?

P: I have no idea. Too much work, perhaps.

Why-chains like these can inspire many different design ideas, depending on where you enter the chain and what values you bring to it. In this example, we could concentrate on improving the work in the manual image archive (new procedures, more rapid feedback to the person sending a request, new forms of communication, making several copies of each image, and so on). For an interaction designer looking at these why-chains, it might be more natural to think in terms of a support system for the archive staff, where the requests are placed electronically and the storage location and loan status of all images are represented, much like the system keeping track of books in a regular library. This type of system could also automatically notify the requesting party if all copies of a requested image are on loan.

It is important to notice that the why-why-why method is a way of probing the problem formulation and *not* a systematic method that infallibly leads to good results. In order to create a useful why-chain, a designer has to be sensible to which paths are promising and which ones are dead ends:

P: I am not happy with the way X-ray images are currently handled at the hospital.

D: Why?

P: Because I am generally grumpy and frustrated.

This why-why-why example illustrates what we discussed earlier—namely, that the result of a method is never better than the people involved in carrying out the process. There are an infinite number of why-question chains leading to completely different conclusions. Therefore, setting up a useful why-chain is a bit like the whole design process in a micro-perspective: it involves designing the problem and the solution in parallel.

In inquiring about a design situation, the designer has to reflect on what kind of information she really needs. Inquiry without intention—that is, without an idea of purpose and outcome—easily becomes a randomly executed examination of the situation. The design of an inquiry, and choice of methods and techniques for doing it, is therefore one of the most important aspects of design.

4.2   Exploration

As we noted earlier, the distinction between inquiry and exploration is by no means clear when it comes to design. However, it seems to make sense to talk about inquiry in the context of finding out the characteristics of the design situation at hand, that is, the study of the existing. If we adopt that convention, we can talk about exploration when we consider the study of the possible, or of what might be.

Some design theorists describe exploration as searching through a space of possible designs or solutions. Whether the space already exists for us to discover, or whether it is in principle infinite and genuinely constructed as we explore it, is a philosophical question that we need not address here. Either way, there is a multitude of methods and techniques in the design literature intended to facilitate this exploration. It is generally seen as desirable in certain phases of explorative work to cover as much ground and generate as many solution ideas as possible. Moreover, the possibilities a designer explores should draw on different foundational principles rather than minor variations of the same basic idea. This diversity of possibilities is known as divergence and is closely related to everyday notions of creativity, lateral thinking, and so on.

We recognize the value of divergence for two main reasons. First, the danger of "design fixation," where all considered possibilities draw on the same basic idea, always implies the risk of overlooking better possible solutions based on other foundations. Second, it is not uncommon for designers to get personally involved with their proposals. In a team situation, such personal involvement makes it hard to discuss the proposal constructively. Comments that are critical of the proposal run the risk of being interpreted as critical of the person behind the proposal. A consciously divergent approach helps avoid this problem, since it is harder for the designer to be personally involved in ten different proposals. Viewing one of your own design ideas as any idea among many—an idea with its merits and shortcomings—is hard. Coming up with ten ideas makes it easier to see that each designer's ideas are, in fact, only a few examples among many.

Divergence, however, has dangers as well. Using methods such as the ones we present here, it is not very hard for a designer to come up with many ideas. The hard part is to come up with good ideas. It can be argued that the generation of many ideas increases the chances of finding the good ones, but then the problem becomes recognizing the good ones. The ability to assess quality and identify fruitful paths for further development can never be exchanged for divergence in the simplistic sense. In other words, quantity is never a substitute for quality. We discussed the notion of quality in some depth in chapter 3 and urge you to keep that notion in mind as we move on to a few examples of methods and techniques for exploration.

4.2.1 Future Workshops

A *future workshop* is a method for participatory social and organizational development (Jungk and Müllert 1987) that has been successfully adapted to work-oriented design of digital artifacts (Kensing and Madsen 1991). The aim of a future workshop is for future users or stakeholders to clarify the common problems in their current situation, create visions about the future, and discuss how these visions could be realized. The future workshop has three phases: critique, fantasy, and implementation.

The *critique* phase is a brainstorming session on problems in the current work situation. Contributions are formulated as brief, critical observations or statements. They are grouped in categories corresponding to problem areas. Participants are then divided into small groups, where each group takes one problem area and formulates a concise and coherent critique of it.

The *fantasy* phase is oriented toward unrestricted ideas on what the future situation could be like. Kensing and Madsen recommend a warm-up exercise where critical contributions from the previous phase are transformed into positive ones. The main creative part of the fantasy phase is a second brainstorming session, this time on future possibilities. It is particularly important that all criticism and judgment of the viability of proposals is postponed during this session. The ideas from the brainstorming session are evaluated by a vote, where each participant chooses five favorites. The seven or eight winning ideas are then collected into a basis for a vision. Participants are divided into small groups again, and each group develops their own refined version of the vision, still without regard to practical and technical limitations. Kensing and Madsen strongly recommend the use of metaphors as a way to summarize and develop the vision.

The *implementation* phase starts when each small group presents its vision. The possibility of realizing different visions under current conditions are assessed in a joint discussion, which also includes an identification of what needs to be changed in order to realize the visions. The future workshop concludes with a plan for further work: what needs to be done, when, and by whom.

In the field of information systems, future workshops are seen mainly as a way to initiate a process of change among future system users. The designer is thought of as a facilitator who makes sure that all participants' view are heard, fruitful metaphors are used, results are documented, and so on. We find it perfectly feasible to use the future workshop method in a design team where developers and designers participate—for instance, in a product development situation where the target audience is not well defined in terms of a specific workplace. A future workshop in that context would be very similar to the *system transformation* method described by Jones (1992): the identification of existing problems, the creation of a "goal state" where the problems are solved, and finally, the construction of a "chain of transformation" from the current state to the goal state.

4.2.2   Brainstorming

Brainstorming is an associative technique that most people have heard about, but not many people have actually used it to its full potential. The aim of this technique is to help a group of people quickly generate and organize a large number of ideas starting from a given question or problem. The technique was introduced by Osborne in the 1950s, but our description here is based on Jones (1992). Brainstorming broadly consists of three steps: collecting a group of people, generating ideas without judgment or analysis, and structuring the results to make them useful for further work.

Collecting a Group of People to Produce Ideas Together   It is, of course, most useful if this group contains some of the people who will subsequently use the results, but it can also be valuable to introduce other relevant people's perspectives. A group size of between three and seven people is the most appropriate.

Generating Ideas   The group gathers around a table or in front of a wall. Each participant has a pen and some pieces of paper. The rules for the generation phase are then reviewed:

•   Nobody is allowed to criticize or question an idea. Everybody must feel comfortable with proposing anything without fearing comments such as, "You can't do that!" Ideas are not to be discussed during generation; discussion and analysis comes later.
•   The group's goal is to produce as many ideas as possible. Do not wait for the best moment—as soon as you get an idea, write it down and present it to the group.

- It is good to combine and build upon the ideas of others. The whole point of brainstorming in a group is that you should be inspired to have new, unexpected, crazy, and good ideas by what other people say.
- Only one idea per piece of paper is allowed. The subsequent analysis and structuring phase will be more convenient if the team does not have to split notes or write new ones.

Then the generation of ideas begins. The question or problem motivating the brainstorming is introduced briefly, without hinting at any particular solution approaches. The initial question or problem is not discussed or elaborated; experience shows that people who are not used to brainstorming can spend hours trying to refine the group's task if they are allowed to, perhaps in an attempt to postpone the unknown and stay in the safe mode of critical elaboration. This should not be allowed to happen in a brainstorming session. A slightly ambiguous or underdefined starting point might make it easier for people to start generating diverse ideas in a brainstorming session.

After introducing the starting point, each member of the group tries to think of ideas and simultaneously react to what other members propose. As a person thinks of an idea, she writes it on a piece of paper and places it on the table or the wall while reading aloud what she has written. After the first few minutes, the group typically goes into a highly intensive phase. Idea generation continues until the energy level begins to wane.

In groups where people do not know each other from before, it might be hard to break the ice at the beginning of idea generation. A reliable alternative in such situations is to start by individual preparation, where group members spend a few minutes thinking about the starting points and writing down ideas. Then the group process is initiated by rounds where all members take turns proposing one idea each. This is usually sufficient to get the ideas going and the energy level up.

Structuring the Results   There are many ways to utilize the idea notes from the generation phase, but a common method is to construct an affinity diagram. The group jointly sorts the ideas into clusters of ideas that seem to belong together. The first round of sorting is also an opportunity to remove duplicates and clarify cryptic notes. When the notes are sorted into categories that feel appropriate, the group tries to name each category and write a new note with the category name. If there are many groups, the next step is to repeat the affinity sorting for the category labels, which should eventually result in a tree structure of ideas with a few levels of headings.

In practice, affinity sorting nearly always leads to overlap, ideas fitting into several categories, and structures that do not seem relevant with respect to the idea generation

poses a new digital storage medium for the X-ray images and all the implications that would entail.

We can also note that the two sub-solutions have rather far-reaching consequences, maybe significant enough to warrant a reassessment of the entire vision. We are apparently no longer thinking only about a support system for the X-ray image archive staff, but rather a change in the larger system where image providers (the archive itself and its staff) and image consumers (the medical staff) are the two main actors.

4.2.5 Various Techniques for Transcending Fixations

Despite the importance of divergence in exploration, it is not uncommon for a designer to get stuck with the idea she happened to think of first. This is particularly true in cases where the problem or the idea seems familiar, and it may cause problems if the first idea is not quite good enough but captures the designer's thoughts to the extent that it is hard for her to go beyond it. Many techniques have been suggested to get out of such a situation known as "design fixation," some of them involving unexpected questions:

- Are there any new technologies I could use?
- What ideas can I find in other areas?
- What are the trends of the field in other countries and cultures?
- What would I do if I were a competitor?
- What would I do ten years from now?
- What would I do if the project budget were ten times larger? Ten times smaller?

Other proposed techniques for avoiding fixation address the idea generation strategy:

- Look for a physical analogy, a biological system, or a metaphor.
- Take a day off and browse a shopping mall or a computer store.
- Make wild and random guesses.
- Take a known idea that is not good enough and ask other people to critique it.
- Take an impossible idea and ask people to critique it.

De Bono (1993) describes *random input,* a strategy-oriented technique using randomly chosen material. It is almost ridiculously simple: Place the problem, or the creative focus where you need new ideas, in relation to a randomly chosen word.

X-ray image system: fair

We then try to develop new ideas from the resulting combination. In this example, we might think of the type of fair where companies present their products, visitors browse the offerings, and talks and seminars are arranged on topics pertinent to the subject of the fair. What if the X-ray image system contained a forum for discussions on diagnoses, second opinions from experienced colleagues, ideas for different treatments, or reflections on the work of diagnostic radiology! This idea feels quite interesting, possibly worth developing further, but most of all it highlights the need to know more about the social organization of the work around X-ray images and diagnostics, and the possibilities to change that organization if appropriate.

In this example, I (Löwgren) got the word *fair* by closing my eyes and pointing at random into a dictionary. De Bono also suggests other ways of acquiring the random input, such as making a list of sixty randomly chosen words, then looking at the second hand of your wristwatch, and taking the corresponding word when you need to generate new input. The list has to be revised occasionally in order to keep the impulses fresh.

The use of random input has been an important factor in the development of Jones's thinking on design theory, starting from his authoritative collection of design methods in 1970 and moving toward experiments with chance-driven processes both in design and in writing design theory. A good example is the collection *Essays in Design* (Jones 1984) where the essays are composed around randomly selected quotes. Inspired by the composer John Cage (among others), Jones devised a system for accessing his own collection of books based on random numbers. The exact means of acquiring random input are perhaps not very important in general, but what is important is that the input is truly random rather than something you try to think up yourself. The technique of random input is based on the idea of adding new impulses to a more or less saturated thought process. The saturated process cannot be expected to provide a new impulse by itself; when you try to think of something new, it will almost certainly be something too close to the previous line of thought.

The real crux of transgression techniques is, of course, to determine that the current idea is not good enough, that you are stuck in a rut, and that you need to actively bypass the fixation. The elusive notion of judgment is apparent again (see chapter 3), as the sense that your current operative image is not good enough is not something that can be easily documented in a systematic method. It might be that transgression techniques in general are most useful in cases where the designer has produced an idea that she believes in, but where subsequent evaluation or assessment have demonstrated it to be inadequate. At that point, we believe that many designers have a tendency to look for incremental improvements to address the problems identified, whereas an attempt to look for entirely new ideas would probably be well worth the effort.

For instance, suppose that we get stuck on the idea of offering the medical staff in the X-ray archive example tools for searching a database of digitized X-ray images. Our first attempt features a fairly conventional database search form. As we test the prototype at the hospital, it turns out that the search form is hard to understand and to use. Medical staff members have trouble performing searches and, even worse, they do not seem interested in the idea. We analyze the data from the small evaluation session and find a number of problems that could easily be fixed: there is a button that should be moved to another window, the labels of a few menu alternatives should be rephrased, and so on. But it does not feel right; we keep thinking about the frustrated look on the head nurse's face as she sat down to try the prototype that we felt so proud of. We spend days tweaking the details of the interface and going over the evaluation data, but it still feels wrong. This is clearly a good time to recognize that we are stuck.

To break the fixation of X-ray database searching, we try to think in terms of metaphors and similes: What is this system like? Since the medical staff uses a light box today to view X-ray images, then maybe the new system is also a light box. It should be used that way, anyhow. An idea! A database system that emphasizes the light box, the images themselves, and the visual and dynamic aspects of handling and comparing X-ray images. There have to be search tools, of course, but the point is that the system should not feel like a database where a medical staff member would type in the query, submit the search, and receive a batch of hits. Rather, it should be a place, a surface where the user looks at X-ray images and handles them. That would also mean that each user should have convenient access to a personal collection where she keeps images that she is working with for the moment. And so we are off on a different track. The fixation is bypassed.

When it comes to transgression, it is also important to recognize that basically no design problems are genuinely new. There are always examples of similar products, research studies concerning the contexts of which our design situation is one example, fiction and science fiction sketching bold ideas in the area, and so on. It would be odd to call literature and market research a method or technique, but it must nevertheless be emphasized how important it is to have a good overview of the design domain. To approach each design situation as a blank slate and work only from first principles is a huge waste of resources. We will not go into the details of how literature and market research is conducted, but we will provide a practical example of how it is used in design processes.

In developing the X-ray example, we stumbled over an ethnographic field study of diagnostic radiology (Ramey, Rowberg, and Robinson 1996).[1] The researchers presented the working processes and conditions of X-ray diagnosis in a rather detailed and accessible way, and we noted two particular findings that served as immediate inspirations for functions in our intended system. First, the study highlights the importance of physically manipulating the images under scrutiny: pointing to them, marking areas, and annotating the images themselves. In terms of interaction design, this could suggest personal collections of transparent sheets that the medical staff can lay over the images, draw and type on, save and later retrieve by association with the images connected to the sheets. The other finding was the importance of being able to combine the overview of a whole series of images with magnified detail views of parts of individual images. This suggests a focus+context approach.[2] This approach could be as simplistic as a two-level presentation where collections of thumbnail images (possibly with significant visual features automatically enhanced) provide the overview and the main work area offers magnification and other operations on a detailed level.

Exploring possibilities is a major part of any design process. We hope to have shown that exploration is not only about using the right methods or techniques, but also about the ability to know what kind of situation you are facing: Is it a lack of alternative solutions, fixation on one idea, difficulty in going beyond the ordinary, or something else? Exploration is therefore not one specific task, but a whole range of tasks. A designer needs to have the ability to recognize the task at hand and to choose and employ a suitable approach, method, or technique.

4.3 Composition

In all design processes, there are situations when the designer has to make a whole out of certain parts. Design is a composition of the existing and the potential, or in other words, of the present and an idea of the future. It is a composition of technological and social systems aspects. It is a composition of function, ethics, and aesthetics. Interaction design requires of the designer to deliberate on all these issues and finally make decisions on the final composition. This is a very personal process that has to do with a sense of balance in structure, material, function, and use. However, there are methods and techniques to support the work of composition.

4.3.1 Functional Analysis

Functional analysis is a technique originating in industrial design, where product development for broad and largely anonymous markets is quite common. Sources of information in such design processes are typically diverse, including studies of competing products, market surveys, interviews with intended users and specialists, field studies of the intended use situation, and so on. The main purpose of functional analysis is to get an overview of this diverse information, structure it, and determine where more information needs to be gathered. As such, functional analysis can be seen as an inquiry technique. However, we choose to include it in the composition section for the following reason: The emerging design is represented in functional analysis on a very high level of abstraction, meaning that it can be recomposed significantly with minimal effort. Functional analysis therefore provides an interesting contrast to most other composition techniques, where the design is expressed in much more detail.

A functional analysis aims at expressing what the emerging design is going to do in terms of its functions, but not how it is going to do it. Functions are typically represented with two words, a verb and a noun. If a function is absolutely crucial for the design to fulfill its main purpose, then it is classified as *essential* (E). If it is useful but not essential, it is deemed *desirable* (D). Finally, if the analysis shows that a certain function should not be in the design, then we call that function *undesirable* (U). Functions can also be classified as unknown (?) if their value is not yet clear.

We can retrace our evolving understanding of the X-ray image example from earlier in the chapter in order to capture where we currently stand in the design process. Bringing the information sources and design ideas together in the functional-analysis structure of verb-noun functions and then classifying the functions yields the following state of the design.

Function	Classification	Comment
Supply X-ray images	E	The core idea of the design.
Search images	D	
Manage images	D	Light box idea, visual and dynamic, focus+ context interface, personal image collections.
Support communication	D	Annotations and markup of X-ray images.
Support communication	?	Professional, work-related forum for mentoring, second opinions, discussions on diagnostics, and so on.

Note that the second sense of the function "support communication" in the bottom row is not classified. The reason is that the quality of the functional idea is unknown at this stage; it could be a very powerful idea, but we need to know more about the social organization of diagnostic radiology at the hospital in question before we can make that assessment. For reasons of brevity, functions that have been discarded (after being classified as undesirable), such as the idea of supporting the X-ray image archive staff rather than the medical staff, are not shown in the table.

Finally, we may note that the concise summary offered by functional analysis demonstrates the early and tentative state of the design process. There are large gaps in the composition, which will need to be filled before the resulting design can be a complete digital artifact. Some examples include functions for acquiring and storing new images, for administration of image databases, and for data security. Another class of functions missing from the design at this stage is the potentially significant contribution of automated image analysis techniques to diagnostic work.

4.3.2 Techniques for Detailed Shaping

A large part of composition work is to move toward a gradually more detailed operative image and eventually form a specification (see the discussion in chapter 2). In interaction design, a whole range of techniques has been introduced for this purpose. We outline the most significant ones here and briefly discuss their scopes and limitations.

Most visual shaping techniques discussed here are illustrated by hand-drawn pictures. This is a conscious choice, which has to do with how the resulting expression is perceived in the design process. If a storyboard, for instance, is drawn by hand in a rather simple and clunky way at early stages of composition work, it is consistent with the state of the process up to that point. People will find it rather easy to criticize such a drawing, since it does not appear to represent a great deal of effort. This is particularly important in interactions with intended users, where there is always the risk that a tidy, computer-generated expression will be interpreted as a final solution. This is a problem for at least two reasons. First, the designer might have intended the sketch as an early probe in an ideation process that is far from finished. A rough hand-drawing is more likely than a detailed machine drawing to stimulate dialogue. The other reason is that a tidy "final" drawing creates expectations of rapid delivery ("It looks like you are nearly done, then. Can we have it on our server by Friday?")

A *scenario* is a story about how the intended system is used. Writing stories is a quick and accessible way of contributing to the shaping of a design. The scenario should be made as elaborate and personal as possible, in order to force the design team to pose and answer questions regarding intended users.

A simple example of a scenario, again using the X-ray image project, might look like this:

Jane is a specialist in oncology with significant experience in diagnostic radiology. She has a few minutes before her staff meeting and decides to take a look at the new images of the patient she met on Tuesday with the suspected liver tumor. She can't remember the name of the patient and does not feel like bothering the nurses. Instead, she logs on to the computer system and requests a summary of the most recent X-ray examinations that she has ordered. Ah, there he is halfway down the list: Eddie Miller, age 68. The summary indicates that the new images are ready. She opens them on the screen and picks out a couple of particularly clear ones. If the shading in the middle of the liver has grown in the last few weeks, it is almost certainly a tumor. Jane locates earlier pictures of the same patient with the same camera settings and places them next to the most recent one. Regrettably, the difference is clearly visible: It has to be a malignant tumor. Jane does not even need to compute difference images to be sure.

A significant advantage of a scenario is that it is highly flexible. In the example of the X-ray database, we do not address the details of how Jane handles the interface of the system, but instead concentrate on the functions or user services available. We could just as well have written a more detailed story in order to shape the detailed interaction techniques of the system.

It is instructive to compare the scenario techniques with systematic specification of the same design information, as follows. Which form of expression provides the best understanding of the design ideas? Which is the easiest to envision and react to?

User role specialist physician
Use context pressed for time
Task diagnostic radiology
System services personal logon; summary of patients for each physician; selection of X-ray images (selection criteria: patient, camera settings, time of capture); image analysis (difference image computation).

Written scenarios are very useful in the early stages of a design process, when work on the operative image primarily concerns the development and grounding of the vision. They are flexible in the sense that the people appearing in scenarios can be closely modeled on results of field studies, or be fictive but highly credible characters, or be fictive and extreme characters. Which approach to take depends on whether the scenario is intended to provide a grounding in the current situation or to explore more remote regions of the design space. Scenarios have great communicative potential, most people can understand them and perhaps even write their own or revise old ones. The main downside to scenarios is their lack of precision, and the amount of administrative work becomes nontrivial when the number of scenarios starts to grow (because of the fact that they are easy to create and revise).

An *interface sketch* is a drawing of what the intended system should look like to the user. Figure 4.1 illustrates an interface sketch from the X-ray image project.

In drawing an interface sketch, the designer is forced to address more detailed questions concerning interaction techniques and spatial structuring. Note, however, that an interface sketch is frequently intended to communicate ideas on deeper levels, including user functions, allocation of work between user and computer, and user needs. In other words, an interface sketch is often used to communicate, develop, and ground visions. This typically requires the designer to actively guide the conversation

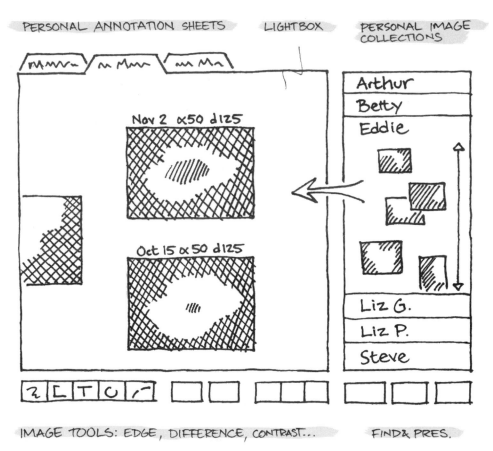

Figure 4.1

An interface sketch, showing the light box, image collections, and annotation sheets.

to those deeper levels, since the sketch deals superficially with issues of detailed interaction and spatial structure. In order to avoid low-level debates at too early of a stage ("I think the image collections should go on the left"), it is important to lead by example and move the discussion to the appropriate level.

Interface sketches are fairly flexible. They can be used to express a wide range of display-based designs, particularly if the sketches are complemented with written scenarios, explanations, or draft user manuals. They are also fairly accessible. One drawback to interface sketches is the hard work that is needed to revise them, unless the designer uses several sheets of semi-transparent sketching paper as an architect would. The main drawback, however, is that an interface sketch cannot really capture the details of a highly interactive, tightly coupled, pliable design (these three terms are defined in chapter 5). It works best for large-grain interactivity using standard interaction techniques and in fact sometimes limits the designer to those possibilities ("I have this really interesting interaction idea, but I can't draw it. Oh well, maybe it's not so important after all.").

A *storyboard* can be seen as a combination of a scenario and an interface sketch. The idea behind a storyboard is simply to draw a series of interface sketches showing how a certain use sequence is played out in the interface. In order to engage the viewer and provide points of identification, it may be suitable to include people who think, react and maybe talk. Figure 4.2 illustrates a storyboard combining the scenario and the interface sketch from the X-ray example used throughout this chapter.

Storyboards combine the advantages of scenarios and interface sketches in that they are expressive, flexible, and accessible. Moreover, they provide good possibilities to shape the intended dynamics of the design, even for animation and tightly coupled animation sequences. The main disadvantage is the amount of work involved in revising a storyboard, since each change typically has to be made in multiple places. A way of partially addressing that problem is to draw the most important parts of the storyboard in detail, while merely sketching the surrounding background.

All the shaping techniques discussed so far were developed in a time when digital artifacts primarily meant a screen, a keyboard, and a mouse. The rapid development of new interaction technologies and infrastructures necessitates new techniques for detailed shaping. It is, of course, possible to draw interface sketches of the small display of a palm-held computer, but those sketches will likely not capture the most important aspects of the design's intended use. We are increasingly looking at design situations of interactional fluency, where the user moves in and out of digital media streams throughout her everyday work and leisure time. Two suitable techniques for such spatial and mobile design situations are role-play (which will be described in greater detail later in the chapter) and movie scenarios.

Figure 4.2
A visual storyboard in which Jane, the oncology specialist, locates the X-ray images of Eddie's liver, selects a couple of them, and places them on the light box to compare them.

A *movie scenario* is a story about how the intended system is used, much like the written scenarios described earlier, but expressed in a movie form. The story typically illustrates how a user or group of users gets something done using currently non-existing digital artifacts. In some cases (e.g., the project illustrated in figure 4.3), the interaction techniques in movie scenarios are quite detailed; in other instances, they might be hinted upon using crude props and prototypes.

The main point of a movie scenario is that rough or detailed design ideas can be placed into a more coherent narrative context. A good movie scenario makes it possible for the viewer to imagine the use of the intended system, or to experience it to a certain extent by proxy. Movie scenarios may sound prohibitively expensive, but they can sometimes be produced on a tight budget using inexpensive recording equipment and regular desktop editing features. The downsides of movie scenarios are mainly that the skills and resources needed for movie production are not always available and that a movie scenario that is too polished might in fact have the same effect as a tidy and final-looking drawing: the viewers may be able to say whether or not they like it, but it does not allow for creative and constructive dialogue. An additional explanation for the paralyzing effect movie scenarios can have might be that we are more or less used to "leaning backward" in the presence of a TV set.

The shaping techniques described so far are biased in the sense that the designer decides what use or interaction sequence to illustrate. This may be good at some stages, since it preserves the focus on the system's intended use, but for the viewer it becomes rather static. A *dynamic paper prototype* is a simple way to illustrate the interactive character of the intended system more expressively (see figure 4.4).

The idea is straightforward: Prepare a number of interface sketches that feature pictures of interaction states that the user might reach. When the prototype is demonstrated and tested, the designer acts as the window manager. The person using the prototype pretends to press a button or type input to a field, and the designer presents the appropriate resulting picture depending on the input that is given. Pop-up menus can be written on sticky notes and placed on the picture when the user presses a particular spot on the interface. Scrollable windows can be arranged by dragging a long strip of window contents under a window-shaped hole. The user can hold a cursor drawn on transparent plastic if the exact pointing location is important to the interface, as is the case with a geographical information system. With some imagination, it is possible to create surprisingly expressive and communicative dynamic paper prototypes with very simple materials.

A benefit of dynamic paper prototypes is that they can communicate a clear sense of the interactive character of the intended system, mainly for designs that use standard

◀ **Figure 4.3**

Stills from a movie scenario. One of the authors (Löwgren) was creative director of this project, which aimed at exploring the design possibilities of video and audio information management. The stills show how we tried to create an impression of a working system in use, by cuts between two views (top and middle) and by faking stylus interaction with a pre-designed animation (bottom) Refer to Andersson et al. (2002) for more on the project.

desktop interaction techniques. They are also simple, inexpensive, and fun to construct and use. A drawback to this technique is that some kinds of interaction are hard to express; for instance, direct manipulation works to a limited extent, but it does not work very well. Moreover, it is quite challenging to prepare and manage all the components you need to communicate the interaction character of a highly dynamic system.

Role-playing generally involves using one's imagination to experience situations that do not yet exist. It can be as simple as a one-person thought experiment placed in the

Figure 4.4

A dynamic paper prototype in use. The user is selecting X-ray images from a personal collection and placing them on the light box.

material world; consider the legendary story of Jeff Hawkins, the inventor of the PalmPilot. His way of assessing the idea of a PalmPilot long before building working prototypes was to fashion a wooden block of the approximate size and weight he was envisioning. He carried that block in his shirt pocket for months, constantly looking for situations where he could take it out and pretend to use it with a stylus. His imagination filled in most of what the prototype lacked in functional detail, and in the end, he was convinced that stylus-operated palm computers would be a feasible idea for personal information management.

More generally, role-playing typically involves a group of people intending to create envisionments of a not-yet-existing situation. For instance, Buchenau and Fulton Suri (2000) describe a design team investigating passenger needs for a new rail service by means of acting techniques. They improvised action in a sequence of focused scenes intended to cover the most important possible activities and situations. They explored different types of travelers, their needs, and various unexpected situations that could come up during specific stages of a train journey. Each scene was introduced with a card containing the scene's rules and explaining the goals and roles of the players. For instance, the role-playing of ticketing started with the moderator giving one of the players the instruction to "buy a return ticket for yourself and a child," while another team member played the role of the ticket vending machine. Subsequent instructions involved different conditions, such as: "now do it with gloves on" or "the machine only takes coins, no bills." Actions leading toward the goals of the scene were improvised, and each scene was followed by a break where the team summarized what they had learned.

The key benefit of role-playing is that it enables designers to experience situations and make discoveries themselves. It is also extremely flexible, in that nearly any situation can be collaboratively imagined, acted, and experienced, at least as long as the players are motivated and the session is facilitated by a moderator skilled in improvisational acting techniques. Sato and Salvador (1999) offer a broad summary of theater techniques for such purposes. However, it must be pointed out that even with all the role-playing in the world, the designer never becomes the person whose role she plays. Empathy mediated through role-playing is a useful complement to, but no substitute for, fieldwork and other activities of inquiry to better understand the design situation at hand.

In many cases, it is quite feasible to construct *dynamic digital prototypes* that look and behave like the intended system to a certain extent. The whole point is, of course, that such prototypes can be constructed more quickly in prototyping tools than by constructing them in the delivery environment; on the other hand, the designer loses in terms of stability and generality. There are also some aspects of a system, such as response times, that cannot be validly expressed in a dynamic digital prototype since they depend on the technical characteristics of the delivery environment.

There are many tools available today for constructing prototypes similar to dynamic paper prototypes. In one such prototype, there could be a screen containing a button. When the user presses the button, a new screen is presented that looks exactly the same except a new element appears. The user's impression is that the pressing of the button created a new element on an otherwise static work area. Another class of tools is the graphical programming environments, where virtually any kind of interaction technique can be illustrated provided that the necessary programming skills and working time are available. In example 5.2, we discuss such a tool (Macromedia Director) in more detail.

Figure 4.5 illustrates a screenshot from a dynamic digital prototype of the X-ray image system, constructed in Macromedia Director. In this case, we have aimed for a prototype that communicates the intended user functions, contents, and structures along with intended interaction techniques, but which is neutral with respect to implementation environment. There are other available prototyping tools based on standard interaction components, which may be preferable if it has already been decided to adhere to the user interface standards of a particular implementation environment.

A dynamic digital prototype offers a more realistic preview of the experience of using the intended system than the other shaping techniques presented here. The trend has been to use dynamic digital prototypes mainly for detailed design work. It is not impossible to discuss user needs and wants on a fairly high level based on a dynamic digital prototype. However, remember the problems that can emerge because of how easy it is to perceive it as something more or less final. This is particularly true for people who do not know how unfinished the prototype really is and how much work that remains before delivery. One possible remedy is to scan hand-drawn visual elements and put them together in a dynamic digital prototype, in order to convey a more tentative character of the work.

Another aspect of dynamic digital prototypes is that they form an undemocratic material, in the sense that you need special technical skills in order to modify the prototype. The digital prototype is different from the paper prototype, where anybody can cut a piece of paper in the shape of a button as well as the designer can. There are studies of participatory design projects where the aim was to co-create dynamic digital prototypes (Bødker and Grønbæk 1989). The intention was to use HyperCard as a tool for participatory envisionment of a new system, but the outcomes were mixed. As long as the prototype under development could be modified using simple direct manipulation techniques, the users were highly involved and active in the participatory process.

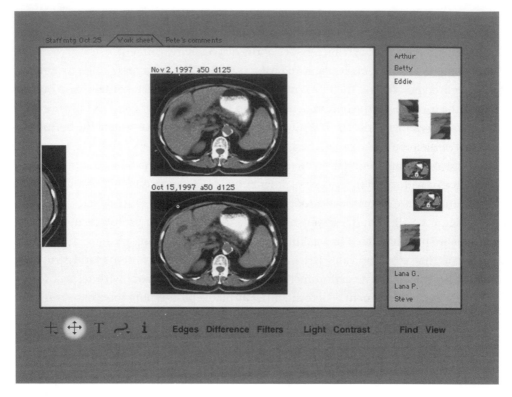

Figure 4.5
The dynamic digital prototype does not have to consist of standard interface components, if the important thing is the contents and the interaction sequences.

However, as soon as programming was called for, then the fluent dialogue between designers and users broke down.

It is necessary to be aware of the asymmetric character of dynamic digital prototypes and use them with these limitations in mind. They do, in fact, require a specialist skill that the designer has but that most other stakeholders in the design process do not have. By making dynamic digital prototypes the vehicle for communication and collaboration, a designer is exerting power of an exclusionary nature.

It is obvious that composition can be viewed at different levels of abstraction and at different stages of the design process. The methods presented in this section can be used in many ways for different purposes. Once again, we have to restate the notion of *intention* when it comes to the use of methods. There is never a situation that demands a specific method or a specific technique. There is never a method that leads to a guaranteed result or even the same result if used by different designers.

Composition is all about trying to bring things together and to create a coherent gestalt of a possible design.

4.4 Assessment

Chapter 2 addressed the trade-off between the contributions of different stakeholders to the assessment of a digital artifact. Most methods in the literature favor the appropriateness of the product or the idea in the intended use situation over the designer's own ethical and aesthetic assessment.

Evaluation has always played an important part in the field of human-computer interaction (HCI), perhaps due to its ancestry in applied psychology and its use of experimental methods to study human interaction with computers. HCI evaluation is strongly focused on the user interface. A common point of view is that the user interface determines the user's possibilities to benefit from the services of the system, and the evaluation aims at locating interference between user and services.

It is probably fair to say that *usability testing* is one of the cornerstones of HCI. Usability testing refers to more or less formal experiments, where intended users try to perform test tasks using the proposed system or a prototype of it. The interaction between user and system is studied, with particular emphasis on performance aspects: how much time it took the user to perform tasks, how many and what types of errors were committed, how often the user consulted the manual, and so on. An excellent introduction to usability testing and related HCI approaches is found in Preece, Rogers, and Sharp (2002).

Usability testing has proven to be very attractive in the software industry. Many companies operate labs where usability tests are performed with invited users and sophisticated technical support for data collection and analysis. One reason for the popularity of this method is that usability testing works very well with requirements-driven systems development. If measurable usability requirements are added to requirement specifications, then the prototype can be tested in the lab and, if necessary, redesigned and tested again until the stated requirements are met. This amounts to a development philosophy known as usability engineering (Nielsen 1993), which is considered as a way to improve control over the notoriously unruly design process. The role of engineering ideals in the history of HCI and the history of design is a topic that we will return to in chapter 6.

A drawback of usability testing is that it might be difficult and costly to find test participants. The field of HCI has developed alternatives known as *inspection methods,* based on the theoretical foundations in psychology (refer to Nielsen and Mack 1994, for a survey).

Inspection methods include the collection of experimental HCI research in guidelines that can be used to assess a proposed design, as well as theoretical models of human information processing that can be used as "substitute users" to indicate likely usability problems in the design under evaluation. Another example of inspection methods is heuristic evaluation, where a number of usability experts independently assess a proposal and point out predicted usability problems according to a set of general rules of thumb.

A general observation is that HCI evaluation methods are focused on the product and on general usability criteria. The individual use situation is less important; a usability problem in the user interface is always a problem, as long as the product is going to be used by the intended user group. Classical usability testing also runs the risk of disregarding the effects and qualities of the system as a whole.

The long-term value of a digital artifact and the users' development over time are also hard to assess in usability evaluation. A usability test is typically short and concentrates on a user's first contacts with the proposed design. Moreover, it rarely considers the user in her everyday social context of colleagues, customers, collaborations, hostilities, interruptions, and multiple competing concerns.

A more contextually oriented evaluation requires time and access to the environments where the artifact is actually used. The last years have seen an increasing interest in methods based on qualitative field studies and ethnographic techniques. In all of these methods, the evaluator enters the use situation with an inquisitive and explorative stance, rather than looking for quick answers to previously formulated questions. The directions of a study are determined by the development of the evaluation; the evaluator assumes the role of an apprentice surrounded by experts, rather than an expert surrounded by novices. Wixon and Ramey (1996) provides several examples of field study methods that can be used for contextual evaluation.

The difference between inquiry in early phases of a design process and assessment in the later stages becomes less important if we think of assessment as a long-term contextual activity. The method of contextual inquiry, which we described earlier, also works to assess the results of a design process. If we add the notion of users as competent professionals (not limited to paid-work professionalism, of course) who are constantly changing and developing, we approach a perspective where the border between design and use is gradually blurred. The product is never really finished, but keeps evolving throughout its lifecycle by the users' own appropriation and modification, or by interventions from the designer based on contextual field studies. Henderson and Kyng (1991) call this *continuing-design-in-use* and sketch a lifecycle starting when a user initiates a change in the artifact to make it fit the use situation better. This change must initially be protected and then gradually be made permanent and as accessible as the previously available parts of the artifact. Knowledge of the change and its use must be disseminated, and the history and reasons for changes must be made available. The next step of the lifecycle is when users learn about the change and incorporate it in their daily work. Finally, Henderson and Kyng emphasize the importance of providing feedback to the initiator of the change.

For our purposes, it is interesting to note that the life cycle of continuing-design-in-use can also be viewed as a model for contextual assessment, where the role of the "evaluator" is to support and facilitate local processes of change rather than assuming an expert position in analyzing the use of the artifact and redesigning it.

This section has indicated the importance of understanding evaluation methods at a rather profound level, as they—like any other method—embody perspectives and underlying values. As we will elaborate in chapter 5, an important design-theoretical perspective is to think of quality as an ongoing discussion. From that perspective, assessment methods include ones that facilitate articulation of intended and actual qualities. One example is the family of methods or techniques evolving around the notion of design-as-argumentation; another concerns the role of the critic in the knowledge-construction system around design.

4.4.1 Design-as-Argumentation

In the early 1970s, Horst Rittel concluded based on his experience of urban planning that design is best understood as negotiation. There is no "right" solution, only a number of more or less good solutions supported by more or less good arguments. He coined the term *wicked problems* to indicate problems that are not amenable to analysis and description before they are solved, and observed that design typically deals with wicked problems (Rittel and Webber 1973). Driven by a desire to make the design process more democratic, he created a simple notation aimed at documenting and making explicit the negotiations underlying a design decision. The notation, IBIS (Issue-Based Information System), consists of the three primitives issues, positions, and arguments. By using relations such as "supports," "objects-to," and "generalizes," a deliberation or negotiation could be captured in a network structure.

Rittel's pioneering work inspired others to develop techniques for articulating design argumentation (refer to the survey by Buckingham Shum 1995), albeit for different purposes. In line with the general trend of the 1980s and 1990s away from political and ideological design, the main emphasis was instead placed on the many solution ideas that typically surface during an explorative design process. An illustrative example is the notation technique called QOC for Questions, Options, and Criteria (MacLean et al. 1991). Figure 4.6 illustrates how our reasoning about different visions for the X-ray image system could be captured in a QOC diagram.

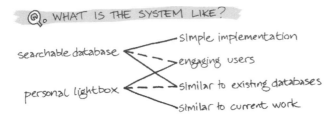

Figure 4.6
Example of a Questions, Options, and Criteria (QOC) diagram. Our work so far has resulted in two alternative answers to the question posed at the top of this diagram. These alternatives are assessed against the same four criteria.

Questions refer to the design questions motivating the deliberation. *Options* are the different alternatives being developed and considered. The options are assessed against a set of supposedly general *criteria*, where a solid line represents a positive assessment and a dashed line is a negative assessment.

The purpose of QOC and similar notations is to document the exploration of the design space and encourage the parallel pursuit of several options. As design work proceeds, a number of questions, options, and criteria are formulated and connected in a complex web; the QOC notation encourages the interrelation of single-question structures to larger networks. The developers of QOC provide a set of guidelines for using the notation, including the following:

- Use questions to generate options.
- Use options to generate new questions.
- Find maximally different options.
- Include criteria that yield positive as well as negative assessments.
- Find alternatives that resolve the negative assessments but preserve the positives.
- Look for general questions to ensure consistency in the work.

Generally speaking, the idea behind argumentative notations is very powerful. Irrespective of whether the diagrams are seen as negotiation protocols (as in the case of IBIS) or as explorations of the design space (QOC), it is valuable to document the design process and, in particular, all the ideas that were considered but never realized. However, practical experience shows that the structures soon become unwieldy and hard to manage. One field study of QOC in use for a medium-sized design project showed, for instance, that the only way to keep the QOC structures up-to-date and useful was to appoint one of the team members to full-time QOC secretary. The secretary's tasks were to make notes during design sessions and then tidy up, revise, interrelate, and summarize the material (McKerlie and MacLean 1993). An interesting question that the study unfortunately did not address is whether the QOC efforts ultimately proved worthwhile.

Argumentative notations can also be seen as personal design techniques, mainly intended to support the individual designer in a parallel, explorative mode of working. Some findings indicate that these notations are useful in the process of learning to work divergently and avoiding premature fixation (Löwgren 1994). They may also be useful tools at decision points where the designer feels the need to summarize her possibilities and requirements. A simple QOC diagram with possibilities as options and requirements as criteria might support the decision or indicate where more information or more work is required before making the decision.

Grudin (1996) underlines the importance of making the ultimate usefulness of argumentative notations visible, since the notations involve additional work not directly contributing to the deliverable object. An obvious analogy from the world of programming is documentation of program code: Everybody knows the importance of good documentation, but when a deadline approaches, documentation is not a priority compared to the production of working code.

4.4.2   Critics and Criticism

When we consider a design discipline as a system of knowledge construction, we can note a number of key roles or functions. The more mature disciplines contain not only the roles we would consider obvious, like designer, client, and user, but also the role of the critic.[3] There are, of course, many anecdotes of "critics" providing little more than personal vengeance or commercially motivated purchase recommendations, but we would like to concentrate for a moment on the principled role of the critic in a design-oriented knowledge construction system.

First, what do we mean by a knowledge construction system? Briefly, the key to understanding this concept is to think of a discipline as an ongoing collective effort to advance its own capabilities. This clearly entails more than designing and delivering artifacts; specifically, it includes the elicitation, refinement, and dissemination of transferable knowledge. The knowledge that is advanced within the discipline has to be accessible and actable to members of the discipline, validated in practice, and elaborated and questioned in the continual discourse that is the core of knowledge construction. Awards, exhibitions, and publications are all important components in such a system, as well as countercultural efforts to provoke and question the mainstream judgments and ideals.

From this perspective—which fits very well with our notions of thoughtful design, articulation of qualities, and personal development of design ability—the role of the critic is an important one. Her task is to analyze existing designs and contextualize them in broader perspectives of history, society, and culture—to point to analogies and explore their scope, to look at ideas from points of view other than their origins, to ask unexpected but clarifying questions, and to point out implications unforeseen to the designer and the users. The knowledge offered by a critic is neither empirical nor deductive; yet it should be highly accessible and actable to members of the discipline. Moreover, the critic serves an important role in maintaining relations between various disciplines of professional practice and the everyday culture and society in which the disciplines are embedded.

Regrettably, the field of interaction design and digital artifacts has not yet evolved a recognized role for the critic. In other words, the attempts at digital artifact criticism that can be found have yet to make an impact on the mainstream modes of knowledge production. In the late 1990s, when technological developments and, above all, euphoric market expectations brought digital artifacts into the higher levels of public awareness, several magazines and websites were launched with the intention to address digital artifacts from cultural and societal standpoints. Most of them, however, went down with the stock market. The most significant exception is perhaps in the field of computer games, where the role of the critic has been recognized for quite some time, both in magazine reviews for general audiences as well as in academic studies.

An important example of digital artifact criticism outside the games community is the book *Interface Culture* by Stephen Johnson (1997), where the aim is to "think about the elements of modern interface design as though they were the cultural equivalents of a Dickens novel, a Welles film, a Rem Koolhaas building—in other words, as works possessing great creative and social import, and having longer-term historical significance than just the latest product review in the high-tech trades" (8–9).

Johnson addresses topics such as the desktop metaphor, multiple windows, links and hypertext, and software agents. For instance, his analysis of multiple-windows environments starts by pointing out how computers have evolved toward a state of fragmentation that more closely resembles our natural modes of daily operation. He then moves on to outline the legal and ethical issues involved in the use of frames in websites and the corresponding possibilities of presenting content in contexts not anticipated by the originators of the content. The broad perspective of the critic, still quite unfamiliar to the field of digital artifacts, provides knowledge that is not typically found in prescriptive method handbooks or field studies of digital artifacts in use, yet is evidently useful and relevant to the interaction designer.

4.5 Coordination

The fifth and final category of our presentation is the meta-level: methods and techniques intended to facilitate the management and organization of the design process, particularly the coordination between multiple participants in the process. This is a central focus of many mainstream methods in human-computer interaction and software engineering, as well as in information systems and organizational development. To broaden the scope by way of an example, we describe a method that is oriented more toward coordination and strategy control for creative design processes.

4.5.1 The Six Thinking Hats

Edward de Bono is an important contributor to the literature on creativity for a general audience. He coined the term lateral thinking, which refers to thinking "sideways," finding other possibilities, and developing new ideas rather than digging deeper into the old ones. De Bono has published several books on creativity and methods for creative thinking in everyday life as well as in business (see, e.g., *Serious Creativity* [1993]). One of his best-known methods is the six thinking hats.

The aim of the method is to identify the perspectives needed in a successful process of design or problem solving, to clarify communication in a group, and to promote collaboration instead of animosity. The six thinking hats refer to six perspectives, which are each assigned a color.

The *white* hat is like paper: a neutral format carrying information or data. What information do we have? What information is missing? What information would we like to have? How can we get it? When all members of a design team put on a white hat, they disregard design ideas and arguments in order to concentrate on the available information and how to fill the gaps in it.

The *red* hat is about feelings and intuition: think of red as in heat and fire. When a person wears a red hat, she can say what she feels without any need to justify it: "I just know that people are going to love this feature." Intuition and feelings can be a composite of several years of experience and very valuable as such, but of course they may also be wrong. Either way, it can be both healthy and creatively productive for individuals to express their feelings in a design process.

The *black* hat is like the robe of a stern judge who makes critical judgments. The job of the person wearing a black hat is to point out why an idea cannot be done, will never be profitable, and so on. "This can't be implemented on the platform we have agreed to use." Nobody wants to make mistakes or do silly things. The black hat is clearly useful and frequently used; however, it should not be used too often or too early in the design process. If all tentative ideas are cut off with black hat criticism, they will never get a chance to develop or inspire other group members to new ideas. The most important function of the black hat in a design process is probably the possibility of limiting criticism to certain phases instead of having it occur throughout the work when it might hamper the creative flow (compare the generation phase in brainstorming, mentioned in section 4.2.2).

The *yellow* hat is like the sun: optimistic and positive. When wearing a yellow hat, an individual looks for the feasibility and logically based benefits of ideas: "Well, we could do it if we could find a development library with 3d-objects." Most people might find it easier to wear a black hat than a yellow one. Finding possibilities and benefits takes more effort, but it can be worthwhile in order to give new ideas a chance to grow.

The *green* hat stands for creativity, new ideas, new alternatives, and possibilities (think of vegetation and rich growth): "Could we do this in a different way? Are there any additional alternatives? We need some new ideas." Putting on a green hat creates time and space in the design process for a concentrated creative effort.

The *blue* hat represents a birds-eye view from the sky. It concentrates on the process, the agenda, the next step, summaries, and conclusions: "We are lost in details—how do we move on? Could we have a summary of your views? I think we should all put on green hats to get some new ideas." The blue hat is normally used by the chairperson or the facilitator of the meeting, but other members can also use it and put forward suggestions.

The six thinking hats is not a method in the sense that it prescribes a sequence of actions. Rather, it can be seen as a framework for discussion and teamwork coordination, to be used in different ways depending on the situation. According to de Bono, it helps move away from adversarial positions towards cooperative exploration since the whole team can wear a black hat at the same time to reflect on the dangers of a project, then all wear a yellow hat to explore the benefits, or a green one to open up new possibilities.

Even though the six thinking hats are typically used occasionally in a larger-scale process as a way to switch the mode of a group's or a group member's thinking, they can also be used in sequence to quickly explore a subject:

White hat: What do we know?
Green: Ideas, suggestions, alternatives.
Yellow: The feasibility, benefits, and value of the ideas.
Black: Dangers and risks of the ideas.
Red: Feelings toward the ideas.
Blue: Decision.

4.6   Remarks on Methods in Design

The final section of this chapter concerns the role of methods in design. Relating back to the introduction of this chapter, it is easy to see that the role of methods and techniques depend on how we view the designer. If we think of the designer as a self-organizing system, then methods are mainly *material for learning*. Learning to use a new method expands a designer's language and repertoire of tools for different situations, but she is not a skilled method user until she can go beyond the method description. When a designer understands why the different steps in a method are performed, when she can adapt the method to the situation at hand, when she can exchange a technique prescribed by the method for another one she is familiar with and get a better result, that is when she knows the method well enough. If a designer can reach that level of sophistication, then methods will work very well in the design process without appearing overly restrictive, rigid, formalistic, or pointless.

Another reason for using (more or less) systematic methods in design is that a designer always works in a larger context. A method can be the common ground that is necessary for clear *communication* between the actors in the design process. A situation where many people are involved in a design project can quickly become untenable unless all actors involved share a common language to some degree. The use of the term "language" here is not limited to speech or text, but refers to any shared form of expression.

A method understood in this sense serves not only as a language for expression, but also for *planning and coordination* purposes. Perhaps the greatest advantage of methods is the one that is most easily taken for granted. It is their potential to help designers organize their work temporally. Design projects are complex and often unpredictable, which means that sometimes they grind to a halt and sometimes they gallop away in excitement and enthusiasm. A method may offer a prescriptive way of organizing and planning activities, a way that has proven useful in other projects.

Methods are bearers of *history* and collectors of *competence*. Even if we do not want to follow prescriptive methods in detail, we may gain invaluable knowledge about how other designers disseminate their experience by studying methods. If we can find the time to reflect upon the foundations underlying a method and reconstruct their underlying rationality, we can then challenge and develop our own assumptions about design work.

However, the authors of this book do not hold great hopes for methods in terms of *quality assurance*. A common ideal is to describe methods in enough detail to make the process repeatable, measurable, and in some senses more objective. Against this, we would simply like to point out that the result of a design process can never be better than the individual designer, irrespective of the method used.

A common argument for detailed methods is that they make it possible to run a process independent of the exact individuals participating in it. If the method can describe and prescribe the process well enough, then the individual designer can be exchanged in any phase as long as the method is maintained. In our view, however, this is not a feasible argument. Even the simplest understanding of design is incompatible with the view of the process that lies behind the independence-from-individuals idea. In this model, the designer is seen as a method operator, which is not a reasonable role in a realistic design process. Every designer is unique in her competence, and a method cannot control an unpredictable process in any given situation.

Methods can be seen as providing comforting support and security for a designer, and perhaps also providing a way to escape some of the responsibility of the design process. Unfortunately, this sense of security is not very durable, as the designer will always eventually face a situation where the method is inadequate. If the designer is not prepared, it is hard to predict the consequences. A better and more thoughtful approach is for a designer to constantly aim to develop her readiness and design ability, where methods and techniques are merely one kind of tool among many others.

5 The Product and Its Use Qualities

As we indicated in chapter 3, the development of a sense of quality and a language for articulating use-oriented qualities is a core element of interaction design ability. It is essential for designers to know what their products are and what they mean. The meaning of a product is never straightforward and unambiguous; it can never be obtained by the use of some objective scale of measurement. Of course, there are qualities that most people recognize and in some cases, there are even majority views on how they can and should be measured. In interaction design, such qualities typically include technical performance and structural features. However, most product qualities of interest to a designer are not that visible or easy to isolate. How do you measure usability and flexibility in a useful and practical way? How about the economical viability and ecological sustainability of a product? Even harder and less noticed are qualities such as social appropriateness, ethical justifiability, and aesthetic adequacy. Of course, researchers and designers have attempted to create means of measuring these and other qualities. In many camps, the ability to measure all relevant product qualities is seen as desirable. The intention is mainly to facilitate the design and deployment process; it can be safely stated, however, that there are no commonly agreed upon approaches for handling the more difficult aspects of digital artifact qualities.

The lack of objective measures does not mean that it is impossible for a designer to ponder product qualities—quite the contrary. A strong awareness and a set of powerful tools-for-thought are essential. A designer is never allowed to skip the question of product qualities by using the argument that nobody knows how these qualities can be measured. In any design situation, all qualities of the product will be determined whether they are measurable or not. It would be preferable if this determination was always the effect of a conscious and intentional design act, but in many cases the outcomes are unanticipated. We simply cannot consider all possibilities and safeguard ourselves against all unpredictable effects. There is only so much time and so many resources available to the design process, and the product ultimately has to be finished.

There are different kinds of design work, but the task for the designer always involves issues of needs, requirements, expectations, contexts, general trends and cultural traits, and even style and taste. A society and a market is always under the influence of a Zeitgeist—that is, a general and more or less shared set of views of what is structurally and culturally possible and acceptable in a specific design situation. It is important for the professional designer to be sensitive to these currents, but it is every bit as important to have a strong personal standpoint on what distinguishes a good product.

It may be worth pointing out in passing that knowing the qualities of everyday products does not necessarily mean knowing the qualities of digital artifacts. We are dealing with a strange material here, one where the spatial and the temporal meet in new ways. Much of our general sense of quality, what we know from handling the physical objects of everyday life, is not adequate when it comes to describing digital artifacts.

Our aim in this chapter is to provide tools-for-thought to help the reader build a sense of interaction design products and their qualities. In view of the inherent difficulties of objectively measuring the interesting qualities of digital artifacts, we advocate an approach based on *articulation*. This is to say that we view a designer's knowledge of product quality as an ongoing debate, a conversation with other designers and design theorists, as well as with design situations and the stakeholders involved in them. Statements are made in this debate through the main vehicles of design and reflection. A digital artifact or a design concept can be seen as a statement about a desirable product quality. Likewise for written or spoken analysis, where a core quality of a certain artifact genre or class of use situations is identified.

Product quality statements as outlined in this section are never generalized in the sense of straightforward application to new design situations. There is a significant amount of work involved in understanding the statement being made, assessing its relevance for the situation at hand, and figuring out what specific design actions it entails or supports (or discourages). By necessity, this work falls on the "reader" of the statement; the "writer" of the statement can make it easier for the reader by articulating the reasoning behind the statement and its possible scope and consequences.

Our approach in this chapter is therefore to provide the reader with a set of suggested, *use-oriented qualities of digital artifacts*. The qualities we propose are not general, but they have a scope of applicability that reaches across individual examples. One set of qualities concerns the users' *motivations* for engaging with the digital artifact, another addresses the immediate *sensation of interacting* with the artifact, and a third set has to do with the *social outcomes* of interaction. There is also a set of qualities pertaining to the *structural features* of the artifact as they manifest themselves in use and a final set addressing the induction of users' reflection upon their situation.

Our method is to illustrate most of the qualities we propose by analyzing concrete examples of digital artifacts in some depth. We want to emphasize the illustrative purpose of choosing these specific examples in the hope of making it clear to the reader not to focus too much on the chosen artifacts in terms of technical sophistication or state-of-the-art, nor as "killer applications" or classical artifacts. The examples are chosen to illustrate different *digital artifact genres* and the important qualities associated with them; they are not necessarily good examples in every respect. In fact, we doubt the existence of such examples since design is always a trade-off between different qualities and interests.

Here is a reasonable question the reader might have at this stage: "I want to be a game designer. Why should I read about the use qualities of an automatic teller machine (ATM)?" We can think of a few reasons why you should. First, a large part of the practical ability to design rests on having a repertoire of formats. As we indicated in chapter 3, formats are solution-oriented ideas, concepts, or examples. A broad collection of formats enables a designer to act more swiftly and confidently in new design situations. Secondly, the meta-skill of articulating product qualities and taking part in the ongoing debate about product quality is equally important in all genres of digital artifacts. Attempting to grasp examples of articulation work helps to build sensitivity to product quality, which is an essential part of design ability in any domain. Finally, and perhaps most importantly, the implicit notion of fixed genres and segmented markets is an obstacle to design innovation. We would argue that it is valuable for a game designer to know about the core qualities of ATM design, not in order to apply them uncritically to her own detailed design decisions, but rather to question and push the tacit boundaries of her work. Speaking of games and ATM design, here is an illustrative suggestion by Jeff Kipnis: "People like to play lotto and people like to use the ATM. Why don't you make it an option in the ATM to say put your money in and say, I'll bet a little bit and see if I can get a little more out, so you ask for twenty dollars, and you push the button, and you could get twenty-five or you could get fifteen" (qtd. in Dunne 1999, 54).

The specific idea may be good or bad, but it clearly has that unmistakable feeling of pushing a tacit boundary. The first time your read it, you might react with instant criticism: "You can't play games with people's hard-earned money! It wouldn't be . . . right." Then you read it again and start imagining what it would be like if your ATM played games with you. You find two days later that you still think about what an ATM-lotto machine would be like and how the idea could be used in other contexts. The tacit assumptions on ATM predictability and reliability have been pushed.

The qualities of digital artifacts we propose are summarized at the end of this chapter and related to other attempts to grasp the notion of quality in design. It should be noted here that the qualities we propose do *not* form a taxonomy. Even though our examples are chosen for their different core qualities, we maintain that the qualities we identify are interdependent in highly complex ways. The final quality and character of a particular digital artifact is *emergent* rather than additive.

A warning: Using the qualities we identify as a checklist for product evaluation would inevitably drain them of meaning. Instead, they should be seen as proposed tools for questioning, elaboration, and making informed choices in thoughtful interaction design. Design is always an act of composition, of shaping a whole and its parts simultaneously. The guiding principle in composition work is judgment of the emerging whole, as the complexity of design is too great for "divide-and-conquer" approaches. The main purpose of product quality articulation is to develop the ability to make such judgments, which constitute a thoughtful approach to understanding the qualities of digital artifacts.

5.1 Example: Automatic Teller Machines (ATMs)

An ATM consists of a computer, a small display screen, a numeric keypad, a card reader, and a cash dispenser. Some ATMs have another dispenser for statements and other printouts, and some feature unlabeled buttons around the display that take on different functionality in different dialogue states. The ATM computer has no internal database and relies on telecommunication with the computer at the current user's bank for balance information and other transactions. The user's ATM card contains the PIN code and identifies the bank. Keypad input is buffered in some situations—for instance, enabling the user to type the desired amount to withdraw before that question is presented on the display.

Using an ATM is like a conversation with somebody who likes to be in control of the dialogue:

ATM: Enter your PIN code!
Customer: 5555.
ATM: You can now withdraw cash, check your balance, or transfer money between your accounts.
Customer: Transfer money.
ATM: From which account?
Customer: 5555 313 2494.
ATM: To which account?
Customer: 5555 176 9921.
ATM: And how much do you want to transfer?
Customer: $100.

The most frequent services require only brief conversations. The buttons along the side of the screen are often used for withdrawal of preset amounts. The card is usually returned before the money and printouts. Some of the first ATMs were designed to dispense the money first, but in testing it was found that many people left their cards in the machine. The explanation is, of course, that the main goal was to withdraw money and when the money appeared, the goal was fulfilled and the card was forgotten.

It is easy to identify some shortcomings of the ATM design in terms of individual use properties, stemming from the rather old-fashioned infrastructure of transaction-based database communication. For instance the user has to go through several interaction steps to specify a transaction before the bank is contacted and the ATM may be notified that there is no money in the account. It would be straightforward (technically speaking) to redesign the ATM to initiate the user interaction and at the same time send for all information that might be needed at later stages of the interaction.

Another observation is that the interaction with an ATM is the same for everybody, even though we may have different uses for it. We already identify ourselves to the machine by inserting a more or less personal card. What if I could customize "my" ATM to offer a cash withdrawal of $50, with no receipt, at one press of a button? Other users might like to always have their current balance presented first, even though it would mean waiting for a few seconds after entering their PIN code.

5.1.1 Social Action Space

The most interesting aspects of the ATM are, however, concerned with issues that are larger than the design of the interface. It is clear that ATM technology illustrates a new way of handling money in everyday life. Before ATMs were invented, a person had to plan her cash needs in advance in order to make appropriate withdrawals while the bank was open. Now, all that person needs to do is make sure that she passes an ATM on her way to the restaurant. Some people rely on this kind of deferred planning to the extent that they depend on finding a working ATM. It is surely the case that a massive breakdown in telecommunications that disabled all ATMs in a city would show up quite clearly when stores in the city add up their sales for the day.

An ATM automates some of the simple bank customer services, makes the services more available to customers, and allows bank clerks to concentrate more on tasks that require skill and human judgment. When a customer walks inside the bank to withdraw an amount of cash, the clerk serves mainly as a mediator between the customer and the database. But to some customers, this mediation and human contact where the clerk personifies the bank is seen as very valuable. Would a bank lose customers if they referred all cash withdrawals to ATMs?

There is a significant trend in everyday life to reduce the use of cash. Some examples are credit cards, store cards, cash cards, postal money transfer, phone banking, and web banking. The main reason is that cash is expensive to handle. A customer transaction over the counter costs the bank roughly five times as much as via the web, and ATMs and manual phone services cost roughly two and a half times the web cost. Reducing the use of cash is also seen as a way to reduce robbery and other crime.

The point is that every product is designed with the (tacit or overt) intention of changing or facilitating change in the way people act. The ATM is a very clear example of how the social action space is designed. The intention is to change the activity patterns of bank customers from always coming into the bank to performing simple tasks by using machines. The design of fees for cash withdrawal over the counter compared to the ATM is also changed to further reinforce the activity-pattern change. However, ATMs also affect our social action space in other ways, some of which are unforeseen and perhaps undesirable. If a person is a deferred planner and finds the ATM closed at 9 P.M. on her way to meet up with friends at a bar, the situation may be characterized as a breakdown. It may in fact be the first time that this person notices the change in her own activity pattern.

It is not difficult for the designer to change users' social action spaces. Any change in the man-made environment, any new artifact, brings with it some kind of change in the social action space. The hard part is to predict the outcomes: the future social activities around the new artifact. For example, a new digital artifact may be designed with the intention of facilitating internal communication in an organization in order to overcome entrenchment and hostility. As it turns out, the new artifact is instead used as a forum for intense and upsetting debates, where employees anonymously voice unpleasant opinions about the organization and each other. This course of events may be good or bad, depending on the detailed context and on the point-of-view, but it is certainly clear that the artifact plays a significant role in shaping the activities in the organization. The social action space that is introduced was previously unthinkable, and apparently larger than the designers anticipated.

If we view changes in social action spaces as an important quality of (certain classes of) digital artifacts, then interaction design becomes more than the mere designation of a bundle of functions and gadgets. A more appropriate characterization might be that interaction design is the design of *conceivable social environments,* or as Terry Winograd puts it (qtd. in Preece, Rogers, and Sharp 2002, 70), "designing a space for people." The ATM is a good example of interaction design that has affected our social action space in many ways, with some expected outcomes and some surprising ones.

5.2 Example: Macromedia Director

Macromedia Director (referred to from now on as "Director") originated as a tool for multimedia productions—that is, interactive presentations made up of text, image, sound, and video, and typically delivered on a CD-ROM. Even though it has expanded significantly, its original intentions are still discernible in its basic structures. Director is based loosely on the model of animated film editing, where a presentation (a "movie") consists of a sequence of frames. All media elements to be presented in the movie frames are stored in one or more "casts." The "score" is an editable representation of the frame sequence, and a basic movie is constructed by placing media elements from the cast into the score.

When the movie is played, each frame is presented with the media elements they contain. There is plenty of support for frame transitions—for instance, having a frame dissolve gradually into the next. Making media elements move is similar to cartoon animation; if you want to make a toy car drive across the stage from left to right, place it to the left in the first frame and move it a little to the right in each subsequent frame. A quicker way of getting the car to move is to indicate its positions at the start and the end of the sequence in "keyframes," then have Director compute the intermediate positions in a process known as "tweening."

Simple interactivity is also accommodated in the film-editing model. You can insert a "behavior" from a behavior library to make the playback pause on a certain frame. In that frame, a media element can be turned into a mouse-sensitive button with a behavior that moves the playback to another frame when clicked. Hypermedia information presentations, such as menu pages with related pages of content, are easy to construct in that manner.

In order to use Director for hypermedia work with simple structures and an emphasis on the multimodal content, the basic model described in the previous paragraphs is perfectly adequate. Historically speaking, that has also been Director's main use: web site prototypes, adventure-style games with branching narrative structures, courseware, information presentations, and so on. But eventually, a designer is bound to come up against situations where the capacities of pure node-link hypermedia structures are too limited for the task at hand. It is at this point that Director's underlying programming language Lingo becomes interesting.

The behaviors mentioned in this example are in reality small, encapsulated scripts; pieces of programming code, implemented in Director's integrated scripting language Lingo. Lingo has grown more or less organically with each new version of Director into a fairly complete and general programming language, capable of much more than merely sending the playback head to specified frames in a score. Specifically, the two-dimensional and three-dimensional graphical primitives in Lingo are reasonably adequate and highly integrated with the film editing model and various drawing tools. Moreover, Lingo is interpreted, which means that any piece of code a programmer writes can be tested and debugged immediately, with no need for compile-link-load cycles. This makes Director (and Lingo) a useful choice for prototyping more advanced interaction techniques. Figure 5.1 shows some main elements of the Director and Lingo authoring environment.

The possibility of making a code template (a class) and creating multiple instances from it also gives Lingo some of the power of general object-oriented programming. A Lingo program created using such techniques does not need to be tied to a specific movie, but stays active in the computer's memory for as long as Director runs. We will not dwell on this subject; refer to Small (1996) for an introduction to the potential inherent in thinking of Director as a general programming environment rather than a multimedia production tool.

5.2.1 Transparency

Director and Lingo, when studied together, provide a good illustration of the quality of *transparency*. Starting to use Director for simple slide shows or website prototypes typically involves learning the film-editing model and working with the sequence of frames in the score. At this stage, Lingo is mostly used (unknowingly) in the form of encapsulated library behaviors to control the playback and perhaps some mouse-over effects. The designer only sees the system as the film-editing model.

As you move on to Lingo programming, the film-editing model becomes more transparent. The designer can see through to the language's underlying layers and finds that there is actually a fairly general programming environment behind the film-editing abstractions. Lingo code is not limited to controlling the playback of the score. One common insight that a budding Lingo programmer has is when she realizes that she can make an object move frame-by-frame not only by score-based animation, but just as easily by programming the motion into a piece of Lingo code. While learning to do this, the programmer typically finds that using Lingo to control the animation gives her much more flexibility and expressive power.

More generally, transparency can be seen as a continuum from the black box to the glass box (Rheinfrank, Hartman, and Wasserman 1992). A *black box* is a completely opaque artifact. The user provides input and the black box provides output, but there is nothing in the design of the black box to indicate what happens between input and output. The view of the black box becomes purely functional. In order to use it, all a person

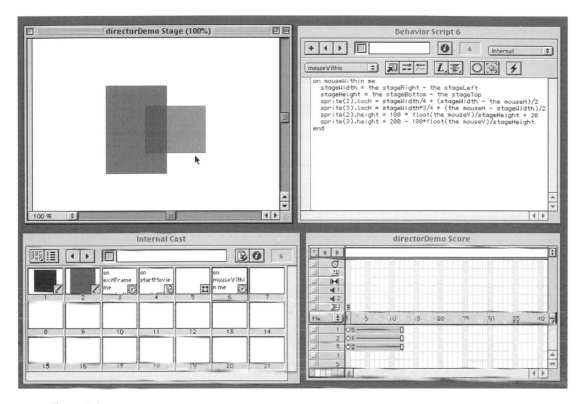

Figure 5.1

The most important parts of Macromedia Director (from the top left and clockwise): the stage, where the final program or presentation is set; the script window, where Lingo code is written; the score, which serves as a timeline for orchestrating playback; and the cast, which contains the elements of the presentation. This example shows a tiny interactive experiment, inspired by the work of Casey Reas, where the position and size of the two squares are related to mouse movements.

needs to know is the relation between what goes in and what comes out, between action and outcome; there is no way of knowing what goes on inside the black box.

The other extreme is the *glass box,* which is completely transparent. The user can see every detail of the artifact through the glass walls, and understand every part of its construction and every transformation in its information processing. The whole process is visible, which potentially leads to a better understanding of the artifact's implications, scope, and ways it can be changed.

Digital artifacts can occupy many possible positions along this continuum, from the totally opaque black box to the glass box where we can see all the way into the quantum physics of the transistors. The ATM is a black box, where the user only sees the relation between input and output, but not much in between. Another, slightly more complex example that exists between the black box and the glass box is the graphical user interface of a contemporary desktop operating system, such as Microsoft Windows. This system is transparent at the level of showing plainly that files are stored in hierarchical structures of directories. Anyone can drag a "document" from one "folder" to another, see it move, and understand the action to some extent. But the layers underlying this overt representation of the action are essentially opaque. For instance, it requires special tools and skills to learn how files are stored physically on the disk.

The designer of a digital artifact always has the difficult task of deciding what level of transparency to create in her design. In the ATM, for example, the intention is that the user should not be able to look inside the box. The ATM is a black box and this is probably a good choice for its purpose. Compared with the ATM, Director appears quite transparent, but in comparison with a traditional programming environment, it is still rather opaque. There are no means for controlling memory and register management, only rudimentary connections to the primitives of the underlying operating system, and so on.

The degree of transparency determines how the artifact can be used—that is, the nature of the resulting action space. An opaque design yields a smaller action space but greater degrees of security and control for the users, whereas a more transparent artifact is more flexible for the users but at higher risk: there is less control of how the artifact will be used and it is more vulnerable to interventions of different kinds.

Returning to the topic of design tools, less transparent designs may be preferable in many cases for novices in a certain field. Considering Director, the most important thing for the novice user to do is to become productive within the boundaries established by the program's outermost layer: simply structured multimedia work. The pleasure of reaching satisfactory results through a program like Director rapidly must not be underestimated. A common design strategy toward this goal is to provide examples, templates, and prepackaged effects for the user to start from, in addition to designing layers of transparency of the digital artifact in a conscious way.

A good example of the rapidly productive strategy is found in the area of bringing nonprofessional users in contact with the pleasures of creative media production. Or, to put it more plainly, helping people deal with their digital photography and home videos. There is a wide range of products offering well-designed templates and small sets of image-processing operations such as cropping, red-eye removal, and image effects. In a few easy steps snapshots of the family on vacation can be turned into nice-looking

Christmas cards. The transparency of these programs is very low—there are no settings for the filters, no general layout functions, no typographic control—and the productivity is instantly high. Image publication on personal web pages is another important niche for opaque and productive tools of this nature. Similar products are easy to find for home video editing as the computing power to capture and manage digital video is moving beyond the professional sphere of the movie business.

The paradigmatic example of rapidly productive tools in the field of three-dimensional computer graphics is Bryce, which was created by Kai Krause and colleagues at MetaCreations (of Kai's Power Tools fame) in the 1990s. The tools from MetaCreations were noticed mainly for their innovative interfaces; however, their main contribution in this context is the level of technical functionality they made accessible to a general audience on desktop computers. Highly automated and sophisticated 3-D modeling, manipulation, and rendering are hidden behind a skillfully designed layer of abstraction, enabling the nonprofessional user to concentrate on the visual results of 3-D graphics and produce stunning original results with little effort.

Unlike the Christmas card programs, Director addresses the issue of users evolving from simple experiments to demanding professional use. An advanced user requires more precision and expressive power from her tools. To meet these requirements, it is necessary to provide greater transparency and flexibility. The solution offered by Director is the underlying programming language Lingo, which is reasonably general and powerful. The general question the designer faces is whether to create a firm boundary between transparent and opaque, or whether to strive for a progressive disclosure of levels as the user's skills and needs develop. There are a few alternatives to consider if the boundary is not firm—for instance, whether the underlying levels of increasing flexibility and complexity should be hidden and require manual unveiling by the user. A trivial example would be the choice of abbreviated versus complete menus in a feature-rich word processor. Some experiments have been made with so-called adaptive interfaces where the underlying levels are hidden but the system discloses them based on independent reasoning about the user's skill level and needs.

The main point here is that all digital artifacts, like most technical systems, have the quality of transparency whether the designer wants them to or not. This is a necessary consequence of the complexity of the artifact. In many cases of interaction design, the quality of transparency is not intentionally designed. Instead, we suspect that it is common for interaction designers to act in accordance with what is considered to be the norm within a certain genre. Intentional and deliberate design requires an awareness of transparency as an important quality of digital artifacts.

5.3   Example: Feather

Feather is a concept designed by Rob Strong and Bill Gaver (1996) for personal communication in situations where one person travels while another stays at home. The aim of the concept is to indicate, simply and expressively, when the traveling partner is thinking of the other.

The system involves two devices: a picture frame carried by the traveler and a sculpture-like structure that remains with the person at home, with a transparent plastic cone containing a single feather and a hidden fan at the bottom. The traveler sends a signal to the partner at home by lifting the picture frame. The signal starts the fan and the feather rises to drift in the air inside the transparent cone, lifting and dipping as it catches the wind.

The Feather concept is exceptionally simple to describe, imagine, and build. It involves only one input and one output. Nevertheless, it has inspired a whole range of other designs and experiments in the emerging field of emotional communication. For instance, one aspect of Feather also identified by Strong and Gaver is the asymmetric nature of the communication. They have proposed a similar design called the "Shaker," where the two devices are identical in function: move one, and the other moves as well. This idea has been elaborated using other communication modalities, such as the White Stone concept: a squeeze of one soft, palm-sized stone heating the other stone slightly (Tollmar, Junestrand, and Torgny, 2000).

5.3.1   Personal Connectedness

In its simplicity, Feather illustrates a foundational quality of digital artifacts in their role as communication media: the possibility to stay in touch, to mediate closeness over a physical or temporal distance. When we think of connectedness in general, we tend to think of sending an email or an ICQ message, or talking to someone on a mobile phone. Feather opens our eyes to other modes of connectedness that are less intrusive and less demanding of our full attention, more subtle, and perhaps more poetic. The lifting of the picture frame gives the interaction a precious feel and the feather dancing in the air reflects the transience and lightness of thought.

There are interesting examples of how our rather crude and attention-demanding contemporary technologies for personal communication are put to innovative uses in search of a more subtle sense of connectedness. For a Scandinavian, the use of mobile phone SMS among young people instantly comes to mind. SMS stands for Short Message Service, a basic function of mobile phone networks where a text message of no more than 160 characters can be transmitted. Inputting text using a ten-key numeric keypad and navigating the message menus of mobile phones are tedious and error-prone tasks that would fail miserably in any proper usability test. Still, among Scandinavian teenagers the number of SMS messages sent significantly outnumbers mobile phone calls. In fact, the use of SMS has been one of the reasons why many Swedish teenagers find regular email unnecessary for their communication needs.

When an SMS message is received, a person's mobile phone typically beeps once. The message stays in her phone until she finds a convenient time and place to read it and possibly to reply to it. An interesting variation, apparently popular mainly among Italian teenagers, is the "drin" or "squillo," which means to dial somebody's mobile phone number, let it ring once, and then hang up. The recipient is aware of this communication code and does not pick up immediately. If the phone stops ringing after only one signal, someone has probably sent a drin. The point is that the call is stored in the phone's list of missed calls, to be viewed later as the equivalent of receiving a gentle thought through a Feather, Shaker or White Stone. Moreover, a non-answered call costs nothing to place or receive, while SMS is normally charged per message sent. This opens for a slightly different protocol in addition to the gentle-thought notion described earlier: If you receive a drin from a friend rather than from a loved one, it might also mean, "Call me, I have no more money on my cash card." Disambiguation is presumably based on personal knowledge of the receiver's relations with different drin senders.

The character of mobile phone communication, particularly among young users, becomes slightly more subtle and ambient, even though its crude interfaces and text-only protocols are still a long way from the interaction techniques illustrated by Feather. What these innovative appropriations of existing technology show is the need for communication not only at the center of our attention, but also on the periphery. There is more to communication than transmitting factual information.

The idea of using digital media as a means to support awareness of people's location and activities is by no means new. An early and influential example of this phenomenon is the work at Xerox Parc and EuroParc in the early 1990s on media spaces. The *in vivo* experiments were based on the idea of placing video and audio equipment in offices and common areas of office buildings that are possibly quite far apart from each other in geographical terms, but close in terms of collegiality, shared concerns, and joint projects. Applications were built for desktop computers that would provide users with peripheral awareness of colleagues in their offices, through thumbnail video presentations and continuous audio. Issues of privacy were identified and addressed by, for example, creating a multi-level protocol whereby a user could signal her availability to her colleagues. The combination of rather low-quality video and continuous audio were quite effective in creating a sense of a cohabited virtual space across geographical distance. Similar ideas have since been developed in several directions, including different forms of ambient displays as well as audio-only channels. The widespread use of instant messaging systems such as ICQ in recent years can be seen as another manifestation of the interest in experimenting with peripheral awareness, albeit adapted to more accessible low-bandwidth and low-technological conditions.

Digital infrastructure is spreading rapidly, with the explosion of the World Wide Web as one significant milestone and recent developments in wireless connectivity another possible milestone. In the digitized parts of the world, we are currently at a disturbing threshold level concerning social availability and awareness. It seems that our communicational practices are not quite adequate for the new infrastructure. Think about the frustration that could occur in a situation where a person sends an important message by email to someone she thinks will read it before the next day, then not getting an answer. At this point, she starts speculating on technical or personal reasons for the communication failure and finally ends up calling the person on the phone, only to learn that this person has taken a few days off. Or think about how something as private as a personal phone conversation or a confidential business discussion have, in a matter of a few years, turned into public performances, to the dubious pleasure of the fellow passengers in a train car, for instance.

We can think of the current communications situation as one where largely technology-led interventions have reshaped our social action space (cf. section 5.1) for personal communication in rather dramatic ways. Local practices evolving in different communities, such as the SMS and drin examples mentioned earlier, can be seen as collective experiments to explore the possibilities of the new social action space. Designers of digital artifacts for personal communication also contribute to the ongoing reshaping of the social action space. Compared to the sender of a drin, the position of the designer is more powerful: the designer's actions and decisions will affect the substrate, the infrastructure, and the potentiality of the action space.

The examples in this section indicate how almost any digital artifact can, and will, be used as a tool for communication and for creating connectedness. Following Dourish (2001), it might even be argued that digital artifacts have an intrinsic impact on personal connectedness (Dourish's first design principle of embodied computing states that computing is a medium). If this is the case, then personal connectedness becomes a more or less general quality in interaction design. Whenever a digital artifact is designed, the designer will affect the degree of connectedness among people as well as between people and artifacts, whether intentionally or unintentionally.

5.4 Example: An Interactive Visualization for Support and Maintenance Planning

A nuclear power reactor runs nearly all of the time. It is shut down for a few weeks out of every year for maintenance and repair work, and the number of tasks that need to be carried out in those weeks is staggering. Hundreds of external experts are hired to help out during this scheduled maintenance period. Security requirements are very high, for obvious reasons. It is important that every task can be traced and verified. Moreover, time is a critical resource. Every day that the reactor is down after the scheduled maintenance period is over costs the power plant large amounts of money in lost earnings.

In the middle of the 1990s, owners and operators of a nuclear power plant in Sweden were exploring the possibility of supporting the maintenance work by means of a workflow system. Previously, all maintenance was managed in a manual system, where work orders and other assignments were represented by paper forms to be signed when a task was completed. The idea was to model the work processes in the workflow system with descriptions of the necessary steps and responsible people. Each task should then be initiated from the computer, which would also provide the information needed to carry out the task.

The maintenance period at the nuclear power plant is planned long in advance and requires close monitoring and managing once it starts. A delayed task can have consequences for a whole series of other tasks. It may be necessary to reschedule tasks, reallocate resources, and make difficult priority judgments. Moreover, security and availability criteria must be fulfilled at all times. The shift supervisor is one of the central actors during the maintenance period. For the shift supervisor, an overall grasp of the situation is essential: what is going on right now, what is the status of critical tasks, and which tasks are planned to start shortly?

In 1996–1997, one of the authors (Löwgren) together with Martin Howard at Linköping University in Sweden designed a support system for maintenance management. The starting points for the design were the large amounts of information (tens of thousands of tasks during a scheduled maintenance period), the need to provide people responsible for certain tasks with a grasp of the whole situation, and our own desire to give the maintenance workers the means to control and plan ahead for their own work situation, rather than merely reacting to orders coming from the workflow engine.

Figure 5.2 illustrates the main ideas of a design concept. The situation is represented in a three-dimensional space with time on the z-axis running toward the observer. Every task is represented by a rectangular shape. The x-axis is divided into functional subsystems, so-called "system numbers," a term which is already a well-established part of

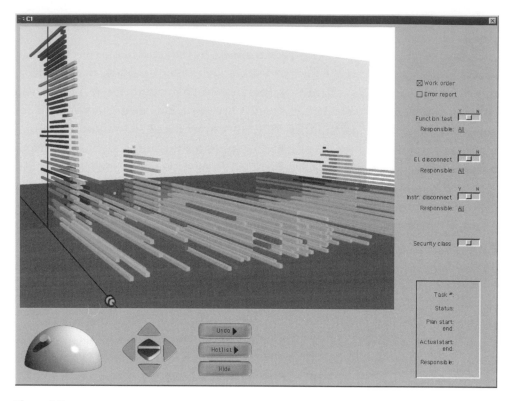

Figure 5.2
A design concept for managing large amounts of workflow information.

the work language at the site. The y-axis presents the number of tasks per subsystem. The semitransparent surface in the x-y plane represents the current time.

The controls to the right of the spatial presentation are filters that operate instantly on the presentation (see figure 5.3). The filter settings control which tasks are presented. For example, if a person only wants to see tasks planned to start tomorrow or later, she drags the planned start time filter to tomorrow's date and all tasks planned to start today or earlier instantly disappear. Filters are combined conjunctively, which means that the only tasks to be presented are the ones that pass through all the filter settings. Figure 5.3 illustrates an interaction sequence where the user first selects all tasks that contain function tests and then the tasks where the person with the initials SBH are responsible. The presentation in figure 5.3 shows that there are only three tasks that fulfil both selection criteria. The controls below the spatial presentation are used for navigation. Tasks can be viewed from different angles, at a distance for overview or close-up

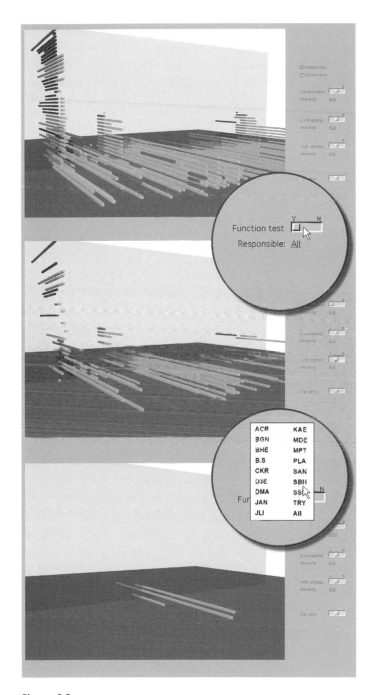

Figure 5.3
Filter settings instantly affect the presentation.

for details on a specific task. Movement is always animated to take the cognitive burden of view reconciliation off the viewer. Tasks can be temporarily hidden if they obstruct the line of vision. The "undo" function makes it possible to back out of an unsatisfactory series of navigation operations. Useful views and filter settings can be saved in a "hot list" and shared with colleagues.

5.4.1 Tight Coupling and Pliability

The information in the proposed maintenance management system corresponds to a relational database with a large number of records and several searchable keys. The filters are equivalent to search criteria for the different fields of records, combined with the logical conjunction "AND." Still, the concept is not very similar to a conventional design based on a database. (Figure 5.4 illustrates a more traditional version of a functionally similar system, with a search form, a summary of search results, and a detailed view of one of the records found.) The main conceptual difference is that this maintenance management database has been turned inside out. A regular database initially shows no contents. After formulating a search query, the user is presented with exactly the results that match the query. Our concept, on the other hand, initially shows all the data in the database when all the filters are disengaged. Activating different combinations of filters cuts away at the presentation until all that remains are the tasks the user needs to see for the moment.

The idea of turning databases inside-out was introduced by Ahlberg, Williamson, and Shneiderman (1992) who call the method "dynamic queries." A subsequent article (Ahlberg and Shneiderman 1994) introduces the use quality of *tight coupling*. The main idea is to minimize the distance between user intentions, user actions, and the effects of these actions. An example is the immediacy of filtering feedback. Any filter manipulation is instantly reflected in the presentation, and the users can gradually work their way toward the intended selection (or toward serendipitous discoveries, as is often the case with the visualization of large data sets). Other means of tightening coupling include providing a reliable undo function to back out of any undesirable interaction state and designing input controls that clearly show their current availability (for instance, graying out inapplicable buttons instead of presenting error messages after these buttons are clicked).

More generally, the quality sought in the interactive visualization described here can be identified as *pliability*. A set of information is pliable to the user if it feels like a responsive material that can be manipulated in an almost tactile sense. Pliability contributes to a highly involved process of exploration where the loop between senses, thought, and action is very rapid and physical rather than elaborate and mental. The

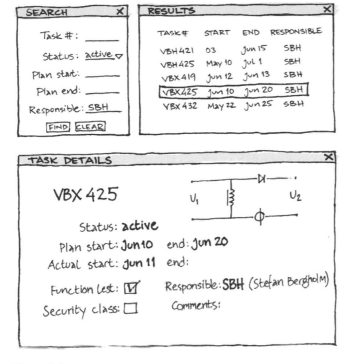

Figure 5.4
A functionally similar design for workflow information, shaped in a more traditional database form with search and presentation windows.

user makes a small quick move, the material shapes and responds, the user notices something new, she makes another move, and so on.

An example of exploring pliability on the micro-level of user-interface sensations is the Sens-A-Patch interaction technique for navigation of moderately sized information spaces (Löwgren 2001).

Sens-a-Patch (see figure 5.5) is based on the idea of spatial constancy—information elements stay in the place they are put on the navigation surface throughout the course of a session and across sessions. In order to fit many elements on to a small surface, the presentation is based on overlapping clusters, one of which is active at a time and the rest of which are visually faded into the background (but still legible). The user experience seems to create a certain amount of involvement, or at least visual or tactile interest. In one case where Sens-A-Patch was used to present all the contents of a medium-sized website, some users were observed to stay on the first page longer than their information needs dictated, in order to play with the sensation of navigating the

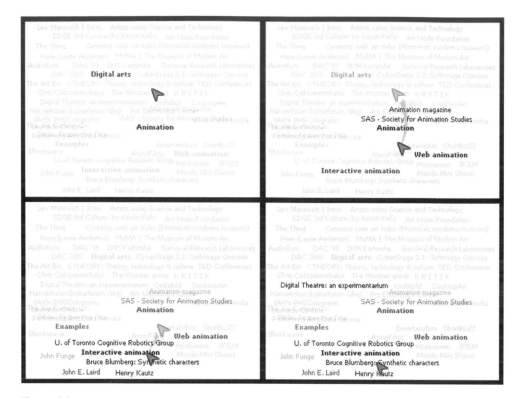

Figure 5.5
Navigating a Sens-A-Patch surface (starting from the top left). Clusters of information are activated and become more clearly visible as the cursor passes over them.

surface. This less goal-directed play at the first page may facilitate the serendipitous discovery of interesting contents.

Moving beyond the surface of the digital artifact, we find that pliability (as opposed to rigidity) is a possible direction in many fields of administrative data processing (Henderson and Harris 2000).[1] It is often the case that the use of administrative systems is unnecessarily restricted and constrained merely because of the underlying database structures used for implementation. A feasible alternative is to aim for more free-form data, basing disambiguation and other technical needs on social mechanisms as appropriate. A simple example is the rediscovery of the margins of paper forms, where annotations can be made and tied to the appropriate context (the form itself) for future interpretation. Most existing databases could easily be augmented with free-form fields similar in function to the margins of paper forms. Similar arguments can be made for the equivalent of sticky notes in "digital paperwork."

Pliability concerns the plasticity of digital "material." A pliable artifact supports exploration and fine-grained control; it is flexible to unanticipated needs and desires. In that sense, pliability can be seen as an attempt to articulate a design direction away from the rigidity that sometimes comes with traditional information systems, in terms of manual handling of the interface and work procedures embedded in the systems.

5.4.2 Control/Autonomy

Returning to the example of the maintenance support system at the nuclear power plant, it may seem odd to a reader skilled in workflow technology that the interactive visualization concentrates so strongly on providing users with the means to manage the maintenance information. Isn't the whole point of workflow systems to provide users with the task requests and other information they need as the workflow engine processes the predefined workflows?

The system design was based on a conscious choice to place a great deal of initiative with users and to offer a tool for their independent work planning and evaluation. The goal was to promote proactive use rather than reactive, which led to a general design principle of providing as much information as possible from the very beginning together with adequate means for accessing and managing it.

In general, what the user experiences as *control* is related to the degree of *autonomy* built into the digital artifact. A strongly autonomous design, an agent, is an artifact that acts on its own in a world defined by the symbols accessible to it. It maintains its own goals, chooses its own means, and can be said in some sense to have a will of its own. To the user, the agent is an actor who can be more or less collaborative.

In the 1990s, the idea of anthropomorphizing agents—endowing them with human traits or qualities—attracted some interest. The Knowledge Navigator future scenario from Apple in 1987 featured Phil, the intelligent desktop agent, who looks like a clever young man with a white shirt and bowtie. The user (a university professor) instructs him through spoken words to perform tasks such as answering the phone and finding all relevant unread articles for preparing a talk.[2] A more recent example of this desktop butler cliché is the character of the so-called Help function in Microsoft Office.

On the other end of the autonomy spectrum, purely nonautonomous artifacts are tool-like in their character. The user wields a tool to process materials and refine them into products of work. The tool is an extension of the hand or the eye—an instrument that facilitates or enables certain actions that remain under the strict control of the user.

The most interesting parts of the spectrum are, of course, between the two extremes of pure agent and pure tool. Virtual spaces are increasingly being used as habitats for artificial-life creatures where the user can affect the course of events to some extent. In some worlds, the user constructs her own creature and then returns later to learn how it has developed during its autonomous life in the virtual world. An example is "The Bush Soul" by Rebecca Allen (1997); artists such as Christa Sommerer and Jane Prophet have also presented work of this kind.

The genres of God-games and Sim-games can also be considered in terms of autonomy. An overall epic or a world simulation runs autonomously on a long-term time scale, where the player modifies local conditions and hopefully the general development of the game world by her actions. Are such virtual spaces and games autonomous or not? Clearly, they occupy places somewhere between the pure agent and the pure tool.

More mundane examples include the search function of a database system. It is an agent in the sense that even though it has been given instructions on a slightly abstract level as to what information to retrieve, it autonomously "chooses" how to carry out the task and which sectors on the disk to visit. However, it is also a tool, since it facilitates the processing of information material that the user would otherwise have to manage, search, and collate manually.

The question of appropriate positions on the autonomy spectrum has been subject to some debate, prompted by work on autonomous web agents in the mid-1990s. Norman (1994) argues for the primacy of user control over digital agents in order to eventually build user trust. If a user cannot trust an autonomous agent, it is of no use—even though it may have been designed to serve. When the user reads all the messages automatically marked for deletion by an email filter, just in case, then she does not save any time after all.

The maintenance support system at the nuclear power plant is an example of a use situation that designers approached with more or less tool-like ideals, where a more conventional workflow system would have been more of an autonomous agent. The general issue of agents versus interactive visualizations is addressed by Shneiderman and Maes (1997), who approach some sort of consensus in the proposition that agents may be suitable for various tasks that occur "behind the scenes," but that the user must still be able to predict and control the externally visible properties of the system. They also note that the debate about positions on the autonomy spectrum sometimes compares apples and oranges, in the sense that visualizations are more appropriate for professional users and structured or semi-structured information spaces, whereas agents are useful mainly for intermittent use and unstructured information such as the World Wide Web. One might ask, however, how Norman's requirement for user trust in agents relates to the idea of intermittent use.

As with the earlier qualities, control/autonomy is not always handled intentionally by interaction designers, even though all digital artifacts have this quality. Control/

autonomy has a significant impact on how people can and will use the digital artifact in question, and how the digital artifact will behave as an actor in a network of actors.

5.5   Example: Tetris

Tetris is perhaps one of the best-known computer games in existence. The basic idea behind it is extremely simple (see figure 5.6 for an illustration). Blocks of different shapes

Figure 5.6
The first Macintosh version of Tetris, released in 1988, running on a vintage Macintosh Plus 1 Mb with the nine-inch screen that this version of the game was designed for.

fall one at a time into a container, and the task is to align the blocks by rotation and sideways movements to fill the bottom of the container completely. Once a "layer" in the container is completely filled, it is automatically cleared to leave room for more blocks. Of course, the pace of the game increases as the player accumulates more points, and eventually the level of not-completely-filled layers reaches the top of the container. Game over.

The game of Tetris may be extremely simple, but it has also proven to be extremely addictive. It has been ported to nearly every computer, game console, and handheld computing device. In fact, most young users of information technology today probably think of Tetris as a typical puzzle game for the mobile phone. At one point, it was the best-selling computer game in the world and it is consistently rated highly on game critics' lists of outstanding classics. The core concept of the game has inspired thousands of clones and variations, including ones with alternative geometries, new block shapes, multiplayer possibilities, and additional functions and features. Given the game's long-standing popularity, it might be useful to sketch a brief outline of the history of Tetris.[3]

In 1985, the two computer engineers Alexey Pajitnov and Dmitry Pavlovsky at the Computer Center of the Moscow Academy of Sciences—who had experimented with making computer games on a mainframe computer—came in contact with high school student Vadim Gerasimov who knew how to program the IBM PC. They decided to team up and after a few months, Pajitnov came up with the original idea for Tetris based on an earlier game of his called "Genetic Engineering." This game in turn was inspired by the block shapes of a classical puzzle called Pentamino. The first prototype of Tetris was developed for the Electronica 60 computer, a Soviet clone of the PDP-11 with a monochrome character-based terminal where square brackets (like these: []) were used to represent the falling blocks. It was then further developed on the IBM PC with colorful DOS graphics.

The creators discussed the possibilities of selling a collection of compelling PC games, including Tetris, but the system of business and governance in the former Soviet Union made this impossible. The game spread by word of mouth and personal contacts around Moscow, and somehow made it to Budapest where it was ported to the Apple II and Commodore 64 by Hungarian programmers. It was brought to the Western audience by Mirrorsoft and Spectrum Holobyte under unclear licensing conditions as the first game to emerge from behind the Iron Curtain, in a new version of the game for the IBM PC filled with Russian-themed graphics and music. It was an instant hit and became the best-selling game in the United Kingdom and the United States in 1988. The rest, as they say, is history.

5.5.1 Playability and Seductivity

If you have ever played Tetris, it is very likely that you have also said "Just one more time!" while staring at the game-over screen. This is a simple way of stating that Tetris exhibits a high degree of *playability* (Minter 1997). Terms like "addictive" are sometimes used to the same effect: to describe the enticing quality of a good game.

More generally, it is obvious that the use qualities of a game cannot be measured with the same yardstick as conventional productivity programs. We might claim that a new accounting system is good if it saves us half an hour that we can spend on more interesting work tasks, but to talk about a game that saves time would almost be a contradiction in terms. To the contrary, a game should be challenging and interesting enough for us to waste lots of time on it (from the point-of-view of our employer or family members).

The accounting program might be designed with the intention of making the user interface consistent and predictable in order to allow the user to concentrate on financial transactions rather than on handling the program. In games, on the other hand, the handling itself can be a vehicle for challenges that might occupy the player for days. This is perhaps best illustrated in an adventure game, where the current task in a traditional goal-oriented sense might be described as simply crossing the bridge. However, the interface is not designed to be transparent and facilitate the rapid execution of the task. To the contrary, there might be several interface puzzles that need to be solved before the bridge can be crossed and the "current task completed" (for example, find the hidden keyhole and figure out how to open it, insert the object that was lying around for no apparent reason in the bat cave three levels ago, activate the mechanism to open the bridge gate by figuring out the appropriate sequence of manipulations, and so on).

How, then, can we understand the mechanisms that make us say, "Just one more time" even at 2:00 A.M. when it is a workday tomorrow and we are already really tired? A crucial difference between games and most work-oriented productivity programs is that we engage with games because we want to, not because of external demands to perform or produce something. The rewards that motivate the game player do not come from the outside, but rather from the joy of playing or the sense of accomplishment involved in reaching a higher score, solving a mystery, or winning a tournament. In short, a game player is driven by intrinsic rather than extrinsic motivation.

Following Thomas and Macredie (1994), we can identify some of the elements contributing to intrinsic motivation.

Challenge   The level of difficulty of the game increases with the player's proficiency.
Fantasy   The player can experience magical events and perform magical actions.
Curiosity   Information is tantalizingly hidden and requires effort to be revealed.

Novelty   The player is continuously presented with new or transformed information and situations.

Complexity   The game is difficult enough to require significant amounts of reasoning in order to make progress.

Surprise   The behavior of the game and the unfolding of events are not easily predictable.

Control   The player not only proceeds through and learns about the game through active participation, but also directs what is going on to some extent.

Competition   The game offers possibilities to compete against oneself, the system, or other players—which provides the thrilling prospect of winning (or losing).

It is clear that the elements of intrinsic motivation are neither necessary in a strict sense, nor simply additive. For example, Tetris must be considered a success in terms of intrinsic motivation even though it draws almost exclusively on challenge, surprise, and competition with oneself. The elements of surprise and control are clearly in a trade-off relation to each other: something unpredictable is outside of player control. The point here is not to provide an epistemologically correct taxonomy, but merely to provide a basis for understanding playability as a use quality.

Another interesting approach is the concept of *seductivity,* which has been proposed as a way of understanding the captivating qualities of certain digital artifacts (Khaslavsky and Shedroff 1999). Seduction is described analytically as a process of enticement (attracting attention and making an emotional promise), relationship (making progress with small fulfillments and more promises, possibly lasting for a long time), and fulfillment (making good on the final promises and ending the experience in a memorable and positive way).

Khaslavsky and Shedroff offer the Visual Thesaurus by Plumb Design as an example of a seductive experience.[4] The Visual Thesaurus is a web application that adds new dimensions to the well-known contents of a traditional thesaurus by virtue of its interactive properties. Instead of database-style lookups, the user explores the synonyms of words and eventually the transient nature of language itself by navigating a beautifully animated network of words and their interrelations. In the analysis provided by Khaslavsky and Shedroff, the Visual Thesaurus offers surprising novelty for most users; goes beyond obvious needs and expectations; creates an emotional response due to its visual and interactional beauty; connects to personal goals through the fascination of words and concepts; promises to fulfill those goals; and leads the casual viewer to discover deeper meanings of looking up a word in the sense of the multidimensional and dynamic relationships between concepts.

It is straightforward to see how the notion of seductivity can be used to further our understanding of playability. For instance, a highly playable game might offer surprising novelty, create emotional responses through its visual and interactional qualities, allow for the formation of personal goals inside the game universe, and offer promises for the player to fulfill those goals.

The analysis in this section identifies qualities that distinguish good games, but does not say anything about how to achieve them. Designers and researchers have addressed the question of how to design a good game, and even though this chapter is not the place for an exhaustive discussion, we can provide a typical example. Pearce (1997) suggests that a game must contain a goal or objective known to all players from the outset; obstacles to create challenges for the player by impeding her progress towards the goal; resources to help the player achieve the goal and overcome obstacles; consequences in the form of rewards and penalties; information that is known to all players, to one player, or only to the game itself; and finally, rules and structure that provide the logical framework for the other elements of the game.

To open up another line of analysis, the classic status of the original Tetris game builds upon its character as a strongly challenging single-player competition with oneself. However, with the emergence of increasingly pervasive digital infrastructures comes the notion of a *game as a social activity,* of playing as doing something together with other people. Many successful single-player games have been developed into multiplayer versions. In fact, a two-player version of Tetris was designed already by Pajitnov and Gerasimov directly based on their work with the initial single-player version. In their two-player version of original Tetris, the container had no bottom. One player's blocks fell from the top down, the other's from the bottom up, and the object of the game was to compete for the space inside. Current plans at the Tetris Corporation, where Pajitnov is affiliated, include the development of software for Internet-based Tetris tournaments.[5]

Virtually all new games produced today—for consoles, personal computers, handheld computers, and mobile phones alike—involve at least some elements of network and social game play. Some are fundamentally social games, whereas most involve a combination of social elements and local, standalone features. A striking observation is that network games entail a new class of motivational factors, based on social interaction rather than on individual psychological considerations.

This is perhaps most obvious in role-playing games such as Everquest. Such games are typically based more or less directly on non-digital role-playing games, where a group of physically and temporally co-located players form a team and set out to perform quests in a fictitious world constructed and maintained by a game master. Or, to be more accurate, the role of the game master is typically to create the space of potentialities in the fictitious world. Its ongoing construction, maintenance, and elaboration is an act of collective narration where the players and the game master have equally important roles. The players act in accordance with their roles within the fiction; the game master takes care of acting for the characters the players meet, the overall unfolding of events unknown to the players, opponents' strategies and actions in battle, and so on. The main point of these games for our purposes here is that they build on social interaction within a fiction, but at the same time encourage a significant amount of social interaction outside the fiction that does not occur unless the fiction is present as a background. In other words, a group of role players can meet once a week for several years and have a great time involving plenty of interaction outside the fiction. But if the group decides to meet without playing the game, it is likely that they will find the conversations empty and something crucial missing.

In the digital versions of role-playing games, the role of the game master is typically automated and the players typically do not occupy the same physical space, but rather meet across physical distances and even from different countries. What emerges over time is a combination of two different game-playing cultures, or two different sets of motivations for playing. Many players engage in the game mainly for the pleasures of collaborative accomplishment (inside the fiction) and social interaction (inside and outside the fiction) together with old and new friends, all people they may never have met face to face. But there are also groups of players who engage in the game mainly to "win." Winning of course means different things in different games, but one good example is Everquest where the rules are based on the traditional family of (non-digital) fantasy role-playing games. A player's character gains points for accomplishments and the points translate into greater powers in the game, learning new skills, withstanding and being able to hand out more physical damage in battle, mastering more powerful magical spells, and so on. "Winning" translates roughly to attaining the highest possible level of player power. Strategies are plotted, alliances are forged, missions are planned—all with the intention of collecting as many points as possible. Everquest also contains a few "epic quests"—missions to accomplish inside the fiction—that somehow represent the ultimate level of achievement in the game universe.

It turns out that playability is a quality with many facets, including intrinsic motivation as well as social aspects. We may note that play, in a more general sense, is a concept with potentially broader scope than the teenage computer game genre. Many areas of everyday life contain aspects of game playing and role playing. Demarcations between work and play are becoming increasingly contrived, and it is in the interest of the thoughtful interaction designer to question them by means of reflective thought and design action.

5.6 Example: Signwave Auto-Illustrator

At first glance, Signwave Auto-Illustrator looks like any other vector-based drawing program. There is a tool palette, a drawing surface, property windows and so on. But once you start drawing, something unexpected happens. When you select the rectangle tool, drag out a rectangular shape on the drawing surface, and let go of the mouse button, the result is not the straight rectangle you would expect. What you get instead looks more like a child's drawing of a house. When you select the pencil and try to draw a curving line underneath the rectangle/house, the line turns into a cursive doodle when you release the mouse button. The text tool inserts nonsense words when you click to position the insertion point on the canvas. You select the house, open the color palette and try to choose a subdued pink color. The color palette would not let you do this, but taunts you for selecting lame colors and instead proposes a really strong, shocking pink. At this point, you start realizing that Auto-Illustrator is not like your average vector-based drawing program (see figure 5.7 for an illustration).

Auto-Illustrator is in fact a work of art, developed by Adrian Ward and awarded several prestigious prizes in the digital arts community. Clearly, it is also a piece of working software, a tool in the sense that it can be used to produce drawings.[6] But its character is much less submissive than conventional drawing programs. The basic shapes, such as rectangles and ellipses, are distorted by one of the autopilots in the program. The shape autopilot has different settings, and in the example above it happened to be set to childish style with average precision (which is between shabby and precise). The pencil autopilot choices range from insipid to cursive, and in the example from figure 5.7, it was set close to the cursive end of the scale. The text tool generates nonsense words with different linguistic traits (one setting is called slightly foreign, and uses numerous diacritical marks in the generated text). There is a tool to create a bug on the canvas—that is, a small dot that starts moving around on its own, leaving a visible trail behind it. There are tools and filters offering distortions one would not expect from a traditional tool, such as the instant Bauhaus style or the conversion of a vector drawing to a connect-the-dots exercise, complete with numbered dots. In short, Auto-Illustrator exercises a greater influence on the final drawings than a typical drawing tool would. The program exhibits a significant degree of autonomy;

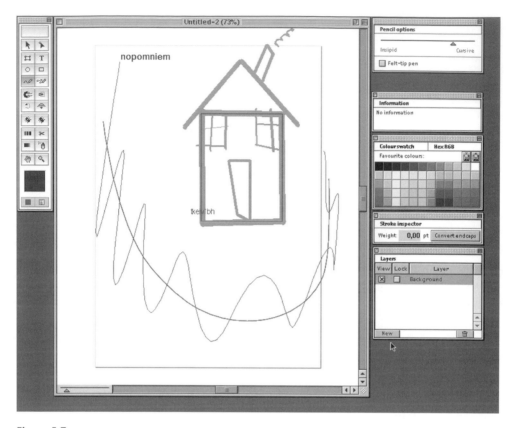

Figure 5.7
An Auto-Illustrator drawing in progress. The gray lines (rectangle and curve) are not part of the drawing; they are superimposed to illustrate the shapes that were actually drawn. (Image by permission of Signwave.)

the drawings are more clearly the results of a collaboration between the user and the program, or perhaps between the user and the designer of the program. In Adrian Ward's own words:

Auto-Illustrator is a semi-autonomous generative vector design application for Macintosh and Windows computers. While parodying existing professional graphic design software, Auto-Illustrator raises difficult questions and proposes new ways of interacting with artwork whose medium is software. As the user operates the software in order to produce a graphic design, the software interferes and makes its own decisions on how the design should look. The final design produced is no longer entirely the hand of the graphic designer, but also that of the software author, who has expressed himself through the use of code. Familiar questions of authorship and authenticity are raised again whilst in an entirely familiar environment—that of traditional desktop software.[7]

5.6.1 Parafunctionality

In the arts, including the digital arts, it is not uncommon for the artist to question what exists and to make the audience question their assumptions, prejudices, and everyday perceptions of life and reality. When this approach is applied to design, we might arrive at a design strategy that Dunne (1999) labels "critical design." In that context, he defines *parafunctionality* as a form of design where function is used to encourage reflection on our relationship with technology, or "how electronic products condition our behavior" (44). Using or attempting to use a parafunctional object creates a heightened sense of distance, mainly because it is conceptually difficult to assimilate into your view of reality. Acknowledging its usability or usefulness is hence also to discover new ways of seeing the world.

It should be noted that not all parafunctional objects can be used. A simple example is the Intolerable Object by Philippe Ramette whose lens would focus the sunlight directly onto the top of your head with possibly fatal consequences. Modeling a use scenario in your mind is in many cases enough to achieve the estrangement effect motivating the parafunctional design. The prerequisite for this to happen is that the proposed artifact is not too strange or else it will be immediately dismissed. It is a question of creating what Dunne and Gaver (1997) call a *value fiction*. If technology in science fiction is futuristic while the social values are conservative, the opposite is true in value fictions: The technologies are realistic while the social and cultural values are fictional or highly ambiguous. The viewer or imaginary user of a value fiction might ask herself why the values embodied in the proposal seem unreal and question the social and cultural mechanisms that define what is real in the first place (Dunne and Raby 2001).

It may seem that the quality of parafunctionality and, more generally, the practice of critical design, is mainly an artistic concern. In a narrow sense, this may be true, but we choose to include parafunctionality here since it illustrates an important aspect of the thoughtful stance. More than any other proposed use quality of digital artifacts, parafunctionality represents the distancing and critical reflection that is necessary for noticing the assumptions we normally take for granted about the role of digital artifacts in society and everyday life. This kind of thinking is every bit as necessary in the design of systems to support office work as it is in the arts.

5.7 An Incomplete Map of Digital Artifact Qualities

In figure 5.8, we have laid out a map of the eight use qualities discussed in the examples given so far. We have also introduced a handful of other qualities that we consider important for the broad picture. This map is by no means a comprehensive illustration of use qualities. Rather, we hope this map and our elaboration of the individual qualities

AMBIGUITY
SURPRISE
☐ PARAFUNCTIONALITY

ANTICIPATION
☐ PLAYABILITY
☐ SEDUCTIVITY
RELEVANCE
USEFULNESS

☐ PLIABILITY
FLUENCY
IMMERSION
☐ CONTROL / AUTONOMY

☐ SOCIAL ACTION SPACE
IDENTITY
☐ PERSONAL CONNECTEDNESS

ELEGANCE
☐ TRANSPARENCY
EFFICIENCY

Figure 5.8
A map of the eight use qualities elicited from the examples in this chapter (highlighted) and ten more that we find important to discuss.

will inspire readers to make their own contributions and to pay attention to these and other use qualities in a more conscious way. The map is our way of grouping use qualities into a structure. Given such a structure, it might be easier to discover blank spots or recognize when too much emphasis is placed on certain aspects. The spatial layout of figure 5.8 does not carry any meaning in itself except that it structures and groups the qualities visually.

The group of qualities on the left of figure 5.8 deals with motivation   Each of the qualities we propose is unique, but what they have in common is that they affect the user's motivation to continue using the artifact.

Playability is the addictive quality of a game that makes the player say "Just one more time!"

Seductivity is the emotional enticement of a digital artifact and its evolving relationship with the user.

Anticipation is a quality of use that has so far mainly been connected with dramatic structures and various forms of plot-driven interaction. In the context of interactive art, Fujihata (2001) describes the interaction process as one of participation and imagination:

In an art of interactivity, one must be stimulated by interaction and enjoy having one's imagination activated. Interactivity is a stimulation of the power of imagination. By the power of imagination, one tries to see what will happen a few milliseconds ahead. This brings a future to the present. It is a bridge between a past and a future. Only interactivity can make such a jump, enabling us to escape from the chronological cage. I believe it is a real creation.

Relevance and *usefulness* are examples of extrinsic motivational qualities, in the sense that the reasons for doing something may very well originate outside the user (even though the user may have internalized them to the extent that she thinks they are her own). Qualities such as these are inherited from work-oriented design of digital artifacts and from academic disciplines such as information systems and human-computer interaction. When a person calls something relevant, and even more so when she calls it useful, there is always the need to orient it toward a purpose: Useful for what? The traditional answer in the realm of digital artifacts is concerned with work tasks. If a system offers the information and tools a user needs to perform a task, then it is a relevant and useful system. The connections to modernist design notions such as "fitness for purpose" should be apparent.

Even though these concepts are typically used in reference to work tasks, it may be noted that the words in themselves do not preclude other applications. For instance, it seems quite sensible to talk about the relevance and usefulness of a website dedicated to fishing. But there are certainly some limits to relevance, usefulness, and other purpose-related qualities. Is Feather a relevant system? How useful is Tetris? At first, these questions may seem strange, but Feather might be relevant as a tool for keeping a friendship alive, and Tetris might be useful as a tool for relaxation or killing time. Such answers, however, border on stretching the concepts of usefulness and relevance beyond recognition.

The group of qualities in the middle of figure 5.8 deals with our immediate experience of interacting with a digital artifact, including our handling and perception of it
Pliability is the plasticity or malleability of the digital material in the hands of the user. Surface pliability is related to the tightness of the loop between the user making a move, perceiving the result, and understanding what she perceives. Deep pliability has to do with possibilities of acting freely and shaping the material, such as when the user annotates the margins of a form to communicate something outside the structured boundaries of the form itself.
Control/Autonomy deals with the distribution of initiative and responsibility in the interaction. Different degrees of a digital artifact's control/autonomy are conceivable, from pure tool to pure automaton.
Immersion deals with the handling of digital artifacts. At the focus of our attention, handling and perception of digital artifacts can become immersive. Digital artifacts offer possibilities for quasi-physical immersion through virtual reality technologies, where

the idea is to fill our sensory organs as much as possible with the "virtual world." The virtual reality artwork Osmose, developed by Char Davies, is a powerful example, where the immersive effect comes from the program's exploiting of our kinesthetic sense of body and motion.[8] Moving around in the Osmose world is accomplished not by making contrived gestures with data gloves, but rather by the user breathing in and out and by shifting her body weight. Technically speaking, there is a sensor around the user's chest that is connected to her own vertical position in the virtual world. The user stands on sensors that are connected to speed and direction of travel. The immersive experience of navigating through the fundamental bodily function of breathing, however, is not reducible to simple technical understandings.

Immersion does not require expensive equipment or sensory-surround stimulation. There is another kind of immersion that comes from a person engaging so deeply in the task at hand that the world around it is forgotten. In terms of digital experiences, such immersion sometimes occurs in creative and explorative activities such as writing, drawing, playing games, or surfing the web. The experience is clearly related to the well-known psychological state of flow. A slightly more passive, but very real, form of immersion can come from being told a captivating story. Perhaps the most immersive activity in the digital realm, however, is programming where complex structures are built in the delicate balance between the programming language constructs and the limits of the programmer's own mental capacity.

Fluency as a use quality of digital artifacts is highlighted by the increasingly pervasive presence of digital infrastructure in our lives. "Use" is not necessarily on or off. It is rather more like a fluent dance among multiple representations. Information streams flow between center and periphery of our attention as we move through the shifting environments of everyday life and work. Transitions need to be graceful and undisruptive.

The group of qualities to the right of figure 5.8 concerns user's interactions with digital artifacts and their outcomes on a broader social level

Social action space is the potentiality for (social) action that is inherent in a digital artifact.

Personal connectedness is the quality of getting in touch, being in touch, and staying in touch with other people in a personally meaningful way. Note how personal connectedness is different from technical connectivity or availability, which deals with connections with little regard for who is connecting to whom and why.

Identity and the constructing and maintaining of identity is central in the use of digital artifacts, which possess symbolic use qualities like any other design objects. The recently emerging culture around skins for accessory desktop applications demonstrates our common desire to project just the right image. Translucent covers in organic shapes have been fitted onto every conceivable computing peripheral since the groundbreaking introduction of the iMac in 1998. But the construction of identity runs deeper than merely picking the right skin (whether it is made of pixels or plastic). The rapidly productive creative tools discussed in section 5.2 are important in this regard. A user with no training or innate talent in the visual arts can produce quite sophisticated results quickly and with little effort—and make a significant contribution to the ongoing project of reconstructing the user's image of herself.

The group of qualities at the bottom of figure 5.8 can be said to represent mediations of structural qualities, or engineering ideals as they are reflected in use qualities
Transparency in the sense we use it here has to do with the user's ability to uncover underlying layers of functionality and complexity as her learning proceeds or her needs evolve. The term is also used in human-computer interaction to indicate the unobtrusive ("intuitive") quality of a user interface that allows the user to concentrate on the task and the objects of the work domain. We do not make a strict separation between user interface and task domain, and rather see transparency as a dimension that can be consciously addressed in a design process.

Efficiency in using a digital artifact is typically connected to performing tasks for external purposes. Efficient use is rapid and error-free. One of the main forces behind the human-computer interaction field has historically been to improve the efficiency of computer-supported work tasks.

Elegance of a digital artifact, in a technical sense, is a combination of power and simplicity (Gelernter 1998). As a general aesthetic principle for engineering, an artifact should perform as well as possible with as simple of a construction as possible. For programming, this translates to creating elements (modules, objects, subroutines, or programs) that compute rapidly in few lines of source code. Note that simplicity itself is not necessarily a simple concept—a highly efficient and compact program can be almost impossible for anyone but a few experts to understand, but still be considered an elegant piece of work by virtue of its "power" and "simplicity."

Elegance in this technical sense is somehow related to the notion of functional minimalism, where the artifact is considered from the user's point-of-view and the goal is to offer appropriate core functions (power) and nothing else (simplicity). This can be seen as an engineering-aesthetic reaction to the exceeding amount of less-than-powerful features found in many mainstream applications. For instance, a word processor would be elegant if it were only good at word processing without also offering poor layout tools and even worse drawing tools.

The group of qualities on top of figure 5.8 deals with the user's creation of meaning in relation to a digital artifact

Ambiguity is generally considered detrimental in human-computer interaction, and it certainly stands in opposition to efficiency and transparency as those concepts are commonly interpreted. However, as Gaver, Beaver, and Benford (2003) argue, ambiguity can also be understood as a resource for encouraging close personal engagement with digital designs.

Gaver, Beaver, and Benford (2003) identify three types of ambiguity—information, context and relation ambiguity—and show how they have all been used to good effect in digital arts and design. One of their examples, Desert Rain, is a mixed-reality installation on the subject of virtual warfare and the blurring of boundaries between real and virtual worlds. The intention is to provoke participants to re-examine the boundaries between reality and fiction. To this end, the boundaries are deliberately ambiguous in that they mix elements of theater, performance, and computer game; the content is a mix of 3-D game-like graphics and video clips depicting real people's experiences of the Gulf War; rain curtains are used for projection, which provide a continually shifting and blurred view of the virtual world.

Ambiguity renders easy interpretation impossible by creating situations in which people are forced to participate in order to make some sort of meaning out of what they experience. An ambiguous design sets the scene for the creation of meaning, but does not prescribe an interpretation. The task of making the ambiguous situation comprehensible falls on the human actor, which may lead to inherent pleasure as well as a deeper conceptual appropriation of the design.

Parafunctionality is the quality of a digital artifact that encourages us to reflect on our relationship with technology, or more generally on the social and cultural values we hold and why we hold them.

Surprise is, of course, an element of parafunctional experience, but it also has interesting implications outside the realm of critical art and design. Holmlid (2002) discusses surprise as a use quality in relation to confusion in traditional work-oriented contexts, pointing out that the surprised user is interested in what she actually did (understanding the unexpected outcomes of an action), whereas the confused user is interested in what she should be doing instead of what she is doing. Surprise and confusion are not seen as errors but rather as natural parts of problem-solving activities, which might involve exploration of action possibilities inherent in the artifact as well as a reconsideration of the initial problem—the reason for encountering the surprise or confusion in the first place.

5.8   The Dynamic Gestalt

The eighteen use qualities we propose, and the structure of the map featured in figure 5.8, are based on our experiences and best understanding of digital design material. There is, however, one quality that we are aware of that we cannot capture in our map and it might be the most important quality of them all. The *overall character* of a digital artifact cannot be described by simply adding up a number of particular qualities. The artifact is more than the sum of its constituent parts; it has qualities that cannot be deduced from the structure and configuration of its parts—that is, it has holistic or emergent qualities. Figure 5.9 shows a very simple example, merely intended to illustrate the difference between additive and emergent properties.

Digital artifacts are every bit as temporal as they are spatial. In order to perceive the whole, or the *dynamic gestalt,* of a digital artifact, we need to experience it as a process, which is to say that we need to try it. The gestalt of a digital artifact *emerges in the interaction with the user over time.* There is no way for a user to get an idea of the dynamic gestalt without interacting with the artifact and exploring different possibilities and courses of events.

This means that the dynamic gestalt of a digital artifact can and must be described and analyzed as a whole, beyond the more particular use qualities we have introduced so far. For instance, interaction with a digital artifact has a temporal flow that can have different feels to it: calm, rapid, or stressful, for instance. Moreover, there is a dramatic structure to the dynamic process that spans across the course of the process from its introduction to its conclusion. This dramatic structure may, for instance, be described as inspiring, boring, obvious, or repetitive.

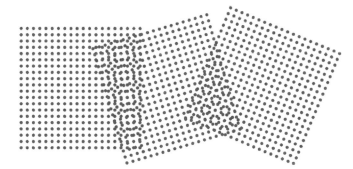

Figure 5.9
A simple visualization of emergent properties. The ring-shaped patterns where the rasterized squares interact are not easily predicted by looking at the squares in isolation, yet stand out clearly when the squares are superimposed. (Adapted from Davies and Talbot 1987.)

The examples of digital artifacts in this chapter are probably deeply unsatisfactory for a reader who has had no previous experience of using the artifacts described. The reader may get a sense from our way of writing that there is something interesting to be experienced in drawing with Auto-Illustrator, for instance, but our dry descriptions and screen shots will never be the same as using the program itself. This discrepancy is (hopefully) not a result of poor writing on our behalf, but rather an illustration of the dynamic gestalt concept. Auto-Illustrator, like any other digital artifact, has a dynamic gestalt that can only be apprehended by actually using it.

The dynamic gestalt of a digital artifact can be understood to some extent by the notion of overall *character*. We form ideas of people's (and artifacts') overall character rather quickly, ideas that are not deductively traceable to the sum of all individual actions and utterances of the person in question. Our idea of the character of a person is, in that sense, a holistic property. It is even the case that we use the notion of overall character to explain apparent inconsistencies in what we observe: "Oh, that is just part of his idiosyncratic character." The dynamic gestalt of a digital artifact is, in this sense, rather like its overall character (Janlert and Stolterman 1997).

There are other ways to characterize the dynamic gestalt of a digital artifact. A great deal of attention has, for instance, been paid to the idea of using metaphors as a means to describe digital artifacts, especially to describe their use qualities. On the other hand, we still find this to be an area that has not received enough attention. It seems as if the question of qualities has been mostly focused on single aspects of a digital artifact, particularly on aspects of an objectively measurable nature. The idea that the digital artifact has an overall character or gestalt that might overrule the effect of a single quality is a problematic—but particularly important—notion. Even though we still have no comprehensive way of characterizing the dynamic gestalt or overall character of a digital artifact, there is no excuse for not attempting to do so. Every interaction design will lead to a product, a digital artifact, that has a unique gestalt. Developing ways of describing, examining, criticizing and categorizing the overall character of such products should be a fundamental priority for our field and for anyone who wants to become a thoughtful designer.

5.9 Other Approaches to Design Quality

Attempts at creating languages to describe artifacts and their qualities are not unusual in traditional design disciplines, quite the contrary. Nearly every design discipline has its examples of such languages, whether they are presented as product semantics, design languages, or simply as the role of the critic in the larger knowledge-constructing system in which the designers and the artifacts also take part.

Krippendorff (1989) defines product semantics as "the study of the symbolic qualities of man-made forms in the cognitive and social contexts of their use and the application of the knowledge gained to objects of industrial design" (10). The primary concerns of product semantics are how artifacts make sense to their users, how they are symbolically embedded in society, and what roles they play in the ongoing self-production and reproduction of culture. Rheinfrank and Evenson (1996) take a designer's perspective on these same issues. They point out how what they call a "design language" can be consciously used by designers to communicate an understanding of intended artifact use to the users, create consistent and desirable images of, for example, a company through the design of its products, and affect a society's developmental trajectories.

A common notion seems to be that designers who are aware of product semantics and participate in the ongoing articulation of artifact qualities are capable of doing their work in qualitatively different ways. Articulation can be seen as a way to share and develop design knowledge, insights, and experiences among designers. Through articulation, designers and critics try to make explicit the qualities inherent in existing artifacts for assessment and appropriation. What we have presented in this chapter is a starting point for moving toward a more elaborate, intersubjective language for addressing the qualities of digital artifacts. Qualities such as the ones we have introduced must be assessed through dialogue, then elaborated, complemented, and possibly rephrased and combined into new formulations. This can be done by analyzing new kinds of digital artifacts and introducing the results into public debate.

This situation hints at the emergence of a new role in the knowledge-constructing system surrounding digital artifacts—namely, that of the *critic* (as introduced in chapter 4). The field of interaction design is well supplied with scientific evaluation of design concepts, and the creative development and dissemination of new design concepts within interaction design also works rather well. However, compared to other design disciplines, interaction design's lack of critics and criticism is obvious. There are occasional examples, such as the efforts by Johnson (1997), to situate the digital artifacts and communication media in a wider cultural context, but much more needs to be done to promote the vitality and progression of this field.

From a designer's point of view, however, there is still something missing. Even a very developed language for describing digital artifacts' use qualities does not in and of itself provide the necessary understanding of the totality created by these qualities as they are merged into a specific design. This totality comprises the basic structure of the artifact, all of its use qualities, and everything else pertinent to the artifact. In some cases, a certain use quality may be more or less irrelevant, whereas in other cases, it may dominate. The totality of a digital artifact is more than the sum of its constituent parts; it has desirable qualities such as flexibility, durability, and stability. A flexible and durable composition has a certain integrity and allows the user to make sense of it both immediately and as her relationship with it develops over time.

A language of use qualities says nothing about how to design an artifact or how to address its totality, but it may support the designer in her ongoing work of developing a repertoire, an articulation language, and a sense of quality. It may help the designer be prepared for new design situations, but it can never be a prescription for action in any specific situation.

6 | Conditions for Interaction Design

Every design field has its own history and future. The existing and future practice is, of course, deeply influenced by earlier practices, ideas, and values. There is always an intellectual tradition manifested in present practice that changes in resonance with a surrounding culture. In the case of interaction design, the intellectual heritage is most clearly present in the form of paradigms and ideas dominating the disciplines related to the shaping of digital artifacts, such as information systems, software engineering, and human-computer interaction. In this chapter, we outline important parts of interaction design's historical heritage as we understand it. We also point to the existence of a more general history of design where the basic assumptions on the nature of design work have been debated and developed for a long time in ways that have implications for interaction design.

In addition to history, the future also affects our understanding of the conditions, limitations, and possibilities for interaction design. Thus, we devote a section in this chapter to a discussion of how interaction designers can relate in thoughtful ways to the rapid technological development of our field and to the future of digital materials.

We believe that the historical sketch, the comparison with other design disciplines, and our comments on dealing with the future, if taken seriously, can be important contributions to the thoughtful development of what it means to be an interaction designer.

First, however, we examine the general relationship between technology and society. The interdependence between the two is an essential condition for interaction design, as well as for any other creative technological work.

6.1   We Shape Technology, Technology Shapes Us

Technical artifacts are highly interconnected with people and the way we live our lives. The nature and meaning of this interplay is a question that has fascinated many thinkers; there are numerous theories on the relations among technology, society, and people. This is not the place for a detailed survey, but it may be valuable to introduce some of the main ideas here. Interaction designers are instrumental in societal development by designing digital artifacts that become part of large and small sociotechnical systems.

We can imagine an axis where the view of people's influence over technology varies from one end of the axis to the other: the who-is-in-charge axis, if you like. One extreme point of the axis corresponds to a view stating that technology is completely neutral morally and ethically; it is the use of technology that determines how we should assess it. A computer may help blind people read the newspaper, but it may also guide an intercontinental ballistic missile. Technology is seen as a collection of tools that are picked up, used, and then returned. Assessments like good and bad cannot be assigned to technology and technical artifacts in themselves. Pfaffenberger (1989) refers to this view as *technological somnambulism* and dismisses it as misguided and dream-like. The main problem with this view, he contends, is that the development and use of technology leads to far-reaching changes in people's behavior and the structures of society. The technological somnambulist disregards such effects.

The other extreme point on the axis—which MacKenzie and Wajcman (1985) indicates is the most influential perspective on the relations between technology, society, and people—is *technological determinism*. Briefly, technological determinism views technology as an independent force in societal development, where technological changes cause societal changes. The strongest version of this theory even pinpoints technology as the most influential force in societal development.

The people developing technical artifacts are of course members of society, but their work is commonly seen as independent and located outside of society. Technology development is usually viewed as applied science: Developers apply new scientific findings, which consist of objective and increasingly detailed insights into how nature really works. The technology resulting from this application of scientific findings is then introduced into society and causes certain societal effects, which are sometimes unpredictable.

It is, however, easy to show that historically technological development and societal effects are not linked in a simple causality. The characteristics of society matter significantly in terms of which technical artifacts are put to use, irrespective of their usefulness and other valuable qualities "in themselves." There are many examples of how one technical artifact has led to different effects under different societal conditions. Consequently, the causal relation between technical artifact and societal conditions is not one-dimensional or strictly logical. Still, it is equally clear that technology does affect society. A famous example is Winner's (1980) discussion of road transportation in New

York. The bridges for freeways leading from New York City to Long Island were designed to allow only regular passenger cars to pass under them. Buses could not pass through these bridges, which meant that the only way to visit Long Island or live there was to be able to afford your own car—a form of technology as social politics.

It seems clear that neither of these two extreme views of the relationship between technology and social conditions above is very useful. Technology is neither value-neutral, nor is it an independent variable with necessary causal effects on societal development. How, then, is the shaping of technology determined? MacKenzie and Wajcman (1985) present a number of possible explanations; the following section is based on their presentation.

We mentioned earlier that science is often seen as a force shaping technology: a view whereby technology is applied science. It turns out that this explanation is inadequate in several respects. Modern sociology of science shows that not even the natural sciences are objective and independent of society. In fact, the choice of problems to research and the choice of research methods are better understood as social constructions determined by political, organizational, and other factors. Moreover, it is easy to demonstrate historically that the development of technology was not always tightly linked to science, and definitely did not always exist in a one-way relationship. Technological development contributes strongly to the development of science; an obvious example is the use of computers, which enables new classes of computational methods in the natural sciences today.

Another valuable explanation of technological development is that technology itself shapes new technology. The main part of all technological development does in fact consist of modifications and additions to existing technological artifacts. Many important inventions were demonstrably inspired by existing technology, perhaps merely transferred to a new domain of application. There are, of course, more factors influencing the shaping of technology than just technology itself, however.

In order to understand the development of technology, and the development of large technical systems in particular, it is important to consider the intended goals of this development. One common goal, in the field of digital artifacts as well as in technology in general, is the economical goal of increased earnings and reduced costs. Moreover, if we acknowledge that existing economic systems and "laws" are not universal but rather closely connected to contemporary society, then we realize that politics, government, and culture also contribute to the development of technology. Pertinent examples from our field might include the politically motivated efforts to introduce information technology in schools and massive military investment in information technology research and development.

A reasonable conclusion is that technology is shaped by societal factors, although not in a unilateral or instrumental way. Society is equally shaped by existing technology and technological development. We shape technology, and technology shapes us. When an interaction designer considers an intranet design for a workplace, it can be attributed to the observation that the workplace accommodates or "needs" such an artifact, but these conditions are equally determined by technological development.

Technology is part of society, and when we act as designers of technology, we also act as members of society. Hence it is important for a thoughtful designer to understand the forces that affect our society and shape our future. Even if these reflections have no direct influence on the practicalities of design work, they do constitute a foundational element in any design activity. Interaction design is part of the ongoing design of our society.

6.2 The Early History of Design

Any form of human activity that can be delimited and given a name has a history. This also holds true for design. Before going into a few examples of design history, we need to ask what a historical perspective might mean for interaction design. The question is particularly relevant considering the very short history of our field. Is there anything to learn?

History can be regarded in many different ways. For instance, we can view it primarily as a way to learn "how it was." Such knowledge may be interesting and valuable in itself, but it may also offer more substantial returns. The most obvious result of design-historical studies is an understanding of design work as part of a larger society, of the cultural movements of the times, and of the ideas, belief systems, and ideologies pervading a specific society at a specific moment in time.

Designs that are perceived as radically avant-garde in a certain culture at a certain time may appear as hopelessly mundane and trivial at another time. Ideas that are technically and socially impossible in a certain cultural context may provide highly innovative openings for new technical possibilities in another time or place. In addition to the descriptive purpose of history, there is also the view of history as part of an ongoing process, where history forms the basis for design decisions we make today. Understanding history means understanding where we come from and understanding the traditions and conceptual "sediments" that shape and influence our current work (Collingwood 1946).

6.2.1 Craft and Design

The original form of creative work is embodied in the idea of the individual craftsman. The distinctive characteristic of craft is that the same person is responsible for the idea, shape, production, and in many cases even the distribution of an artifact. In the really traditional scenario, a craftsman is also the eventual user of the artifact. People create their own tools and everyday artifacts, which in themselves satisfy functional as well as aesthetic and cultural needs. Traditional craftsmen do not separate design from production in the way we do today in most disciplines. Neither do they separate client from producer, nor client from consumer. The craftsman has often been used as a symbol for the total design process, where all aspects of design and production are synthesized into a natural whole.

The development from craft to modern design and production has proceeded at different paces and occurred at different times in the various sectors of society. One of the first areas introducing this division of labor was architecture. The building process became hard to manage as the buildings were made larger and more complex. A person was needed to take overall responsibility for a building's shape and design—and the role of the architect was born.

We can see the same development in many other areas. As long as products and their production process are simple and manageable, then they are performed as crafts. When the complexity of the process increases, or when demands necessitate mass production, then divisions of labor and responsibility are introduced. There are several possible explanations for such developments, ranging from simple arguments about work complexity to more ideological and political perspectives.

What is important to us here is that division of labor has occurred, and we are in a situation where the work of creation is separated from production in most fields. The need for specific design competence has grown accordingly. The understanding of design competence and what it entails, however, differs strongly across fields. There are still fields where craftsmanship—a strong connection between design and production—is emphasized, but also fields where design work is entirely separated from traditional craft and production.

The same general trend can be seen in the field of digital artifacts, albeit on an entirely different timescale.[1] In the early years, around 1940–1950, computer use was a craft. The people using computers were also the ones designing and coding the programs they needed. There was rarely any division of labor. Gradually, the field has expanded and diversified to the current situation in systems development where a multitude of professions and competencies are involved between the start of a development process and a final product.

Wroblewski (1991) explores the implications of looking at interaction design as a craft. One of his conclusions, perhaps not surprisingly, is that we need more appropriate tools and responsive materials for interaction design. Wroblewski also raises the more interesting question of what research (or, more generally, knowledge construction) in the field would be like if the model were design rather than experimental methodology. One of his suggestions is that the interaction design researcher assumes the role of the *articulate craftsman,* responsible for determining the factors shaping digital artifacts in a way that has practical meaning and relevance. It is particularly important for the articulate craftsman to identify the trade-offs underlying important design decisions. Examples of such trade-offs that should be of interest to other practitioners are information versus time, ease of learning versus efficiency, and information in the "head" versus information in the world.

The work of Wroblewski and others has led to a rediscovery of Alexander's ideas from the 1970s on a pattern language for architecture (see, e.g., Alexander et al. 1977) In recent years, some attention has been devoted to applying the notion of patterns to interaction design (even though it seems to have been most successful for structural patterns in software engineering). A typical example is the massive collection by Van Duyne, Landay, and Hong (2002) of patterns for e-commerce websites. Casaday (1997) was among the first to explore the idea with some attention to Alexander's original intentions. In Casaday's approach, a pattern identifies the context of a design problem, the contradictory intentions that need to be weighed against each other, the specific problems following from the trade-off, and finally ways to solve the problems. One of Casaday's patterns is called the airport passenger.

Context   An interactive system requiring high-skill performance on first encounter.
Forces   Efficiency, reliability, and immediate learning of particulars are all required.
Problem   Balanced satisfaction of all requirements.
Solution   Standardize components and procedures, leaving only unavoidable case-to-case variation. This solution can be seen in airports around the world, and in the consistency of graphical user interface (GUI) elements across platforms. (Casaday 1997, 290)

It may be worth pointing out here that our notion of design as a knowledge construction system—with related concepts such as articulation, paradigmatic examples, use qualities, digital artifact genres, the possible role of the critic, and the development of design ability—is closely related to Wroblewski's idea of an interaction design researcher as an articulate craftsman.

There are several conclusions to draw from the reasoning presented here. We may note that digital artifacts must always be designed, irrespective of the environment we are considering. Whether we are thinking of craftsmanship or a strict division of labor is irrelevant. The job must be done—a design must be devised. Furthermore, we observe that the existing division into different professional roles is not a static situation, but rather a process of continuous change subject to new modes of working, new responsibilities, and new technology. This change is not likely to slow down in the near future—in fact, it seems rather that we are still in the early stages of a quite radical evolution. Significant changes are to be expected in what we know today as "interaction designer." It may divide into increased specialization, where each subfield has its own competence profile. We might expect a course of development similar to what we have seen in other design disciplines, which means that interaction designers are likely to face changes in their professional roles and will need to make many career decisions in the years to come regarding area of specialization, project role, and so on.

However, evolving professional roles and competence profiles are not the only conditions for interaction design. Historical studies also show the emergence, development, and obsolescence of different design-theoretical ideologies and styles. The short period of time corresponding to the history of interaction design exhibits similar traits.

6.3   The History of Interaction Design

Even though we cannot address the whole design history of the field of digital artifacts, there are some interesting lines of development that provide a deeper understanding of our intellectual tradition. Human-computer interaction (HCI) and the Scandinavian school of systems development are the two fields that we find most relevant; they are both strongly focused on the use qualities of digital artifacts, and they exhibit interesting similarities over time.[2]

6.3.1   Usability and Human-Computer Interaction (HCI)

There is no question that usability is a central concept in the field of Human-Computer interaction (HCI). One of the main goals of the field is to contribute to the development of more usable digital artifacts; historically, it is easy to demonstrate how the meaning of the usability concept has shifted quite significantly over its relatively short lifetime.

The field of HCI has its roots in what was in the late 1970s called software psychology (Shneiderman 1980), a discipline with a strong basis in experimental psychology methods and the scientific tradition. The phenomenon of study was a human interacting with a computer, and the intention was to accumulate empirical knowledge through controlled experiments. The scientific methodology would ensure that the knowledge was true—within statistical limits—and applicable to other instances of human-computer interaction. It also formed the basis for more general theories concerning human thought and action in front of a computer. These theories were not only capable of explaining observed phenomena, but ideally also useful in predicting what would happen in new situations. One of the most famous theories, the Model Human Processor, was presented in 1983 by Card, Moran, and Newell in *The Psychology of Human-Computer Interaction*. The preface indicates the intended role of the theory, as follows: "The domain of concern to us . . . is how humans interact with computers. A scientific psychology should help us in arranging this interface so it is easy, efficient, error-free—even enjoyable" (Card, Moran, and Newell 1983, 1).

Within the framework of these general theories, usability was seen as the degree of fit between system properties and general human psychological characteristics. The goal for the designer was, obviously, to maximize the fit. There is still a strong element of psychological science in HCI research, but its impact on professional systems development has been rather limited.

The demands of professional systems development for cost-effective and manageable modes of working paved the way for a new approach known as usability engineering. It is clearly inspired by the foundational work in experimental psychology, but the crucial difference is that usability engineering concentrates on practical information rather than on general facts and theories. The following passage summarizes the ethos of usability engineering:

Usability engineering is a process, grounded in classical engineering, which amounts to specifying, quantitatively and in advance, what characteristics (and in what amounts) the final product to be engineered is to have. This process is followed by actually building the product and demonstrating that it does indeed have the planned-for characteristics. Engineering is not the process of building a perfect system with infinite resources. Rather, engineering is the process of economically building a working system that fulfills a need. Without measurable usability specifications, there is no way to determine the usability needs of a product, or to measure whether or not the finished product fulfills those needs. If we cannot measure usability, we cannot have a usability engineering. (Good et al. 1986, 241)

Usability engineering apparently hinges on the possibility of specifying the usability of the future system in measurable terms, and then measuring the usability throughout the development process to determine if the specified levels have been obtained. Measuring methods have been adapted from earlier HCI studies: experiments in laboratories, but without scientifically rigorous demands on sampling and size of the group of participants. The aim was to achieve as credible information as possible within the time and resource limits of the engineering project. Ideas on what to measure were also adapted from earlier research, including the following:

- User performance on specified tasks, measured in terms of task completion rate, completion time, or number of errors
- Flexibility of the design (measured by the proportion of users in a heterogeneous group able to perform the test tasks)
- How easy the design is to learn, measured by changes in task completion rate, completion time and errors committed over time (One can also measure how well the participants retain what they have learned and how often they need to consult the instructions or help functions.)
- The users' preference and degree of satisfaction, measured by subjective estimates or studied through structured interviews

Usability engineering has proven to be a viable approach in professional as well as academic contexts. Its focus on early specification and measurable requirements goes well with the general ideals of development processes in many companies, particularly ones where an engineering culture is prevalent. However, usability engineering's focus on measurable usability has also been the target for increasing criticism. There is always the danger that a measurement-oriented development process is drawn toward aspects that are easy to measure—such as superficial questions concerning the user interface or time efficiency for contrived test tasks in lab environments that do not have much relevance for real use situations—at the expense of considerations that are more important for long-term outcomes. Two of the originators of usability engineering, John Whiteside and Dennis Wixon, were among the first people to recognize these limitations. In a highly personal conference paper from 1987, they wrestled with the inadequacies of treating usability as an objective property of the product as illustrated in the following passage:

For us, software usability refers to the extent to which software supports and enriches the ongoing experience of people who use that software. This direct emphasis on experience is at variance with "standard" definitions of usability that concentrate on, as primary, measurable manifestations of usability such as productivity, preference, learnability or throughput. Although these may be interpreted as important properties of usability, for us they are not primary. Primary is the person's experience at the moment experienced . . . If the [usability] goals are not grounded in something really meaningful to the users, then the resulting product will be useless to them. (Whiteside and Wixon 1987, 18, 20)

This more subjective view of usability was gradually refined into a development philosophy known as *contextual design* (Beyer and Holtzblatt 1997). Broadly speaking, contextual design is a cyclical process where the phases of requirements generation, design, implementation, and evaluation are performed as many times as the project resources allow. Contextual inquiry, which is a field study method based on ethnographic techniques, is used to help designers develop an understanding of a use situation that reflects the views of users and customers as well as possible (see chapter 4). Diagrams, modeling techniques, and simple prototypes are used in a collaborative process to design the new way of working with support from digital artifacts. Ideas are gradually evaluated through contextual inquiry and the degree of detail increases along with the shared understanding, proceeding from computer-implemented prototypes and eventually through a deliverable system.

As we will see later in this chapter, there are obvious similarities between contextual design and the development philosophy that had earlier emerged within the Scandinavian school of systems development under the name of *participatory design*. Even though the first publications on contextual design and similar approaches overlooked this connection, there is clear evidence of a growing interest in the early Scandinavian sources within the HCI community, starting around 1990. Participatory design techniques have been appropriated and further developed by quite a few HCI researchers, but interestingly most often for reasons other than their original intentions. Participatory design in Scandinavia in the 1970s was essentially an ideological movement, founded in dialectic materialism and core issues concerning the right to work and the value of work. Most HCI work on participatory techniques in the 1990s on the other hand, has concentrated on the possibility of increasing user and customer acceptance, on a broader concept of usability, and on giving designers tools to better understand the intended use situations. (Refer to Spinuzzi 2002 for further discussion on the relation between Scandinavian participatory design and contextual design.)

6.3.2 Systems Development and Scandinavian Themes

Much of the early work in systems development in Scandinavia was influenced by Herbert Simon's ideas about a design science, a science of the artificial (Simon 1969). Using engineering as his example, he argued that many professions address the design of artifacts, which requires knowledge that traditional basic subjects—mathematics, physics, and so on—cannot offer. On the other hand, he was critical of design practices at the time, which he found "intellectually soft, intuitive, informal, and cookbooky" (57). His solution to the dilemma was to present the problem of designing artifacts in a way that was amenable to logical and mathematical treatment, much like in the natural sciences.

Simon's science of the artificial tells us that computers are complex, hierarchical systems—much like the organizations where computers are used. Systems development is equivalent to dividing these complex systems into their constituent parts and defining functions separately for each part. Scientific methods from logic and mathematics are proposed to facilitate the search for and assessment of different design alternatives.

The field of software engineering, which formulated its first mission statements in the late 1960s, was based on similar assumptions. In this field, computer programs are seen as mathematical objects that can be derived from abstract specifications. The correctness of programs can be guaranteed by methods for formally transforming the specifications step-by-step into executable code.

An early and influential example in Scandinavia was the information systems theory of Börje Langefors (1966), which aimed at analyzing the information needs in an organization and breaking them down into atomic units. This analysis would then form the basis for the design of a new and optimal, or at least adequate, information system and the specification of the necessary computer support.

To summarize, the first generation of systems development research concerned rationality and systematic, scientifically grounded systems development methods. A crucial assumption was that intended users would be capable of providing exhaustive and explicit descriptions of their needs and wants. The analysis preceding construction of the information system was seen as an objective collection and evaluation of facts. During the 1970s, a new view on systems development emerged, partly as a reaction to the rationalism of the first generation of methods. The new philosophy, *participatory design*, concentrated on the human, social, and political contexts where information systems were developed and used (Bansler 1989).

The first research projects on participatory design were strongly positioned as political projects, intended to facilitate work life democracy. Where rationalistic approaches used information technology as yet another instrument of management and control, participatory design researchers instead aimed at using systems development processes as a way to increase the influence and co-determination of the workers. One of the pioneering projects, by Kristen Nygaard in collaboration with the Norwegian Metal Workers' Union, began in 1971 and its results were described on a clearly political and social level:

As a result of the project we will understand actions carried out by the Iron and Metal Workers' Union, centrally or locally, as a part of or initiated by the project. In this strategy knowledge was acquired when actions had made the need for new knowledge clear. It was realised that successful initiatives at the national level had to be based on discussions and actions at the local level. The strategy towards design and use of information technology aimed at creating a process which would build up knowledge and activities at all levels, with the main emphasis on the local level. (Nygaard 1979, 98)

Numerous projects followed, many of them in collaboration with different trade unions and all driven by political ideals concerning worklife democracy. Generally, it is fair to say that the participatory design projects of the 1970s were stronger on political levels than on design methods; the results were primarily found in negotiations, legislation, and regulations. Further research and development in the 1980s and 1990s has resulted in a stronger theoretical grounding of participatory design, as well as an impressive suite of tools and techniques for the practical work of doing participatory design. This is not the place to give an exhaustive summary; however, it might be useful to provide a more contemporary view of participatory design in Scandinavia based on work by Ehn (1988):

- Participatory design is a process of mutual learning, where designers and users learn from and about each other. Truly participatory design requires a shared social and cultural background and a shared language. Hence, participatory design is not only a question of users participating in design, but also a question of designers participating in use. The professional designer will try to share practice with users.
- By understanding design as a process of creating new design practices that have a family resemblance (in Wittgenstein's sense) to the daily practices of both users and designers, we really see design as skill-based participation, a way of doing design that may help us transcend some of the limits of formalization. Setting up these design practices is a new role for the designer. Hence, the creative designer is concerned with the users' daily practices in organizing the design process, understanding that every new design practice is a uniquely situated design experience. Paradoxical though it may seem, there are no requirements that the design practice makes sense to users and designers in the same way, only that the designer sets the stage for a design practice so that participation makes sense to all involved.
- Practical understanding is a type of skill that should be taken seriously in a design practice, since the most important rules we follow in skilled performance are embedded in that practice and defy formalization.
- Creativity depends on the open-textured character of human "rule-following" behavior—how we enact and sometimes even invent the rules in a certain context as we go along. Hence, focus on traditional skill is not at the expense of creative transcendence, but a necessary condition. Supporting the dialectic between tradition and transcendence is at the heart of design.
- Traditional systems descriptions are not sufficient in a skill-based participatory design approach. Design artifacts should not be seen primarily as a means for creating true or objective pictures of reality, but as a means to help users and designers discuss and experience current situations and envision future ones.

- Setting the stage for shared design practices using engaging design artifacts makes it possible for ordinary users to express their professional competence when participating in the design process. With "design-by-playing" approaches, such as the use of organizational games and other role-playing techniques, designers can make useful interventions into the social interaction and construction of an organizational reality. With "design-by-doing" approaches, such as the use of mockups and other prototyping design artifacts, it is possible for users to get practical hands-on experience with the technology being developed.

- No matter how much influence participation may give in principle, design practices must transcend the boredom of traditional meetings if the design work is to be a meaningful and engaging activity for all participants. Hence, formal democratic and participatory procedures for designing computer artifacts for democracy at work are not sufficient. Design practices must be organized in a way that makes it possible for users not only to utilize their professional skills in design work, but also to have fun while doing it.

The Scandinavian school of systems development represents an important field in the development of interaction design. This section has merely provided an introduction, but the relevance of, for example, participatory design as part of the intellectual tradition within interaction design should be clear. We also hope to stimulate prospective interaction designers to cross disciplinary boundaries in their search for competence. The examples we have discussed in this chapter are only a few out of many possible ones. There are similar connections and relationships to be drawn from other related fields of research and practice. A thoughtful design stance is not a predetermined and stable position, but rather an ongoing examination of ideas and thoughts from closely related as well as more distant fields. Thoughtful design does not take history as ready-made: instead, it sees history as an ongoing project.

6.4 Lessons from Design History

Interaction design is a comparatively young field, but it can nevertheless be understood as a design discipline. As such, it has relations to other design disciplines and to developments in areas of design, even those that existed long before the first computer was constructed. In this section, we would like to point out three interesting parallels where concepts and developments from other design disciplines offer relevant insights into the nature of our own work in interaction design.

6.4.1 The History of Design Studies

Since the early 1950s, there has been an interest among researchers in the common traits of design work across disciplines. The interdisciplinary research field known as design studies comprises disciplines such as industrial design, engineering, architecture, urban planning, and perhaps also interaction design. The overall aim of design studies is to understand design and to prescribe better ways of working.

Based on the history of design studies, Cross (1984) describes the emergence of design studies in terms of four generations. The first generation, "The Management of the Design Process," present mainly in the 1960s, viewed design as a process of systematic problem solving that proceeded hierarchically by dividing problems into smaller subproblems. The process as a whole was divided into analysis, synthesis, and evaluation. The designer was seen as an objective, scientifically trained expert; there were already experiments in the 1950s where measurable usability goals were used in product design in order to gain control over the iterative development process. A systems perspective was prevalent, and the primary aim of this perspective was to adapt the product to its intended environment by means of unbiased analysis followed by shaping and evaluation.

The second generation of design studies, "The Structure of Design Problems," was prevalent in the late 1960s and 1970s. It criticized the first generation's simplified view of design problems and emphasized the interplay of emerging problem formulations and solution ideas throughout the process. A key concept was user planning, implying a role for the designer as a catalyst who had the task of liberating the users to fulfill their own requirements and ideas. However, practical experiments demonstrated the dangers of an overly passive designer in terms of solutions of inadequate long-term use quality and durability. One example was Lucien Kroll's new buildings for the University of Louvain where the indoor climate turned out to be unbearable. The reason was that the amount of window surface on the walls of the building did not follow established building norms. Instead, window surface specifications were decided by users, who did not have the professional architectural knowledge needed to make sound decisions.

The second generation of design studies was also distinguished by an increasing interest in empirical studies of authentic design processes, where the most important findings included the importance of an early vision and the observation that professional designers are more solution-oriented than problem-oriented. A general conclusion of the second generation of design studies was that the systematic methods of the first generation were poorly suited for use in practical design.

The third generation, "The Nature of Design Activity," which belongs to the late 1970s and the 1980s, is mainly characterized by inquiry into the nature of design knowledge. A gradual recognition evolved that large parts of relevant design knowledge are tacit and situated, which led to a focus on the designer's thinking and competence. Design was seen as a particular mode of thinking, and researchers looked for psychological and philosophical theories to better understand and explain what the design mode of thinking really meant. Important questions included the true nature of design, the skills and knowledge necessary for design, who is really a designer, and what the central concepts of design are.

Cross describes the fourth generation of design studies as "The Philosophy of Design Methods," in the sense that it addresses a number of different research themes growing out of all three of the previous generations. Researchers develop normative models for how the design process should be arranged, as well as performing empirical studies of authentic design work alongside philosophical reflection on design and design research.

For our purposes, it is interesting to compare the historical sketch of the four generations of design studies with the history of interaction design that we outlined in sections 6.3.1 and 6.3.2. It would appear that our field has passed through phases quite similar to the first two generations of design studies, albeit unknowingly: the faith in systematic, scientific methods and unbiased analysis, followed by a growing interest in participatory design in HCI as well as in systems development.

The question is then whether we in interaction design can extend the comparison to design studies and predict a new phase in the development of interaction design theory where we turn to introspection, and questions concerning the nature of design knowledge and the philosophy of design methods, which would be analogous to the third and fourth generations of design studies. In a way, this book is an example of such an inward turn, with its recurrent discussions of design ability and how to develop it, its perspective on design as a knowledge construction system involving a repertoire of examples and a language for articulating qualities, and so on. It remains to be seen whether our approach will be an insignificant footnote to the theory of interaction design or whether it can serve as a sign pointing to promising new avenues of inquiry.

6.4.2 Design for Office Work

Interaction design, as a child of information systems and software engineering, has a strong tradition in work-oriented digital artifacts, perhaps particularly geared toward office work and so-called productivity applications. For this reason, it may be interesting to take a brief look at the broader design history of office work. Adrian Forty (1986) indicates a line of development in the design of office environments that strikes us as also relevant to interaction design. Toward the end of the nineteenth century, offices looked more or less like you would expect the office worker's home to look (particularly if the worker in question had a slightly more elevated position in society and the workplace).

Then, various theories on efficient and scientifically based work organization gained popularity in the wake of modernism. The most noted example is, of course, Taylor's "scientific management," where the basic idea was to analyze work tasks all the way down to single manipulations, restructure them on detailed levels, and then evaluate the expected improvements by timing and other performance measures.

Through the influence of this trend, which was originally intended mainly for manual labor in industry, offices changed as well. Office landscapes became the norm, typically with an office manager at a desk physically raised above the rest of the main office floor. In other words, the hierarchical structure of the company or organization was reflected in the layout of its office space. Large desks with drawers and binders were considered obstacles to efficiency and control—hence, they were replaced by clean flat surfaces where the manager could more easily see what office workers had in front of them. Recorders, copiers, typewriters, and other office equipment looked like machines in the classical, black-iron-and-visible-mechanism sense of the word. The "office factory" became the ideal.

A reaction against this office structure came through the domestication of offices in the 1950s and 1960s. The goal became to make offices as different from factories as possible, by offering employees personal spaces that they could furnish and decorate individually. There was also a significant development toward increasing personalization of work content and organization.

We may think that the digital artifacts we design today for office work are personal, adaptable, flexible and domesticated, but consider examples such as workflow systems, management access to employee email, shared file archives with complete access only for a few centrally placed people, information views based on work roles, the standardization of file formats and application programs . . . Could it be that we are in fact involved in building information factories? And if this is the case, then what can we learn from the historical development of office work?

6.4.3 Functionalism and Aesthetics

To stay with the theme of information factories, we may note that many digital artifacts, particularly the ones intended for work-related situations, are developed with aims such as efficiency, utility, rationality, and control. The field of interaction design does not really have a developed notion of styles, but a quick examination of design history shows that concepts like efficiency, utility, and fitness-for-purpose are strongly connected with modernism and functionalism. Louis Sullivan's famous maxim that "form follows function" is often used to symbolize the spirit that is considered as characteristic of modernism, particularly its love for the machine. The architect and artist Le Corbusier (Jean Edouard Jeanneret) is cast as the typical functionalist with his ideas on the city as a machine for living, the bed as a machine for sleeping, and the overall aesthetic elevation of mechanical production: "If houses were constructed by industrial mass-production, like chassis, unexpected but sane and defensible forms would soon appear, and a new aesthetic would be formulated with astonishing precision" (qtd. in Lambert 1993, 21).

The critic Willi Lotz wrote a review of the 1927 exhibition "Die Wohnung," in which he gave a clear-cut expression of functionalism: "Objects which are designed not for the sake of appearance but to fulfill their function as well as possible, will arrive at the form which most clearly expresses the function. The aim set by our generation is to make form an expression of function, not the expression of a self-justifying aesthetic" (qtd. in Lambert 1993, 23–24).

Lotz clarifies, however, that this method does not entail a quest for the definitive form: "No one would maintain that *the* chair or *the* bed could ever be finally constructed or that it will actually emerge from a process of natural selection. For if there were such a thing as *the* definitive form, it could only be for a specific period of time and in a specific material" (qtd. in Lambert 1993, 24).

The functionalistic spirit expressed in the quotes cited here probably feels quite familiar and "true" for most students and professionals in information systems, software engineering, human-computer interaction, and similar fields: there is a particular value in realizing a design function suitable to its purpose. We might even posit that if there were a notion of styles of digital artifacts, then functionalism would be strongly dominant. But the point here, as Lambert shows, is that not even the most explicit functionalists proposed causal relations between function and beauty—or even suggested that functional form was an equivalent alternative to beautiful form. Le Corbusier addressed this aspect of functionalism:

When a thing responds to a need, it is not beautiful; it satisfies all one part of our mind, the primary part, without which there is no possibility of richer satisfactions. . . .

You employ stone, wood, and concrete, and with these materials you build houses and palaces. That is construction. Ingenuity is at work. But suddenly you touch my heart, you do me good, I am happy and I say: "This is beautiful." That is architecture. Art enters in.

My house is practical. I thank you, as I might thank railway engineers, or the telephone service. You have not touched my heart. But suppose the walls rise towards heaven in such a way that I am moved . . . These shapes are such that they are clearly revealed in light. The relationships between them have not necessarily any reference to what is practical or descriptive. . . . By the use of raw materials and *starting from* conditions more or less utilitarian, you have established certain relationships which have aroused my emotions. (qtd. in Lambert 1993, 24–25)

Now try LeCorbusier's thought experiment, but substitute information technology for stone and wood, and interaction design for construction and architecture. What would it mean to design digital artifacts that touch the user's heart?

The idea seems more strange when we talk about information technology than when we talk about buildings and architecture. This could be a sign of just how deeply rooted naive functionalism is in our field. Or else the comparison is simply misguided. Either way, it deserves some thought. For an interesting example of this kind of reflection, refer to Alben's (1997) discussion of the nonutilitarian core values of interaction design.

6.5   When History Becomes Future

The fragmentary glances in the rearview mirror of design history that we have compiled in this chapter demonstrate several relevant and interesting connections between general design history and interaction design. Moreover, they also indicate the existence of larger trends and movements in the relationship between design and society. Design does not develop in isolation. To the contrary, it is one of the activities that constitutes and shapes society, while also mirroring its time and its culture. Hence, it is necessary for a designer to have a broad interest in contemporary issues, the development of society, and the culture that creates both the backdrop and the conditions for all design efforts.

An attempt to interpret history is a look into the past that provides a designer with the energy and inspiration to look forward. In every design, we compose and designate a future. The material we use and the ideas influencing our work all carry their own history. Even if we think of ourselves as unique individuals with freedom to design what we want, we have to accept that our "unique wants" are strongly influenced by our context, culture, and history.

Engaging with this history is a way to open new design possibilities. It may also help us identify the design limitations built into a culture, particularly the ones that should be challenged. In this view, historical studies are a strongly future-oriented approach. History provides the power for innovation and for recognizing the foundational assumptions that shape our own thinking.

6.6   Technological Futures

An interaction designer may feel that she is in a "poor" field, since it has such a brief history. Moreover, it is hard to relate to a history that has not yet become distant. But it is even harder for an interaction designer to think of the future. It is true that as designers we are part of shaping the future, but we are always dependent on and influenced by the material we use. So—what is the material of interaction design? How will it develop in the next few years? Does it have any qualities that will last beyond the waves of individual technological fads?

We are all concerned by the seemingly rapid development of technology. We might even experience a kind of *technology stress* where we constantly worry about not keeping up, or about using aging technology that causes extraneous work, or about competitors who have already made the shift to more current solutions. It is evident that as interaction designers we must keep up to date on the development of technology, but how do we do that? Is it even possible? Can we keep up with the pace of change?

The short history of our field already provides examples of how professionals have been imprisoned by aging technology. In the 1960s and 1970s, many administrative systems were built on mainframe computers using the programming language Cobol. A large group of professionals were typecast as Cobol programmers. This group had, and still has, the responsibility for many important systems in banking, corporate administration, and public, and government organizations. The work involved in building these systems was complex and time-consuming; it required all of these programmers' effort and energy, and they were almost completely occupied with the work at hand and hence unable to develop their skills in more strategic, future-oriented directions. Many organizations faced a "competence crisis" in the mid-1980s when they "discovered" that the new generation of information technology demanded new and different skills from its creators. In some organizations, Cobol programmers were dismissed and more recently trained people hired to replace them.

However, the situation today is to some extent reversed. Large administrative systems are still based on mainframes and Cobol—in many cases, the core still consists of the code that was written twenty or thirty years ago—which means that there is still a need for Cobol programmers to maintain and develop systems. A special case was the issue of handling dates in relation to the coming of the new millennium (the so-called Y2K problem), which even saw many senior Cobol programmers come back from retirement to work on the old systems.

This example goes to show how hard it is to manage and predict the development of technology. Our field is certainly characterized by a rapid pace of development, but also by very strong conservatism in the sense that we carry a massive load of older systems that have to work not only in themselves, but also in relation to all the new systems being constructed around them. The future of information technology is shaped against the backdrop of existing technology. However, there are occasional examples of leaps or sidetracks when new possibilities open up and are explored without being constrained by old legacy technology. The rapid breakthrough of multimodal systems is one example where entirely new technology and uses have emerged, more or less without friction against previously existing technology.

The most interesting leap to consider in terms of information technology development is the 1990s transformation of digital artifacts from tools and information processors to communication media. The clearest sign of this transformation is the Internet, a network virtually linking most computing devices in the world together and, above all, dominating many people's perception of what information technology really is. Our aim here is not to predict the most popular web browser in two years time or evaluate the latest trends in mobile broadband. That would obviously be pointless in terms of dealing with technological development. Still, there are valuable lessons to be learned about the nature of a thoughtful design stance from analyzing the Internet's shift from tool to medium in a little more detail.

Due to the Internet, or, more accurately, the widespread dissemination of software and hardware that uses the Internet for communication, information technology has come to be viewed primarily as a communication medium. Access to the Internet is assumed, increasingly by means of wireless networks or mobile phone distribution, which means that the pervasive nature of the new medium is even more apparent. Information of all kinds, from scientific findings to advertising, is found on the web along with productivity applications, games, shopping, and entertainment. Synchronous forms of communication, such as chat channels, multi-user domains (MUDS), and interactive Web sites create possibilities for social interaction in spite of geographical obstacles. Asynchronous communication, as found in email and bulletin boards, occupies a new intermediary position somewhere between the phone and the written letter. The key insight in this development is that information technology represents a new medium that cannot be assessed by simple comparisons with more established media.

It is a mistake to dismiss information technology with the argument that it will never replace the experience of taking a good book to bed. It was never intended to replace the book in that respect. What we have seen over the first ten years of widespread Internet dissemination is merely the first tentative experiments with a new medium. Some insights are starting to emerge concerning the qualities of the new medium, where its potentials are, and what ideas about the medium are less appropriate. Functional and economic qualities are covered well in the literature and in the everyday practice of most professionals in the field. Concerning the aesthetic qualities of digital media and developments in computer art, we may point out in passing that most interesting artists today are not concerned with digitizing paintings or musical compositions to distribute them through a web page, but rather engage in the kind of art that actually requires information technology to exist. Visual artists learn programming in order to explore algorithmic visual structures. Musicians like Brian Eno do not compose final pieces, but rather produce raw materials and tools for the audience to create their own unique musical experiences. Many artworks are presented on the theme of inter-activity and the transformation from onlooker to co-creator.[3]

We should note that it may be misleading to talk about information technology only as a communication medium. The Internet has many faces: a repository for infor-mation, a shopping mall, a meeting place, an entertainment arcade, a worldwide phone book, an application server, a traveler's guide to an unfamiliar city, a way of treating di-abetes in your own home, and so on. An early attempt to analyze the nature of the In-ternet on a more principled level is Stefik's (1996) identification of four fundamental metaphors in the discussion of the Internet and its use. The metaphors are the digital li-brary, the electronic post office, the electronic market, and the digital world.

The *digital library* metaphor reminds us that we are a communicating species with a unique ability to store, use, and build upon knowledge from peers and from earlier generations. With the digital library, the Internet is seen as a way to collect and preserve knowledge for ourselves and the ones who will come after us.

The *electronic post office* addresses our communication needs, as individuals as well as members of one or more communities.

The *electronic market* metaphor is based our need to act in order to live and de-velop. In our society, actions are often made up of business transactions, and the Inter-net is seen as an interesting arena for such transactions to take place.

The metaphor of the *digital world* is about places where we can go to have experi-ences of various kinds. The places can be populated or desolate, full of different kinds of things or empty until we fill them ourselves.

One of Stefik's points is that these four metaphors are connected to archetypes deeply embedded in our culture: the knowledge collector, the communicator, the mer-chant, and the traveler. They represent what we see in ourselves and others; therefore, they should be discussed in order for us to make better decisions on information tech-nology and its use.

The metaphor of information technology as a digital world or virtual environ-ment, combined with the communicational capabilities afforded by the medium, has particularly far-reaching implications for our views of ourselves and of society. A good illustration is the kind of digital artifact known as a MUD. The acronym originally meant multi-user dungeon, a kind of multiplayer game set in a system of virtual caves where the goal was to slay as many monsters as possible. Today, the most common interpretations are multi-user domain and multi-user dimension, and the focus has shifted from monster slaying to social interaction. Contemporary MUDs use the Internet as their communication channel and typically offer synchronous text interaction. The main difference from regular chat channels, and the reason for bringing them up as examples of digital worlds, is the possibility of creating virtual spaces and artifacts. The player in a classical text MUD is represented as a so-called avatar, with a screen name and a textual description of the avatar's personal characteristics. The avatar also has a room or a house created by textual descriptions and open for other avatars to visit. Some MUDs offer the possibility for advanced players to program artificial avatars that act autonomously. With the dissemination of broadband Internet access and more powerful desktop computing comes graphical muds, based on pictures or 3-D graphical models of avatars and environments. The basic elements of synchronous text communication and player-created spaces are, however, largely the same.

Turkle (1995) has studied MUD players and the social processes of MUDs extensively, and offers many illustrations of players using MUDs for social experiments. For instance, it is quite common for male players to create and play as female avatars. Experienced players frequently maintain several avatars with different personalities. What is really real when a MUD player, while acting simultaneously in several MUDs in different windows on the screen, says that material reality is merely one of his windows and normally not the best one? What does body and physical presence mean for our identity when another MUD player gets to know, courts, and finally marries a woman he has never seen? The digital worlds, and, more generally, digital culture illustrates the postmodern emphasis on communication, opacity, and experimentation with surfaces as a way of knowing.

Turkle's own analysis relates the development of digital artifacts—from computation to simulation—to the general development of society and culture from profundity and rationality to superficiality and communication. Taylor and Saarinen (1994) introduce what they call a "media philosophy" to describe the simulation culture and its views on knowledge and action: The following passage captures the essence of their view of the contemporary media society:

In the media, one-liners are everything. Impressions are everything. Style, personality, and timing are everything. There is no possibility—and this cannot be emphasized too much—of ruling out the scholar's nightmare of ambiguity and, even more shocking, radical, outraged, emotionally charged misunderstanding. For those who still believe in the dream of transparent intersubjectivity or an ideal speech community of the experts who trade clear and distinct ideas, essences and concepts, misunderstanding constitutes an abiding fear. But misunderstanding can release energy. The law of media is the law of dirty hands: you cannot be understood if you are not misunderstood. (Taylor and Saarinen 1994, 5)

Parting with Taylor and Saarinen, an even more contemporary and more elusive understanding of technology is the notion that we are not only "using technology" but "living with technology" (compare this to the discussion by Hallnäs and Redström, [2002], on the development from use to meaningful presence) When our everyday activities are intertwined and blended with digital artifacts in intricate ways, it might no longer be possible to separate them from the immediate experience of our life-world. Digital artifacts take on a role similar to our homes. We rarely say that we "use" our home. We live in it. Maybe digital artifacts in a more virtualized environment will have the same status as other things with which we live. How this will further change our understanding of digital artifacts is still unknown. But the history of information technology and interaction design, however brief it may be, strongly suggests that our everyday understanding of technology will continue to change radically.

To summarize, we note that understanding technical details is probably not the most important way for an interaction designer to understand the Internet or be prepared to act in the rapidly changing landscapes of ubiquitous, pervasive, and embodied computing. Of course, it is necessary for the interaction designer to grasp the required programming techniques and tools if she is involved in the creation of an Internet-based artifact, but it is more important to think about the social and cultural contexts of the artifact. An interaction designer working in the future of the Internet and digital culture has to ask herself some foundational philosophical questions. What does the emergence of a new digital world mean? Who will create it? How should it be created? What should it be like? How do local and regional values relate to the presumed globalization of the digital world?

Technological developments create new kinds of considerations for the interaction designer. Should all digital artifacts be designed as parts of the ubiquitous digital world, or should some systems be kept separate? How can we be prepared for future development and adaptation to new situations? We are facing increasing virtualization, which is to say that more and more aspects of our physical reality are transformed into or complemented by digital existences. Future design questions are overwhelming in terms of their scope and complexity, but are also amazing and challenging in terms of their potential.

The example of the Internet, of the fundamental shift from tool to medium, prompts a more general question: What is a sensible stance for an interaction designer toward technological development? First, it is important to realize that digital technology is the material that sets the conditions for all manners of interaction design. It is necessary to be curious about technology, technological possibilities, and technological development. Even when an interaction designer is fully occupied with a certain technical approach, be it older or modern, it is important to stay informed about current developments. This kind of curiosity obviously requires an open mind toward the new and unknown, but also a strongly critical eye assessing all new advances against contemporary society and historical knowledge.

An interaction designer's greatest challenge is to discern the technology with long-term importance from the temporary fads in the stream of new technology. Our field has repeatedly demonstrated a tendency to fixate on a new technological idea for a short period of time and greatly overestimate its potential, only to forget all about it when something else comes along. This flocking phenomenon makes it unnecessarily difficult to identify the real news in the technology stream and understand what will be significant on a longer timescale.

In order to make such judgments, it is necessary to assess technology on a sufficiently abstract level, which requires an understanding of its core and its general structure. It is impossible to keep up-to-date on all technological developments, except perhaps in a narrow field of specialization. Instead, it helps to think of new technological ideas as variations of previously known ideas, or concrete implementations of theories and concepts that are already familiar. This makes it possible to discern the qualitatively new elements in the stream of variations and modifications. At this level, change is not as frantic as it sometimes seems on the level of individual technological advances. It is possible to keep up reasonably well, as illustrated by the extended discussion earlier in this chapter on the transformation of information technology from tool to medium.

We end up with the same basic idea again: managing technological development means being *prepared*. Curiosity together with critical thinking can keep you reasonably far along on the stream of development. When an interaction designer encounters new technology in a design situation, she is not paralyzed, instead, she confidently approaches new technology by looking for its core, principles, benefits, and shortcomings. Being prepared also means placing technological ideas in relation to the development of society and culture, and more general philosophical considerations. Even the most groundbreaking technology may be unthinkable given a certain order of culture or society. Technology always depends on its context.

The view of the future that we have outlined here again brings back the notion of information technology as a material without qualities. Over time, however, all the interaction design, all the digital artifacts together form an internally coherent, albeit complex, picture of a material that actually exists and actually has certain qualities. They were not there when we started, but they exist now as a result of our dreams of good technology. In the same way, the technology of the future will be shaped by our ongoing efforts. There are no predetermined outcomes of this development. It is through design that it will become real.

7 | Thoughtful Design

Ultimately, a designer is responsible for her own competence. Sustaining and developing design ability is all about making personal and independent choices about one's fundamental assumptions. This means that what we have presented here cannot be taken as a recipe for unreflective use, but rather as a collection of tools for thought: concepts and ideas that can be used for thinking about design and design quality.

It is perfectly possible that this book seems diverse and incoherent so far. A conceivable question at this point might be "OK, but what is the best way of doing interaction design?" Our purpose has been to compose a book that supports committed readers in their own thinking and their own attempts to become confident designers. Part of that purpose is, unfortunately, the inability to give a simple answer to the question about the best way of doing interaction design. What we can do in this final chapter is merely to tie the threads together in a more concise and coherent picture of the tools we offer for thoughtful design.

The idea of information technology as a material without qualities, in a figurative sense, has been with us since the introduction. It was inspired by the Austrian author Robert Musil and his novel *The Man without Qualities,* which was published in several parts during the 1930s. It was his life's work and he spent many years working on it. Unfortunately, he died in 1942 before he was able to finish it. It is a highly ambitious work combining societal criticism and an account of contemporary life, moral philosophy and romantic ideals, satire and theoretical dissertations, burlesque, and autobiography. The text is full of humor and melancholy, and Musil possessed an extraordinary sensibility for his time in all its details as well as its development of technology and ideas.

We find surprisingly many connections between our own ideas and Musil's work. Obviously, he does not address interaction design or digital artifacts, but his interpretations of thinking and creation are remarkably familiar and timeless. Hence, we choose to illustrate the topics about interaction design that we pull together in this chapter with quotations from Musil's novel.

7.1 A Repertoire and a Language

For interaction design, as for any other design discipline, it is essential to address examples of artifacts and their qualities. This holds true not only for the discipline as a knowledge construction system, but also for the individual designer who needs to develop a repertoire of examples that are exemplary in some sense. This repertoire construction requires an articulation language that is suited for describing and analyzing artifacts and their qualities. We have introduced a number of examples from different genres of digital artifacts and attempted to identify particularly important qualities for each example. Musil addresses the use qualities of trolley cars in Vienna as follows:

While busy with all this he [Ulrich] was watching the passing trolley cars, waiting for the one that would take him back as close as possible to the center of town. He saw people climbing in and out of the cars, and his technically trained eye toyed distractedly with the interplay of welding and casting, rolling and bolting, of engineering and hand finishing, of historical development and the present state of the art, which combined to make up these barracks-on-wheels that these people were using.

"As a last step, a committee from the municipal transportation department comes to the factory and decides what kind of wood to use as veneer, the color of the paint, upholstery, arms on the seats and straps for the standees, ashtrays, and the like," he thought idly, "and it is precisely these trivial details, along with the red and green color of the exterior, and how they swing themselves up the steps and inside, that for tens of thousands of people make up what they remember, all they experience, of all the genius that went into it. This is what forms their character, endows it with speed or comfort; it's what makes them perceive red cars as home and blue ones as foreign, and adds up to that unmistakable odor of countless details that clings to the clothing of the centuries." (1996, vol. II, 943–944)[1]

Musil presents the placement of the armrest and the color of the exterior as decisive for the traveler's impression of the use qualities of the trolley car. However, he also emphasizes the importance these details have for the character of the cars, that is, contributions to their overall gestalt. We would add that the use qualities are shaped by functional, structural, and ethical aspects—and we suspect that Ulrich would agree. If the trolley cars had extremely well-placed armrests, but did not serve the southern part of the city, would the citizens of the southern suburbs perceive them as having "speed and comfort?"

A repertoire of examples and an articulation language must be capable of handling specific details as well as the whole of the artifact (its gestalt). The whole is decisive in the final assessment of any artifact, much like the interplay between the (highly visible) details and the (less visible) whole in the case of the trolley car.

7.2   The Nature of the Design Process

We regard the design process as complex and highly dynamic, where visions interrelate to operative images and specifications in a context of individuals, social structures, and organizational structures. This is in line with Musil's view of the subject:

Unfortunately, nothing is so hard to achieve as a literary representation of a man thinking. When someone asked a great scientist how he managed to come up with so much that was new, he replied: "Because I never stop thinking about it." And it is surely safe to say that unexpected insights turn up for no other reason than that they are expected. They are in no small part a success of character, emotional stability, unflagging ambition, and unremitting work. What a bore such constancy must be! Looking at it another way, the solution of an intellectual problem comes about not very differently from a dog with a stick in his mouth trying to get through a narrow door; he will turn his head left and right until the stick slips through. We do much the same thing, but with the difference that we don't make indiscriminate attempts but already know from experience approximately how it's done. And if a clever fellow naturally has far more skill and experience with these twistings and turnings than a dim one, the slipping through takes the clever fellow just as much by surprise; it is suddenly there, and one perceptibly feels slightly disconcerted because one's ideas seem to have come on their own accord rather than waiting for their creator. This disconcerted feeling is nowadays called intuition by many people who would formerly, believing that it must be regarded as something suprapersonal, have called it inspiration; but it is only something impersonal, namely the affinity and coherence of things themselves, meeting inside of a person's head.

   The better the head, the less evident its presence in this process. As long as the process of thinking is in motion it is a quite wretched state, as if all the brain's convolutions were suffering from colic; and when it is finished it no longer has the form of the thinking process as one experiences it but already that of what has been thought, which is regrettably impersonal, for the thought then faces outward and is dressed for communication to the world. When a man is in the process of thinking, there is no way to catch the moment between the personal and the impersonal, and this is manifestly why thinking is such an embarrassment for writers that they gladly avoid it. (1996, vol. 1, 115–116)

In this passage, Musil concentrates on the necessarily difficult relationship between the form of thinking and the form of an individual thought, which we in interaction design would consider in terms of the relationship between vision and operative image. The dilemma (and essence) of the design process is to move from diffuse and partly inconsistent visions to more specific and explicit operative images, in order to communicate and debate understandings of problems and solutions.

7.3   Design Ability and Ways to Develop It

On a general level, we can view design ability as a constructively intentional intelligence, a kind of intelligence oriented toward performing actions and creating things for certain purposes. This is related to what Musil calls the sense of possibility:

But if there is a sense of reality, and no one will doubt it has its justification for existing, then there must also be something we can call a sense of possibility.

Whoever has it does not say, for instance: Here this or that has happened, will happen, must happen; but he invents: Here this or that might, could or ought to happen. If he is told that something is the way it is, he will think: Well, it could probably just as well be otherwise. So the sense of possibility could be defined outright as the ability to conceive of everything there might be just as well, and to attach no more importance to what is than to what is not. The consequences of so creative a disposition can be remarkable, and may, regrettably, often make what people admire seem wrong, and what is taboo permissible, or, also, make both a matter of indifference. (1996, vol. I, 10–11)

It is not the case that some people lack design ability or sense of possibility, but their aptitude may, of course, be distributed differently across the aspects of design ability. Some may find it easier to be rational and communicative, whereas others are creative and analytical. Some may be more aware of their values and ideals, while others are gifted in shaping and composition.

Perhaps the most important lesson here is that we are all individuals with unique talents and abilities. Developing design ability must, first and foremost, be grounded in a firm understanding of what we as individuals have already mastered and what we need to improve. Design ability cannot be taught to everybody in the same way using the same material. As designers, we have to recognize the need to be sensible to what Musil labels "possibilities" and discern what it takes from us to create and develop such a sensibility.

7.4   The Role of Methods in Design

Design methods are tools for thought, nothing more or nothing less. A skilled designer is capable of assessing the applicability and effects of a method, appropriate it among other tools for thought, and use it in suitable situations in the way afforded or dictated by the circumstances. The dangers of unskilled method use are illustrated by Musil as follows:

Hagauer himself was unable to believe that these things were really happening. Back from his daily obligations, he had sat that evening in his "deserted home," facing a blank sheet of paper much as Ulrich had faced one, not knowing how to begin. But in Hagauer's experience the tried and true "buttons method" had worked more than once, and he resorted to it again in this case. It consists in taking a systematic approach to one's problems, even problems that cause great agitation, on the same principle on which a man has buttons sewn on his clothes to save the time that would be lost if he acted on the assumption that he could get out of his clothes faster without buttons. The English writer Surway, for example, whose work on the subject Hagauer now consulted, for even in his depressed state it was important for him to compare Surway's work with his own views, distinguishes five such buttons in the process of successful reasoning: (a) close observation of an event, in which the observation immediately reveals problems of interpretation; (b) establishing such problems and defining them more narrowly; (c) hypothesis of a possible solution; (d) logically developing the consequences of this hypothesis; and (e) further observations, leading to the acceptance or rejection of the hypothesis and thereby to a successful outcome of the thinking process. Hagauer had already profitably applied a similar method to so worldly an enterprise as lawn tennis when he was learning the game at the Civil Service Club, and it had lent considerable intellectual charm to the game for him; but he had never yet resorted to this method for purely emotional matters. (1996, vol. II, 1030)

Musil's Hagauer was not using a method skillfully in this instance. He turned to the button method by routine, maybe because it suited his way of thinking, but it clearly did not suit the task of composing a letter to his wife, who had recently left him, to try to convince her to come back. The outcome eventually was what you might expect: He did not complete the task successfully, and his wife chose to live on her own.

The point of this quote, which may seem far from the everyday concerns of interaction design, is to illustrate the seductive sense of security that methods seem to offer some designers. We want to argue that although our example may seem far-fetched, there will always eventually be a design situation where the customary method is inadequate. At that point, the designer who is free to choose among several different methods and techniques, and is aware of their shortcomings and limitations, is better prepared to act. Freedom of choice in relation to methods requires insights into your own ability as well as the nature of the design process.

7.5   Society and Technology

Is technological development the same as societal development and progress? Are we in control of the technological development, or is it in control of us? Musil's discussion pinpoints some important positions on this issue:

But Ulrich was enjoying himself. "Is the modern house, with its six rooms, maid's bath, vacuum cleaner, and all that, progress, compared with the old houses with their high ceilings, thick walls, and handsome archways, or not?"

"No!" Hans Sepp shouted.

"Is the airplane progress, compared with the mail coach?"

"Yes!" Director Fischel shouted.

"The machine compared with handicrafts?"

"Handicrafts!" from Hans, and "Machine!" from Leo.

"It seems to me," Ulrich said, "that every step forward is also a step backward. Progress always exists in only one particular sense. And since there's no sense to our life as a whole, neither is there such a thing as progress as a whole."

Leo Fischel lowered his paper. "Would you say that it's better to be able to cross the Atlantic in six days rather than having to spend six weeks on it?"

"I'd be inclined to say that it's definitely progress to have the choice. But our young Christians wouldn't agree to that, either." (1996, vol. I, 528)

In our opinion, it is not a feasible position to view technological development as independent from society or as a driving force in societal development. Neither is the naïve opposing position tenable: Technology is not merely a neutral instrument of our wills and desires. We understand the situation as one of mutual influence: We shape technology, and technology shapes us. Again, Musil's thoughts are highly prescient for the field of interaction design:

"Do you ever go to see a film? You should," he [Arnheim] said. "In its present form, cinematography may not look like much, but once the big interests get involved—the electrochemicals, say, or the chromochemical concerns—you are likely to see a surging development in just a few decades, which nothing can stop. Every known means of raising and intensifying production will be brought into play, and whatever our writers and aesthetes may suppose be their own part in it, we will be getting an art based on Associated Electrical or German Dyes, Inc." (1996, vol. I, 704)

The development of the field of digital artifacts is clearly driven by technology to a great extent. The large companies, consortia, and other technology developers play more or less the same role for us that Associated Electrical and German Dyes play for the movie business in Arnheim's vision of the future.

If you share our opinion that we shape technology as technology shapes us, then it follows that interaction designers cannot passively accept current conditions. A sensible strategy to prepare for the endless changes of technological development is to search for more persistent values and ideals, which can then be expressed more or less successfully using the technology that happens to be today's fashion. Design history is an important source of material for such a search. The rapid pace of technological development and the uncertainty of the future can be handled in similar ways by looking for the really significant shifts in the stream of incremental innovation. It will become apparent that such shifts take place on an entirely different, and much more manageable, timescale.

7.6 The Material without Qualities

Interaction design is about shaping digital artifacts. It is about giving structure and form to human environments and activities. Interaction designers create spaces for action in which parts of people's working lives and private lives take place. The material we use is not entirely without qualities, but its limitations are relatively few. There are many degrees of design freedom that come with the material. Such freedom may appear difficult to grasp, complex to approach, and perhaps even slightly frightening. On the other hand, it may appear as a positive challenge and a source of great creative potential.

7.7 Being Thoughtful

We have emphasized the importance and responsibility of interaction design. To handle this responsibility, our recommendation to interaction designers is to be prepared: prepared to act in a design process, encounter new design situations, learn and develop as designer, and understand historical developments and future technological trajectories. This is a complex and ongoing strategy, and it is made even more complex by the nature of the design material at our disposal. We have seen many examples of design processes becoming more or less paralyzed when designers realize the full scope of the design situation and respond by trying to collect more and more information: more fieldwork, research, analysis of competing products, and so on.

What is needed to deal with the complexities of design, however, is not necessarily more information, but rather a bit more conceptual clarity from the designer. A thoughtful designer, equipped with appropriate tools for reasoning, will be more able to sort out what is important, make necessary judgment calls, distinguish true needs for more information from better-safe-than-sorry approaches, and identify fruitful directions in the exploration of possible futures that is called design. The ideas we have presented in this book are intended to serve as such tools for reasoning. The responsibility of using these tools skillfully will always rest with the designer.

Notes

4 Methods and Techniques

1. Stumbling over highly relevant material in this way happens surprisingly often in design, by the way. The explanation is probably that working with a particular design situation sensitizes a designer to notice other material pertaining to her current focus of attention (much like a person does not notice how many baby carriages there are on the city streets until her first child is born).

2. Focus+context is a concept from information visualization, where it refers to the idea of presenting a potentially large information set in such a way that the material of immediate interest is presented in all its detail (focus), while the surrounding material is still visible, albeit in a more abstract or summarized form (context).

3. The critic also plays a significant part in the knowledge construction system of most of the fine arts.

5 The Product and Its Use Qualities

1. The view of pliability, or malleability, as a deep quality of administrative systems is well elaborated by the Pliant research group at www.pliant.org (accessed Mar. 12, 2004).

2. The Knowledge Navigator video was produced by Apple Computer in 1987 and is proprietary. The design of Phil is discussed in Laurel 1990.

3. The historical background on Tetris is based on an account by Vadim Gerasimov, one of the three original designers (vadim.www.media.mit.edu/Tetris.htm, accessed Mar. 12, 2004), a news article (www.sfgate.com/cgi-bin/article.cgi?file=/examiner/archive/1998/09/24/NEWS7742.dtl, accessed Mar. 12, 2004), and an independent chronicle of the financial complications concerning the rights to Tetris on different platforms (atarihq.com/tsr/special/tetrishist.html, accessed Apr. 16, 2003).

4. The Visual Thesaurus is available at www.visualthesaurus.com (accessed Mar. 12, 2004).

5. Our source on current plans for the Tetris Corporation is their Web site at www.tetris.com, accessed at Apr. 16, 2003.

6.   An Auto-Illustrator user forum is found at www.auto-generation.com (accessed Mar. 12, 2004). Here there are discussion lists of features, bug fixes, and support issues one would expect to find in any product user forum, as well as a gallery with examples of how people have used Auto-Illustrator for their graphic designs.

7.   Adrian Ward's statement on Auto-Illustrator is found at www.adeward.com/swai.html (accessed Mar. 12, 2004). More information about the software product Auto-Illustrator, including retail, is at www.auto-illustrator.com (accessed Mar. 12, 2004).

8.   Osmose is an artwork designed by Char Davies in 1995. It is described at www.cyberstage .org/archive/cstage21/osmose21.html (accessed Mar. 12, 2004).

6   Conditions for Interaction Design

1.   Rheingold (1985) provides a useful historical sketch of early stages in the development of digital technology, structured around a number of key people.

2.   The presentation in this section is mainly based on Ehn and Löwgren 1997.

3.   There is no room here for a more extensive discussion of digital aesthetics. The interested reader is referred to Holtzman 1997, Bolter and Gromala 2003, new media theory such as Bolter and Grusin 1999, or contemporary catalogues such as Leopoldseder and Schöpf 2001.

7   Thoughtful Design

1.   This Musil quotation and the rest of the quotations in this chapter are taken from Musil 1996, the English paperback edition of the novel.

References

Ahlberg, C., C. Williamson, and B. Shneiderman. 1992. Dynamic queries for information exploration: An implementation and evaluation. In *Human Factors in Computing Systems* (CHI '92 Proceedings), 619–626. New York: ACM Press.

Ahlberg, C., and B. Shneiderman. 1994. Visual information seeking: Tight coupling of dynamic query filters with starfield displays. In *Human Factors in Computing Systems* (CHI '94 Proceedings), 313–317. New York: ACM Press.

Alben, L. 1997. At the heart of interaction design. *Design Management Journal* 8(3):9–26.

Alexander, C., S. Ishikawa, M. Silverstein, M. Jacobson, I. Fiksdahl-King, and S. Angel. 1977. *A Pattern Language*. New York: Oxford University Press.

Allen, R. 1997. The bush soul. Available at emergence.design.ucla.edu (accessed Oct. 9, 2002).

Andersson, O., E. Cacciatore, J. Löwgren, and T. Lundin. 2002. Post-hoc worknotes: A demonstration of video content management. In *Proc. 10th ACM Int. Conf. Multimedia* (MM02), 670–671. New York: ACM Press. Video and paper submission.

Bansler, J. 1989. Systems development in Scandinavia: Three theoretical schools. *Scand. Journal of Information Systems:* 3–20.

Beyer, H., and K. Holtzblatt. 1997. *Contextual Design: Defining Customer-Centered Systems*. San Francisco: Morgan Kaufmann.

Bødker, S., and K. Grønbæk. 1989. Cooperative prototyping experiments: Users and designers envision a dental record system. *Report DAIMI PB-292*, Department of Computer Science, Aarhus University, Denmark.

Bolter, J., and D. Gromala. 2003. *Windows and Mirrors: Interaction Design, Digital Art, and the Myth of Transparency*. Cambridge, Mass.: The MIT Press.

Bolter, J., and R. Grusin. 1999. *Remediation: Understanding New Media*. Cambridge, Mass.: The MIT Press.

Buchenau, M., and J. Fulton Suri. 2000. Experience prototyping. In *Proc. Designing Interactive Systems* (DIS '00), 424–433. New York: ACM Press.

Buckingham Shum, S. 1995. Design argumentation as design rationale. In A. Kent and J. Williams, eds., *Encyclopedia of Computer Science and Technology.* New York: Marcel Dekker.

Card, S., T. Moran, and A. Newell. 1983. *The Psychology of Human-Computer Interaction.* Hillsdale, N.J.: Lawrence Erlbaum.

Casaday, G. 1997. Notes on a pattern language for interactive usability. In *Human Factors in Computing Systems* (CHI '97 Extended Abstracts), 289–290. New York: ACM Press.

Collingwood, R. 1946. *The Idea of History.* Oxford: Oxford University Press.

Cross, N., ed. 1984. *Developments in Design Methodology.* Chichester U.K.: John Wiley & Sons.

Cross, N. 1995. Discovering design ability. In R. Buchanan and V. Margolin, eds., *Discovering Design: Explorations in Design Studies,* 105–120. Chicago: The University of Chicago Press.

Curtis, B., H. Krasner, and N. Iscoe. 1988. A field study of the software design process for large systems. *Communications of the ACM* 31(11):1268–1287.

Dahlbom, B., and L. Mathiassen. 1993. *Computers in Context: The Philosophy and Practice of Systems Design.* Cambridge, Mass.: NCC Blackwell.

de Bono, E. 1993. *Serious Creativity: Using the Power of Lateral Thinking to Create New Ideas.* London: Fontana.

Dourish, P. 2001. *Where the Action Is: The Foundations of Embodied Interaction.* Cambridge, Mass.: The MIT Press.

Dunne, A. 1999. *Hertzian Tales: Electronic Products, Aesthetic Experience and Critical Design.* London: Royal College of Art.

Dunne, A., and W. Gaver. 1997. The pillow: Artist-designers in the digital age. In *Human Factors in Computing Systems* (CHI '97 Extended Abstracts), 361–362. New York: ACM Press.

Dunne, A., and F. Raby. 2001. *Design Noir: The Secret Life of Electronic Objects.* Basel: Birkhäuser.

Ehn, P. 1988. *Work-Oriented Design of Computer Artifacts.* Stockholm: Almqvist & Wiksell.

Ehn, P., and J. Löwgren. 1997. Design for quality-in-use: Human-computer interaction meets information systems development. In M. Helander, T. Landauer, and P. Prabhu, eds., *Handbook of Human-Computer Interaction,* 2nd ed., 299–313. Amsterdam: Elsevier.

Elster, J. 1983. *Sour Grapes: Studies in the Subversion of Rationality.* Cambridge: Cambridge University Press.

Fitzgerald, B., N. Russo, and E. Stolterman. 2002. *Information Systems Development: Methods-in-action.* New York: McGraw-Hill.

Forty, A. 1986. *Objects of Desire: Design and Society 1750–1980.* London: Thames & Hudson.

Fujihata, M. 2001. Understanding the world. In H. Leopoldseder and C. Schöpf, eds., *Cyberarts 2001,* 80–85. Wien, Austria: Springer-Verlag.

Gaver, W., J. Beaver, and S. Benford. 2003. Ambiguity as a resource for design. In *Human Factors in Computing Systems* (CHI '03 Proceedings), 233–240. New York: ACM Press.

Gelernter, D. 1998. *Machine Beauty: Elegance and the Heart of Technology.* New York: Basic Books.

Good, M., T. Spine, J. Whiteside, and P. George. 1986. User-derived impact analysis as a tool for usability engineering. In *Human Factors in Computing Systems* (CHI '86 Proceedings), 241–246. New York: ACM Press.

Grudin, J. 1991. Interactive systems: Bridging the gap between developers and users. *IEEE Computer* (April): 59–69.

Grudin, J. 1996. Evaluating opportunities for design rationale capture. In T. Moran and J. Carroll, eds., *Design Rationale: Concepts, Techniques and Use,* 453–470. Mahwah, N.J.: Lawrence Erlbaum.

Hallnäs, L., and J. Redström. 2002. From use to presence: On the expressions and aesthetics of everyday computational things. *ACM Trans. Computer-Human Interaction* 9(2):106–124.

Henderson, A., and J. Harris. 2000. Beyond formalism: The art and science of designing pliant systems. In K. Kaasgard, ed., *Software Design and Usability.* Copenhagen: CBS Press.

Henderson, A., and M. Kyng. 1991. There's no place like home: Continuing design in use. In J. Greenbaum and M. Kyng, eds., *Design at Work: Cooperative Design of Computer Systems,* 177–210. Hillsdale, N.J.: Lawrence Erlbaum.

Hillman, J. 1996. *The Soul's Code: In Search of Character and Calling.* New York: Random House.

Holmlid, S. 2002. Adapting users: Towards a theory of use quality. Ph.D. Dissertation No. 765, Linköping University, Sweden.

Holtzman, S. 1997. *Digital Mosaics: The Aesthetics of Cyberspace.* New York: Simon & Schuster.

Janlert, L.-E., and E. Stolterman. 1997. The character of things. *Design Studies* 18(3):297–314.

Johnson, S. 1997. *Interface Culture: How New Technology Transforms the Way We Create and Communicate.* New York: Basic Books.

Jones, J. C. 1984. *Essays in Design.* Chichester, U.K.: John Wiley & Sons.

Jones, J. C. 1992. *Design Methods.* Second edition. New York: Van Nostrand Reinhold. First published in 1970 under the title *Design Methods: Seeds of Human Futures.*

Jungk, R., and N. Müllert. 1987. *Future workshops: How to Create Desirable Futures.* London: Institute for Social Inventions.

Kensing, F., and K. H. Madsen. 1991. Generating visions: Future workshops and metaphorical design. In J. Greenbaum and M. Kyng, eds., *Design at Work: Cooperative Design of Computer Systems,* 155–168. Hillsdale, N.J.: Lawrence Erlbaum.

Khaslavsky, J., and N. Shedroff. 1999. Understanding the seductive experience. *Communications of the ACM* 42(5):45–49.

Kraut, R., and L. Streeter. 1995. Coordination in software development. *Communications of the ACM* 38(3):69–81.

Krippendorff, K. 1989. On the essential context of artifacts or on the proposition that "design is making sense (of things)." *Design Issues* 5(2): 9–38.

Lambert, S. 1993. *Form Follows Function? Design in the 20th Century.* London: Victoria & Albert Museum.

Langefors, B. 1966. *Theoretical Analysis of Information Systems.* Lund, Sweden: Studentlitteratur.

Laurel, B., ed. 1990. Interface agents: Metaphors with character. In *The Art of Human-Computer Interface Design.* Reading, Mass.: Addison-Wesley.

Lawson, B. 1980. *How Designers Think.* London: The Architectural Press.

Leopoldseder, H., and C. Schöpf, eds. 2001. *Cyberarts 2001.* Vienna: Springer-Verlag.

Löwgren, J. 1994. Empirical foundations for design rationale as user-interface design support. In R. Opperman, S. Bagnara, and D. Benyon, eds., *Proc. 7th European Conf. on Cognitive Ergonomics* (ECCE 7), 305–310. GMD-Studien no. 233. St Augustin, Germany: GMD.

Löwgren, J. 2001. Sens-A-Patch: Interactive visualization of label spaces. In E. Banissi, ed., *Proc. Fifth Int. Conf. Information Visualization* (IV2001), 7–12. Los Alamitos, Calif.: IEEE Computer Society.

MacKenzie, D., and J. Wajcman. 1985. Introductory essay. In D. MacKenzie and J. Wajcman, eds., *The Social Shaping of Technology: How the Refrigerator Got its Hum,* 2–25. Buckingham: Open University Press.

MacLean, A., R. Young, V. Bellotti, and T. Moran. 1991. Questions, options and criteria: Elements of design space analysis. In *Human-Computer Interaction* 6(3–4):201–250.

McKerlie, D., and A. MacLean. 1993. Experience with QOC design rationale. In *Human Factors in Computing Systems* (InterCHI '93 Adjunct Proceedings), 213–214. New York: ACM Press.

Minter, J. 1997. Computer gaming's new worlds. *Computer Graphics* 31(1):12–13.

Musil, R. 1996. *The Man without Qualities.* Vol. I and II. New York: Vintage Books.

Nelson, H., and E. Stolterman. 2003. *The Design Way: Intentional Change in an Unpredictable World.* Englewood Cliffs, N.J.: Educational Technology Publishing.

Nielsen, J. 1993. *Usability Engineering.* Boston: Academic Press.

Nielsen, J., and R. Mack. 1994. *Usability Inspection Methods.* New York: John Wiley & Sons.

Norman, D. 1994. How might people interact with agents. *Communications of the ACM* 37(7):68–71.

Nygaard, K. 1979. The iron and metal project: Trade union participation. In Å. Sandberg, ed., *Computers Dividing Man and Work.* Malmö: Swedish Center for Working Life.

Pahl, G., and W. Beitz. 1988. *Engineering Design: A Systematic Approach.* London: The Design Council. Originally published in German in 1970 under the title *Konstruktionslehre.*

Pearce, C. 1997. *The Interactive Book.* Indianapolis, Ind.: Macmillan Technical Publishing.

Pfaffenberger, B. 1989. Fetishised objects and humanised nature: Towards an anthropology of technology. *Man* (N.S.) 23:236–252.

Poltrock, S., and J. Grudin. 1994. Organizational obstacles to interface design and development: Two participant-observer studies. *ACM Trans. Computer-Human Interaction* 1(1):52–80.

Preece, J., Y. Rogers, and H. Sharp. 2002. *Interaction Design. Beyond Human-Computer Interaction.* New York: John Wiley & Sons.

Ramey, J., A. Rowberg, and C. Robinson. 1996. Adaptation of an ethnographic method for investigation of the task domain in diagnostic radiology. In D. Wixon and J. Ramey, eds., *Field Methods Casebook for Software Design,* 1–15. New York: John Wiley & Sons.

Rescher, N. 1988. *Rationality: A Philosophical Inquiry into the Nature and Rationale of Reason.* Oxford: Clarendon Press.

Rheinfrank, J., and S. Evenson. 1996. Design languages. In T. Winograd, J. Bennett, L. De Young, and B. Hartfield, eds., *Bringing Design to Software,* 63–80. New York: ACM Press.

Rheinfrank, J., W. Hartman, and A. Wasserman. 1992. Design for usability: Crafting a strategy for the design of a new generation of Xerox copiers. In P. Adler and T. Winograd, eds., *Usability: Turning Technologies into Tools,* 15–40. New York: Oxford University Press.

Rheingold, H. 1985. Tools for thought: The people and ideas of the next computer revolution. Available at www.rheingold.com/texts/tft, accessed Mar. 12, 2004.

Rittel, H., and M. Webber. 1973. Dilemmas in a general theory of planning. *Policy Sciences* 4:155–169. Partially reprinted in N. Cross, ed., *Developments in Design Methodology,* 135–144. Chichester, U.K.: John Wiley & Sons, 1984.

Sato, S., and T. Salvador. 1999. Playacting and focus troupes: Theater techniques for creating quick, intensive, immersive and engaging focus group sessions. *Interactions* 6(5):35–41.

Schön, D. 1987. *Educating the Reflective Practitioner: Toward a New Design for Teaching and Learning in the Professions.* San Francisco: Jossey-Bass Publishers.

Shneiderman, B. 1980. *Software Psychology: Human Factors in Computer and Information Systems.* Cambridge, Mass.: Winthrop.

Shneiderman, B., and P. Maes. 1997. Direct manipulation vs. interface agents. *Interactions* 4(6):42–61.

Simon, H. 1969. *The Sciences of the Artificial.* Cambridge, Mass.: The MIT Press.

Small, P. 1996. *Lingo Sorcery: The Magic of Lists, Objects and Intelligent Agents.* Chichester, U.K.: John Wiley.

Spinuzzi, C. 2002. A Scandinavian challenge, a U.S. response: Methodological assumptions in Scandinavian and US prototyping approaches. In *Proc. ACM Conf. Computer Documentation* (SIGDOC '02), 208–215. New York: ACM Press.

Stefik, M. 1996. *Internet Dreams: Archetypes, Myths and Metaphors.* Cambridge, Mass.: The MIT Press.

Stolterman, E. 1991. Designarbetets dolda rationalitet: En studie av metodik och praktik inom systemutveckling. [The hidden rationality of design work.] Ph.D. Dissertation UMADP-RRIPS 14.91, Umeå university, Sweden.

Strong, R., and B. Gaver. 1996. Feather, Scent and Shaker: Supporting simple intimacy. In *Videos, Demos and Short Papers of ACM Conf. Computer-Supported Cooperative Work* (CSCW '96), 29–30. New York: ACM Press.

Taylor, M., and E. Saarinen. 1994. *Imagologies: Media Philosophy.* London: Routledge.

Thomas, P., and R. Macredie. 1994. Games and the design of human-computer interfaces. *Educational and Training Technology International* 31(2):134–42.

Tollmar, K., S. Junestrand, and O. Torgny. 2000. Virtually living together: Using multiple-method design in the search for telematic emotional communication. In *Proc. Int. Conf. Designing Interactive Systems* (DIS '2000), 83–91. New York: ACM Press.

Turkle, S. 1995. *Life on the Screen: Identity in the Age of the Internet.* New York: Simon & Schuster.

Van Duyne, D., J. Landay, and J. Hong. 2002. *The Design of Sites: Patterns, Principles and Processes for Crafting a Customer-Centered Web Experience.* Reading, Mass.: Addison-Wesley.

Whiteside, J., and D. Wixon. 1987. The dialectic of usability engineering. In H.-J. Bullinger and B. Shackel, eds., *Human-Computer Interaction—Interact '87,* 17–20. Amsterdam: Elsevier.

Winner, L. 1980. Do artifacts have politics? *Daedalus* 109:121–123.

Wixon, D., and J. Ramey. 1996. *Field Methods Casebook for Software Design.* New York: John Wiley & Sons.

Wroblewski, D. 1991. The construction of human-computer interfaces considered as a craft. In J. Karat, ed., *Taking Software Design Seriously.* Boston: Academic Press.

Annotated Bibliography

Given the many academic fields involved in the intellectual tradition of interaction design, the amount of potentially relevant literature is staggering. Here, we provide a small selection of pointers, books that we have found useful and that we think the reader might benefit from as well.

Bolter, J., and D. Gromala. 2003. *Windows and Mirrors: Interaction Design, Digital Art, and the Myth of Transparency*. Cambridge, Mass.: The MIT Press.
As one of few examples in the literature, this book addresses the aesthetic qualities of interaction design. It consists of a set of essays composed around selected exhibits from the SIGGRAPH Art Gallery in 2000. The main thesis is that interaction is culturally reflective as much as efficiently transparent, and the book offers several important insights for interaction designers.

Bolter, J., and R. Grusin. 1999. *Remediation: Understanding New Media*. Cambridge, Mass.: The MIT Press.
There is an increasing interest in digital media within the field of media studies. Among the growing literature, this book stands out by striking a successful balance of analysis between the genres and practices of traditional media and the particularities of new media.

Borgmann, A. 1999. *Holding on to Reality: The Nature of Information at the Turn of the Millennium*. Chicago: The University of Chicago Press.
Borgmann presents a historical overview of information, how it has been transformed through time by the introduction of new technology and especially digital technology. Borgmann shows what this development means to our contemporary society. He argues that as we enter a world that is becoming more virtual, we will lose our close connection with reality, which in turn will lead to a deprivation of our life experiences. This is a must-read for anyone concerned with the information society.

Brown, J. S., and P. Duguid. 2000. *The Social Life of Information*. Boston, Mass.: Harvard Business School Press.
This book is one the most referenced books today when it comes to the future of the information society. The authors present an understanding of the new digital technology and of information that is based on the notion of the social networks. Information cannot be seen as free from its social networks. The authors' claim that information has a "social life" changes the preconditions for

how we should develop new information technology. This book will help anyone involved in the world of information to reflect on the role and nature of information and technology.

Cooley, M. 1980. *Architect or Bee? The Human/Technology Relationship*. Boston, Mass.: South End Press.
This is a book about the technologization of work and its potentially harmful consequences: Taylorism, unemployment, alienation, degrading of professional skills, and so on. It serves as a useful reminder of the general responsibility involved in designing for professional use.

Dourish, P. 2001. *Where the Action Is: The Foundations of Embodied Interaction*. Cambridge, Mass.: The MIT Press.
This book illustrates the value of foundational concepts, not only for abstract reasoning but also for practical design. Dourish introduces the notion of embodiment, based mainly in phenomenological philosophy. By way of definition, embodied interaction is taken to be the creation, manipulation, and sharing of meaning through engaged interaction with artifacts. Embodiment integrates the fields of tangible computing and social computing; Dourish covers many existing examples and outlines fruitful directions and principles for future interaction design.

Dunne, A. 1999. *Hertzian Tales: Electronic Products, Aesthetic Experience and Critical Design*. London: Royal College of Art.
Dunne outlines the position of the artist-designer and a manifesto of sorts for critical design, where a key concept is parafunctionality (see chapter 5). His examples cover broad fields of electronic products and art practice, and the work is an important source of inspiration for interaction designers.

Dunne, A., and F. Raby, 2001. *Design Noir: The Secret Life of Electronic Objects*. Basel: Birkhäuser.
This book builds upon *Hertzian Tales* and goes beyond it in articulating the values and intentions of critical design, or design as a way of creating distance and posing questions. One of the main questions concerns the relationship between people and domestic technology, which is addressed in the better part of the book in the detailed story of the fascinating Placebo project.

Fitzgerald, B., N. Russo, and E. Stolterman, 2002. *Information Systems Development: Methods-in-action*. New York: McGraw-Hill.
For anyone who needs to know about systems development methods, this is the book to read. Apart from its presentation of the historical background, the book also deals with new methods and approaches, such as Rational Unified Process (RUP), Xtreme Programming, open source, Web design, and so on. The book has a strong focus on the actual use of methods and presents a framework for method use.

Fogg, B. J. 2003. *Persuasive Computing: Using Computers to Change What We Think and Do*. San Francisco: Morgan Kaufmann.
There has been a growing interest in studying the social psychology of human-computer interaction, where it can be demonstrated that people treat computers as other people in many respects. Fogg builds on previous work, most notably by Nass and Reeves, and takes it further into a study of computer persuasion in different domains. The book is an eye-opener for readers who tend to think of digital artifacts mostly as value-neutral tools or communication media.

Forty, A. 1986. *Objects of Desire: Design and Society 1750–1980*. London: Thames & Hudson.
The author's goal is to relate design history to social and cultural history rather than depicting individual designers as artists. It is important for interaction designers to think about digital artifacts in terms of social and political contexts; Forty provides excellent examples of this kind of thinking.

Gelernter, D. 1998. *Machine Beauty: Elegance and the Heart of Technology*. New York: Basic Books.
Engineering has strong aesthetic elements, whether or not engineers would think of them as such. Gelernter describes the engineering-aesthetic aspects of digital artifacts from an insider's perspective, concentrating on technical elegance as a combination of power and simplicity.

Greenbaum, J., and M. Kyng, eds. 1991. *Design at Work: Cooperative Design of Computer Systems*. Hillsdale, N.J.: Lawrence Erlbaum.
Participatory design and other socially oriented development approaches have a long history in systems development and interaction design. This book is an excellent introduction to the practical techniques of participatory design. The philosophical underpinnings and other more general issues are addressed in Schuler and Namioka (see entry in this bibliography).

Grudin, R. 1990. *The Grace of Great Things: Creativity and Innovation*. New York: Ticknor & Fields.
A beautifully written book where the philosophy of creativity is addressed from unusual angles. The author demonstrates the close relations between creativity and ethics, since "creativity is dangerous." The insights into innovation and the potential conflicts between responsibility and self-actuation make the book valuable reading for interaction designers.

Heim, M. 1998. *Virtual Realism*. New York: Oxford University Press.
Heim offers a thoughtful discussion of what "virtuality" means. Building on a number of examples of virtual technology, Heim suggests ways of living with technology and possible ways of harmonizing computer use with culture. Even though the book is based on existing examples of new technology, Heim builds a philosophical approach to virtual technology that might work as a foundation for criticism and evaluation of new technology to come.

Heskett, J. 2002. *Toothpicks & Logos: Design in Everyday Life*. New York: Oxford University Press.
Heskett reveals how the design of "simple" objects, such as toothpicks, reflects the culture of the country that produced it. The book argues that design combines form and meaning of practical objects by manifesting the identities and aspirations of users. Heskett also has an ambition and a belief that design can play an important role in the future, especially in its role in humanizing new technology.

Hughes, B. 2000. *Dust or Magic: Secrets of Successful Multimedia Design*. Harlow, U.K.: Addison-Wesley.
This book provides a highly interesting account of interaction design from the perspective of a truly reflective practitioner. Hughes discusses core issues in the design of digital artifacts—including judgment ability, creative processes, and qualities of the material—with a strong base in personal experience.

Johnson, S. 1997. *Interface Culture: How New Technology Transforms the Way We Create and Communicate*. New York: Basic Books.
This is one of very few examples aimed at exploring a critic's possible position in interaction design. Johnson addresses topics such as links and hypertext, multiple windows, and the desktop

metaphor, and manages to provide knowledge that is useful for designers as well as other parties in the knowledge community.

Jones, J. C. 1992. *Design Methods*. Second edition. New York: Van Nostrand Reinhold. First published in 1970 under the title *Design Methods: Seeds of Human Futures*.
This is more or less a Bible on methods within the field of design studies. The main part of the book is a collection of thoroughly described methods from various design fields, but the three prefaces (from 1970, 1980, and 1992) are equally interesting as an illustration of how Jones's own view of methods has developed since the first edition.

Jordan, P. 2000. *Designing Pleasurable Products: An Introduction to the New Human Factors*. London: Taylor and Francis.
The field of human factors has traditionally been oriented toward usability, efficiency, and other aspects of goal-oriented use of technical artifacts. Jordan attempts to widen the scope of human factors by introducing pleasure and pleasurable use as a more general framework, based on physical, social, cognitive/emotional, and value-oriented pleasures. His examples are mostly drawn from industrial design, but the approach should also be relevant for digital artifacts.

Kurzweil, R. 1999. *The Age of Spiritual Machines: When Computers Exceed Human Intelligence*. Harmondsworth, U.K.: Penguin.
Moore's law, stating roughly that computer performance doubles every eighteen months, is well known in the field of digital artifacts. Kurzweil draws on many years of experience in artificial intelligence to extrapolate a scenario of a near future where computers reach and exceed human levels of intelligence. At that stage, important questions arise concerning consciousness, responsibility, and the boundaries between humans and machines. Whether or not Kurzweil's predictions are accepted, the general issues are worth pondering.

Laurel, B. 1993. *Computers as Theatre*. Wokingham, U.K.: Addison-Wesley.
According to Laurel, the idea of user interfaces and computers as tools is unnecessarily limiting. She advances the notion of computers as arenas for human action. Based on dramatic theory, she develops a perspective on interaction design and a set of design principles concerning communication, agency, and use experience. The book is highly relevant as a starting point for thinking about virtual realities and other communication-oriented ways of viewing information technology.

Laurel, B., ed. 1990. *The Art of Human-Computer Interface Design*. Reading, Mass.: Addison-Wesley.
This is a collection of articles by different authors, which represents one of the first examples of a design perspective within human-computer interaction (HCI). Reflections on the design process and recommendations on how to manage it are brought together with visions of the future and examples of (at the time) innovative interaction design ideas. The book is still inspirational and serves as a useful complement to the prevalent focus on analysis and evaluation in HCI.

Laurel, B., ed. 2003. *Design Research: Methods and Perspectives*. Cambridge, Mass.: The MIT Press.
The topic of this collection—design research—is broad enough to cover field study methods, explorative design, market and brand issues, as well as trend research and strategies for design research in professional settings. It provides an excellent overview of useful concepts and techniques available to the designer in what we refer to in chapter 4 as inquiry, exploration, and assessment activities.

Lawson, B. 1990. *How Designers Think*. Second edition. London: Butterworth Architecture. First published in 1980.
The author discusses design thinking, design processes, and design strategies in architecture, but his ideas are quite general and relevant to interaction design. A rather well-known part of the book is the discussion of design as solution-oriented—that is, focused on heuristic transformations of solutions proposed early on, rather than systematically analyzing the problem until a solution emerges.

Maeda, J. 2000. *Maeda @ Media*. London: Thames & Hudson.
John Maeda is an artist and graphic designer who has accepted the challenge of the digital media more profoundly than most of his colleagues. In his case, it has led to a focus on the artistic possibilities particular to digital material, including time-based aspects and generative art where the programming capabilities of the computer are used.

McCullough, M. 1996. *Abstracting Craft: The Practiced Digital Hand*. Cambridge, Mass.: The MIT Press.
McCullough offers a carefully articulated craft perspective on the shaping of digital materials. His attention to the fine details of the craft and the qualities of the digital materials viewed as craft materials illustrates a fresh, yet at the same time historically well-founded, perspective on our field.

Meadows, M. 2003. *Pause & Effect: The Art of Interactive Narrative*. Indianapolis, Ind.: New Riders.
If digital design material is temporal as well as spatial, then questions of narrative become crucial for interaction design. Meadows discusses a wealth of narrative projects with a fair grounding in traditional media theory and its encounters with the specific qualities of the digital materials.

Mitcham, C. 1994. *Thinking through Technology: The Path between Engineering and Philosophy*. Chicago: The University of Chicago Press.
Even though this book does not explicitly address design history, it is an excellent introduction to the changing understanding of technology over the course of history. It is useful reading for anyone interested in our relationship with technology and how we shape it.

Mullet, K., and D. Sano. 1995. *Designing Visual Interfaces: Communication Oriented Techniques*. Englewood Cliffs, N.J.: Prentice Hall.
It is not uncommon to think about graphic design as a task of communication. This perspective underlies Mullet and Sano's approach to interaction design, or perhaps more accurately: interface design. The presentation is highly accessible and the examples are chosen effectively.

Nelson, H., and E. Stolterman. 2003. *The Design Way: Intentional Change in an Unpredictable World*. Englewood Cliffs, N.J.: Educational Technology Publications.
This book makes the case that design is its own tradition distinct from science and art. It is an attempt to bring forward a broad and generic view of design. It covers many issues discussed in our book, with a focus on design thinking, judgment, composition, and wholeness, but also covers the splendor and evil of design. To anyone interested in a deeper understanding of design as a universal human activity, this book is recommended.

Ong, W. 1982. *Orality and Literacy: The Technologizing of the Word*. London: Routledge.
This book is a classic on the topic of how the word was technologized and how written language and printing has changed our relations to language and communication. For interaction designers, it is an excellent example of how a particularly relevant technology can be understood and analyzed.

Papanek, V. 1984. *Design for the Real World: Human Ecology and Social Change.* Second edition. London: Thames and Hudson.
Papanek is beautifully explicit on the role of design and the responsibility of the designer: This responsibility is far-reaching and cannot be avoided or denied. His discussions of real-world issues (with examples from urban planning, architecture, and politics) are highly relevant for interaction design in today's world where digital artifacts increasingly pervade our everyday lives.

Pesce, M. 2000. *The Playful World: How Technology Is Transforming Our Imagination.* New York: Ballantine Books.
The boundaries between physical and virtual worlds are increasingly blurred, which is a phenomenon open to multiple interpretations. Pesce chooses to concentrate on the play and toys based on the toy designs made possible by technological innovations, but also draws out more general threads regarding the intersection of artificial intelligence and ubiquitous computing.

Petroski, H. 1992. *The Evolution of Useful Things: How Everyday Artifacts—From Forks and Pins to Paper Clips and Zippers—Came to Be as They Are.* New York: Alfred A. Knopf.
In this classic book, Petroski takes a look at artifacts that most of us never pay attention to. He offers a well-developed theory of technological innovation based on the idea that it can be understood as a response to perceived failures of existing products. His main idea is that irritation, and not necessity, is the mother of invention. This book provides a number of examples of what can be achieved through thoughtful reflection on everyday designs.

Pye, D. 1978. *The Nature and Aesthetics of Design.* London: The Herbert Press.
This is an excellent book by a furniture designer who also engages with more profound questions concerning the nature of the design process. He discusses how design is "actually" performed and provides interesting examples from many disciplines. The book's main contributions lie in its deep understanding and aesthetic perspective on craft and skill.

Schön, D. 1987. *Educating the Reflective Practitioner: Toward a New Design for Teaching and Learning in the Professions.* San Francisco: Jossey-Bass Publishers.
The concept of reflection-in-action has been very influential in contemporary design theory, even though Schön does not delimit himself to design and addresses all kinds of professional practice. This book is not only a useful summary of *The Reflective Practitioner* (1983), but also a discussion of what the model implies for the education of skilled professionals.

Schuler, D., and A. Namioka, eds. 1993. *Participatory Design: Principles and Practices.* Hillsdale, N.J.: Lawrence Erlbaum.
This book includes a collection of philosophical issues, techniques, and case studies concerning participatory design. A main issue throughout the book is the applicability of participatory design outside its specific Scandinavian context of origin, and in particular the differences compared with participatory design in the United States.

Shedroff, N. 2001. *Experience Design 1.* Indianapolis, Ind.: New Riders.
Shedroff approaches experience design as a multidisciplinary field involving digital artifacts as well as many other materials. A particularly interesting aspect of the book from our point of view is

Shedroff's attempt to articulate qualities of use experiences, in a manner related to what we present in chapter 5.

Winograd, T., et al., eds., 1996. *Bringing Design to Software*. Reading, Mass.: Addison-Wesley. This collection represents an early attempt to articulate a design-theoretical perspective on information technology by drawing together chapters from many of the pioneers of the field. The book is highly relevant as an orientation to different "ways of seeing" and understanding interaction design.

Zuboff, S. 1988. *In the Age of the Smart Machine: The Future of Work and Power*. Oxford: Heinemann. This is a book about computerization of work and its possible consequences in terms of changing power structures, erosion of professional skills, and so on. Zuboff argues against the tendency to automate in favor of what she calls the "informate" approach. The book serves as a useful reminder of the interaction designer's responsibility.

Index of Names

Index of Subjects

Absolute particular (every design process is an absolute particular in its combination of designer, resources, and design situation), 9, 44

Actors (in a design process), 33

Adaptive system (a digital artifact that modifies its properties autonomously based on the user's behavior), 111

Adequate design, as opposed to optimal design, 55

Aesthetics (design is an aesthetic activity), 10, 53–54, 160–161
  digital, 160–161

Affinity diagram (a way of structuring the results from a brainstorming), 72

Agent (a digital artifact exhibiting a high degree of autonomy), 121 122

Anthropomorphic, 121

Ambiguity (a use quality of digital artifacts), 136

Analytic ability, 46, 51–52

Anticipation (a use quality of digital artifacts), 132–133

Appropriation (users making existing artifacts their own and using them in unexpected ways), 113

Argumentation (seeing design as argumentation), 93–95

Articulate craftsman (a possible role for a design-oriented researcher), 146

Articulation (a fundamental element in a knowledge-constructing design culture), 2, 96, 102–104, 139, 146

Assessment (the critical examination of a design proposal, idea, or artifact), 65, 91–96, 148–149

Asynchronous communication (one of the action spaces afforded by the Internet), 160

ATM (automated teller machine, an example of a digital artifact related to social action spaces), 104–105

Attention (authentic attention, which is needed in a design process), 24

Auto-Illustrator (from Signwave, an example of a parafunctional digital artifact), 129–130

Black box
  seeing the designer as a, 64
  seeing a digital artifact as a, 108–110

Brainstorming (an explorative design method), 71–73

Bryce (an example of an opaque-and-productive tool), 111

Chance (using chance in a design process), 75–76

Character (a holistic assessment of a person or artifact), 138

Client (a role in a design process), 7, 12, 26–27, 33, 36, 39, 50, 55

Communication (in a design process), 20, 29, 34–35, 50–51, 59–60, 82–83, 89–90, 99, 167